The Secularization
of Early
Modern England

The Secularization of Early Modern England

From Religious Culture to Religious Faith

C. JOHN SOMMERVILLE
University of Florida

New York   Oxford
OXFORD UNIVERSITY PRESS
1992

Oxford University Press

Oxford   New York   Toronto
Delhi   Bombay   Calcutta   Madras   Karachi
Petaling Jaya   Singapore   Hong Kong   Tokyo
Nairobi   Dar es Salaam   Cape Town
Melbourne   Auckland

and associated companies in
Berlin   Ibadan

Library of Congress Cataloging-in-Publication Data
Sommerville, C. John (Charles John), 1938–
The secularization of early modern England :
from religious culture, to religious faith /
C. John Sommerville.
p. cm. ISBN 0-19-507427-0
1. Secularism—England—History. 2. England—Religion.
I. Title. BL2765.G7S66 1992 261—dc20 91-29817

2 4 6 8 9 7 5 3 1

Printed in the United States of America
on acid-free paper

For Henry

Acknowledgments

Authors have no one to blame but themselves for choosing topics on which there are few experts to whom to turn for advice. Naturally, it makes one's debts that much more important. Professors Richard Greaves, Robert Webb, David Martin, and Henry Horwitz offered much-needed help and encouragement at crucial points, whatever misgivings they may have had about the project. Professors Richard Fenn, Jeffrey Cox, Paul Seaver, James Amelang, Gerald Aylmer, Ira Clark, Robert Hatch, Eldon Turner, and Patrick Geary also made suggestions, on the study or the manuscript, which I have tried to incorporate.

I am also glad to acknowledge the alert and sympathetic hearing which my department afforded me, as well as forums which the University of Florida's Department of Religion, the Southern Region of the Conference on British Studies, the Conference on Faith and History, and the editors of the *Journal of Religious History* offered for presenting my case. The latter have kindly given permission to use material that first appeared in that journal under the title, "The Destruction of Religious Culture in Pre-Industrial England," 15 (1988), 76–93. A Faculty Development Grant from the University of Florida was much appreciated. And the faith, generosity, and good humor of my family were unfailing supports. Finally, the very professional efforts of many at Oxford University Press, and especially Nancy Lane, have my sincere gratitude.

In a work of this sort, I am also mindful of an unusually large debt to other historians—eight hundred or more of them, not all acknowledged in the notes—who could not have foreseen their work being quarried for ideas and materials for a work on secularization. No doubt readers will think of others whose research might have been used to enlarge the edifice. Indeed, it is partly to that end that the book is now published.

Contents

The Secularization
of Early
Modern England

1

The Study of
Secularization

There are several ways of expressing what this book is about. It is about the
change from a religious culture to a religious faith. It describes the secularization
of English culture and society, in the sense of a separation of almost all aspects of
life and thought from religious associations or ecclesiastical direction. Rather
incidentally, it will show how thoroughly religion had permeated English culture
before these changes, and how differently we must think of religion in such a
context. We will see which aspects of life were first affected by the marginalization of religion, and which maintained their religious associations long-
est. And the study will try to show who or what was responsible for this momentous change, and when it was effectively completed.

To avoid misunderstanding, we need to be just as clear on what the book is not
about. It is not only about Christianity, however that is defined. We are certainly
not discussing the decline of Christianity, for English religion might be said to
have become more specifically Christian during the period. Rather, this is a
discussion of how religion (something larger than Christianity or the Church)
changed its character, and how it changed its position in English society.

Obviously, much depends on the definition of several terms, and most especially "religion," "faith," and "secular." In his classic study of *Religion and the
Decline of Magic*, Keith Thomas remarked that secularization has not been much
studied.[1] The reason for that is not a lack of interest in such a fundamental
change. Mostly, it is that "secularization" has seemed such a broad, diffuse,
tautological, or even contradictory concept that sociologists and historians have
become impatient with it. They cannot do without the term, but they use it very

gingerly. Scholars complain, quite rightly, that the common notion of a unitary, linear, and inevitable decline of religion is only an assumption, and one which falsifies the evidence.[2] They acknowledge that there has been some kind of religious decline over the past several centuries, but their discussions have foundered because of lack of agreement or consistency in definitions of secularization and of religion.

In approaching the task of definition it is helpful to imagine two ideal-typical extremes, to give substance to those definitions. At the one extreme we may imagine a people whose religious rituals are so woven into the fabric of their life that they could not separate religion from the rest of their activities. Many such groups do not even have a word for their commerce with occult powers. Even some complex societies like Old Kingdom Egypt were thoroughly "integral" in this way. Egypt was considered to be the center of the universe. The king was descended from the greatest god and spoke with divine authority on all subjects in both politics and religion. Indeed those terms are anachronistic in reference to the regime, for the separation of state and church was not recognized; the king's ministers were also priests. Even he was not free to change law as he saw fit but ruled by customs and traditions which were themselves considered sacred. Everything in life had a religious dimension, or to put it the other way around, religion was about the "real world" and not some other realm. Perhaps religion offered nothing to people as individuals, but immortality was promised to the nation. The king, at least, was immortal, and his pyramid tomb was a symbol of the stability of the civilization, an intersection of time and eternity.[3]

At the other extreme we may imagine a society in which religion is a matter of conscious beliefs, important primarily for the times of one's most philosophical and poetic solitude. It would hardly occur to anyone to attempt to "legislate his religion," for religious ideas and institutions are thought to refer to an altogether different realm of "spiritual" concerns. Those who favor a functional definition of religion might look to see whether such a society developed any quasi-religious symbols of collective identity or asserted social goals that would transcend the individual's mundane interest. This would indicate that society still wanted to view itself *sub specie aeternitatis*, from some higher perspective. If not, this truly secular state would have to resolve conflicts without arguing the justice of its decisions, since that would imply its submission to transcendent moral standards, and it could not call for individual sacrifices without implying the almost sacred value of social solidarity.

Probably such an "overdeveloped" society is no more than an ideal type. Perhaps all enduring social contracts are "religious" in the sense already suggested. Even those states which have most proudly proclaimed their secularity have kept up the rituals of social solidarity to the point of maintaining the tombs of their leaders as shrines. They have encouraged a kind of charisma around leaders who unite power and ideology in their persons, just as the pharaohs must have done. For they have sensed that true social decadence, when it means institutional autonomy, class dissolution, and entropy, is a bleak prospect.

Actual societies move back and forth on a continuum between these ideal extremes. Several different processes are involved in moving from the former toward the latter position, and any of them might be called secularization. (It will be best to adhere to ordinary usage in definition, so that we do not end up with an arbitrary or academic usage, which might be impervious to criticism but of no general interest.) Historians have not always recognized that "secularized" has different meanings depending on whether it is being used to describe a society, an institution, an activity, or a mentality. First, as applied to a society, secularization is best understood as the process of institutional differentiation. This means that separate organizations take over tasks once handled by what Robert Redfield called the "primitive fusion."[4] Such differentiation has the effect of confining religion to ever-fewer areas of life, for, except for the church itself, the proliferating institutions will always have a less religious (more "secular") character than the original religio-political regime.

The secularization of a particular institution means giving an institution which was originally religious in character a more temporal purpose, as when the Y.M.C.A. becomes a nonsectarian social-service organization. Even a church can be secularized in this sense, like certain denominations which are now essentially forums for the discussion of current issues. Inanimate objects, such as lands and buildings, can be secularized in this sense, as happened in Henry VIII's seizure of the monastery estates and churches. Ideas can be secularized as well, and intellectual historians such as Hans Blumenberg use the term to refer to such a transformation of concepts from a religious to a clearly temporal reference.[5] This sort of transformation might be called desacralization.

The secularization of a particular activity would refer to its transfer from a religious institution to an obviously less religious one. An example would be the English state's assumption of poor-relief activities, once administered by the Church, or the transfer of literary patronage from ecclesiastics to the laity. This might be termed profanation, since it involves bringing something formerly regarded as sacred into the area of the profane (literally, outside the temple).

The fourth meaning, the secularization of belief or mentality or thought, would indicate that one was not as likely to look to ultimate ends as to proximate, instrumental ones. To avoid confusion, we will refer to this not as secularization (pure and simple) but as the decline (or straining or loosening) of religious belief. Such a decline may take the form of ignoring the religious dimension, or it may involve an active doubt or open disbelief.

The current equation of secularization with declining church membership or attendance is hardly applicable to the early modern period, in which religious devotion took such a variety of forms. Church attendance was by no means the most common form of religious behavior at the beginning of our period.

There is an obvious sequence in the relation between these forms of secularization. Differentiation of religious institutions from others is necessary before it is possible to transfer activities from the former to the latter. Likewise, it is only after such differentiation that it would be possible to transform recognizably "religious" institutions for other uses. One would also expect that these various processes would have the effect of making religion more self-conscious, exposing it as only one part of culture rather than the basis of all. This marginalization of religion would make it easier to ignore, and as religion becomes more self-conscious there arises the possibility of actual unbelief. Indeed, the lag of intellectual change behind institutional change will be a theme of this study.

One need not assume that these processes can move in only one direction. The Middle Ages had seen the Church subsume a number of activities, often by default, which earlier states had performed. Church composers sacralized popular musical styles for use in worship. There was a movement toward the reintegration of political and religious institutions. As late as the fourteenth century, Edward III took a lead from the French in clothing the English monarchy in sacred trappings, issuing "cramp rings" for epilepsy by way of demonstrating his sacred character. Edward's chancellor (a churchman) opened his last parliament with the claim that England was the new Israel and the heir apparent was God's vicar on earth.[6]

The question therefore arises whether we should assume that this reintegration of institutions means that religion is in the ascendant or is being compromised. Was Edward's state acquiring a religious character or dragging the Church down to its level? No general answer can be given. Particular judgments in this area will depend on how well the Church maintained her dignity in the process. Was the activity genuinely hallowed in the minds of contemporaries, or did the Church compromise her character by associating with what had been secular? Depending on the answer, one might term such a change either a sacralization of the activity or a secularization of the Church. To take an obvious example, kings might declare a divine right in their exercise of power, asserting a religious position rivalling that of the Church. In England's case, kings found the Church able to maintain the traditional distinction of sacred and secular in this area and block such pretensions. No one worshipped Henry VIII as cosmocrator or was taken in by seeing James I apotheosized in some court masque.

At times, indeed, the Church saw the need to draw a line between sacred and secular spheres in order to emphasize its superiority or distinctiveness,[7] and it did so by emphasizing the secularity of other institutions. Fencing off the holy and protecting the things of religion from profane handling is an instance of differentiation. So the Church can contribute simultaneously to the secularization of society and to the intensification of a sense of the holy.

In such discussions it is easy to get confused into arguments over what areas of life are intrinsically secular or religious. But there is no agreed-on list: even cooking may be governed by religious rules. A thoroughly integrated culture relates every aspect of life to its religion. There are no areas of life that are intrinsically secular; the boundary is culturally relative. But if we cannot define the secular can we at least define the religious?

Definitions of religion tend to fall into two categories. Sociologists often favor definitions in terms of the functions for which they believe religion exists— encouraging devotion to the common good and justifying the demands of society, providing a common ideology, aetiological myth or metaphysical system, or narcotizing exploited groups with the promise of a better life hereafter.[8] Theologians may also favor functional definitions, as Paul Tillich did in equating religion with one's personal orientation or "ultimate concern." It follows from such a definition that religion cannot decline, since such functions are essential. Religion can only change its disguises, and in fact it is more effective when it is not recognized or labelled as "religion." The most effective religions are simply accepted as self-evident truth. The study of religion, understood in this sense, would be a study of those changing disguises—including modern ideologies.[9] While useful for many types of study, such definitions would defeat the historian who is interested in tracking the curve of religious commitment, as ordinarily understood.

A more useful definition for our purposes would be a more substantive one. Anthropologists may prefer such definitions, which make religion that which gives access to supernatural powers or to the presence of such powers.[10] In a typical formulation, religion is "any system of values, beliefs, norms, and related symbols and rituals, arising from attempts by individuals and social groups to effect certain ends, whether in this world or in any future world, by means wholly or partly supernatural."[11] Including the simple access to the presence of these powers takes account of the phenomenological studies which make "a sense of the holy"—involving awe, fascination, and dependence—the essential characteristic of religion. Such studies always emphasize the concept of power; feelings of remoteness, "otherness," and dependence derive from an awareness of a wholly alien power.[12]

The advantage of a substantive definition is partly that it is closer to the common sense of both the sixteenth century and the twentieth. (We will see in chapter 4 how contemporaries defined religion and how definitions changed in line with secularizing trends.) But there is the added advantage that we will not prejudge what the functions of religion were at any particular time by using a functionalist theory more appropriate to another situation. Even the supposed function of religion in promoting "order" may be called into question; anthropologist Victor Turner believes that the importance of religion concerns "both the maintenance and radical transformation of human social and psychical structures," and social historians sometimes acknowledge that religion often introduces disorder and capriciousness.[13] Finally, although it is not our purpose to trace some general decline of religion, a substantive definition will keep things from getting so slippery that we would not even notice such a decline.[14]

It is worth emphasizing that we have been considering "generic" rather than "normative" definitions of religion. We are not taking sides. It will not be assumed that Christianity is more religious than what historians quaintly call "superstition." We will give no more favorable notice to an "elevating" religion than a mundane one. It is possible for duties to be performed selfishly or for worldly advantage and still be fully religious by this generic definition. Religion will not have to be ethical, church-approved, or monotheistic to merit our attention. Eventually, of course, the folk piety of medieval semipagans lost out to Puritan reformers. History is written by the winners, and historians have accepted the Puritans' view of what is acceptable in religion, with its threefold distinction of essentials, useful ceremonies, and superstitions. But in order to understand the times, we need to pay some attention to those superstitions—for what they were and not just for what they were not.

This will not be easy to remember. It violates our tendency to side with the forces of progress. But we should be open to the possibility that superstition (a word we should avoid) is actually more religious than Christianity (even if we accepted some favorable definition of the latter). "Superstition" may offer more avenues of access to the supernatural than a more refined faith. Numerous scholars and theologians have recognized that the Judeo-Christian tradition, and especially Protestantism, is a secularizing religion.[15] That is not a self-contradiction; it only means that this tradition wants to separate religion from other aspects of life—for the sake of purifying religion. There will be abundant evidence of the secularizing effect of Protestantism in the pages that follow. But the purity or quality of religion is only one of our concerns. Quantity is another.

Most earlier discussions of secularization have become entangled in these normative considerations. Some have argued against secularization on the grounds that Western religion has improved since the "Age of Faith." It is easy for them to contrast the venality of some medieval clergy with the selfless devotion of some latter-day missionaries and philanthropists and postulate a general progress. But this is beside the point; secularization does not simply mean decline or corruption, but also a change in religion's placement. Other studies have limited the scope of the subject by normative definitions. French historians have recently traced the de-Christianization of French society before and during the Revolution.[16] That posits a uniformity of belief and practice which may be even harder to find in Protestant societies. More suggestive for our purposes are the broader studies of popular piety or "local religion" such as those on Spain by William Christian, Jr., on France by A. N. Galpern and Natalie Zemon Davis, and on Italy by Richard Trexler. But there are no close parallels to the kind of study undertaken here.

Our title may raise suspicions that favor will be shown to religious culture over religious faith, or the reverse, so they too need definition. "Culture" is taken to mean the shared practices, values, meanings and symbolic forms of a society. It constitutes the ways of living and thinking which are shared and preserved by a given group. A religious culture is one which offers unmediated access to the realm of supernatural powers, from almost any type of activity or line of thought. In a secular culture, on the other hand, it would take real thought to make the connections between any activity and one's religious ends. To put it another way, in a thoroughly religious culture translations of the whole range of activities into religious concepts are unnecessary. These activities are not just guided by religion, they are the religion itself. By contrast, in a thoroughly secular culture it would seem absurd to try to relate most activities to one's spiritual concerns. Most areas of life are seen as autonomous; religion could only provide a comprehensive symbolism which would pull things together for more reflective individuals.

Religious "faith" need not be defined normatively either. We will not concentrate on the rise of an "authentic" faith, as theologians might describe it, but only mean something more like belief or mental assent and less like ritual or religious activities. Faith suggests a reasoned confidence in doctrines or practices, an affirmation of the other world and God's power. As is often observed, faith sometimes flies in the face of doubt, and almost presupposes doubt. Tennyson braced himself with the lines, "There lives more faith in honest doubt,/Believe me, than in half the creeds." But such an appreciation of faith does not make it more religious than a religious culture.[17]

There is no doubt that we live on one side of a great divide, where religion is something one thinks about rather than something one does. Our histories of religion are often actually studies of theology, which is discussion of religion and not the thing itself. The fact that we can so easily confuse the matter justifies the present study of how religion came to be immured within the mind. How have we come to value religious faith over religious culture, when it involves so many questions and doubts? Was it a choice or inevitable? Was it the evolution of a higher outlook, or a retreat? Did faith only prove to be the most resilient aspect of religion? After all, religious faith is still with us, whereas religious culture is not. A privatized faith has shown even more likelihood of survival than the ideological substitutes for religion of the last two centuries.[18] So it would not contradict the thesis of this study to consider the movement from culture to faith as constituting "religious evolution" as well as secularization.[19]

We should not reify the concepts of culture and faith beyond their descriptive usefulness. The difference between them might even be thought a matter of degree. They can both be shared. They both exist in the mind—faith being more conscious of itself and culture more a matter of mental habit. And yet the self-consciousness of faith does contain an important element of freedom, compatible with individualism. Doubtless this forms the theoretical link between institutional secularization and the shaking of belief.

In particular, we would be guilty of reification if we equated religious faith with Protestantism and religious culture with medieval usage. To be sure, it was the intention of Reformers to make religious beliefs more explicit, being confident that religion could sustain itself in this new mental environment. But by the end of our period they were fabricating elements of a Protestant religious culture to shore up a more exposed intellectual structure. One could not call the result a pluralistic religious culture, since by definition religion can only be part of a pluralistic culture and not its basis. Religious subcultures did survive on the margins of society, but the emerging national culture was to rest on more secular ideological foundations.

Several minor points need clarifying here to avoid misunderstanding later. Given human ambivalence toward the sacred, we should remember that religion will sometimes take the form of protection against supernatural powers—against God's judgment. That is, a positive attitude toward religion may actually involve a hostility toward the gods. Religion can amount to techniques for domesticating God and reducing the terror of the numinous. Medieval men and women had enough real dread to want to build up defenses. The rood screen enclosing the holiest area of a church might be seen as a cage to keep God in, where priests ventured, as into the lion's den. Medieval religious culture may seem like so many lilliputian fetters on God, so that worshippers could control divine actions, judgment, and favors. Indeed Luther complained that by his day religion had become a form of rebellion against God—an effort to create a personal righteousness in defiance of God's offer of free grace. Thus we need not suppose that a vital religion will necessarily involve the love of God. Indeed, more secularized individuals might be on better terms with the divinity.

Another possible misunderstanding would be to assume that the demonic or the sacrilegious belong in the category of the secular. The devil is as much a part of the realm of the supernatural as is God. The secular or profane realm contains only everyday beings, not those remarkable for their diabolic character. An inversion of religion in sacrilege, desecration, or sorcery is not evidence of secularization, however bad-mannered. In medieval England, hostility toward some aspect of religion was often expressed in religious terms. The evidence of thoroughgoing secularization, on the other hand, is to be found in indifference, even though it might be respectful to the Church.

Throughout this study it will be taken for granted that a conscious faith is more open to doubt and final disbelief than the piety which is wrapped in a religious culture. Self-consciousness is the loss of innocence, a fall from one kind of grace. To be sure, doubt does not necessarily lead to disbelief; it may lead to a more mature faith. And we have already acknowledged that a chosen faith can show great resilience, while a birthright religion can crumble quickly in an experience of cultural confrontation. Generally speaking, however, we expect a heightened consciousness of religion to result in its erosion, as assumptions become beliefs, then thoughts, and finally ideas. Related to this is the view that an interest in religion is not itself an expression of religion. Indeed, we will take the advent of theories about religion to be the final stage of institutional secularization.

The method of this study will be to find when and how various aspects of life and thought were divorced from religious values or from the direction of the Church, and secondarily, how that process was related, temporally, to religious belief. That is, we will attempt to measure or date the growing differentiation of religious symbols and institutions from all areas of English society and culture and to see the effect of that differentiation upon thought. Finally, the response of religious leaders will be of interest, as they abandoned the security of ecclesiastical establishment in favor of an appeal to public opinion. Any such refoundation of religion is evidence that belief is ceasing to be taken for granted and is rising into consciousness, where it begins to seem doubtful and requires some defense. This will be evidence that a religious culture was changing into religious belief, evidence of the emergence of faith as a "leap"—in Kierkegaard's apt metaphor.

Naturally, there is no archive that holds the evidence for such a pervasive change. A synthetic study of this kind will depend on the work of many other historians, most of whom did not have "secularization" in mind. Where existing treatments are thin, contemporary evidence will be sought, scattered though it may be. In the end, the question will not be whether the picture is complete—as it could never be—but whether it is sufficient to establish the point.

Such a study will intersect with several other approaches to the study of religious and cultural developments in early-modern England. It has been usual to speak of a religious "Reformation" then, either in terms of an act of ecclesiastical politics or as a clash of theologies. A danger in that approach is to see the sides in this struggle as symmetrical; our study will often have to take note of the secularizing effect of Protestantism rather than treat it as an exact equivalent of medieval religion. Others have described the religious changes as a triumph of the laity in society and within the English church itself; this will be a part of our approach as well.[20] Some have treated the changes as an elite repression of popular traditions.[21] Many have seen these developments as part of a general rationalization of politics, economic life, and science and have puzzled over the part that religious changes had in this process. A study of secularization will draw on all these approaches and offer something to them in return, and it will show how such matters as iconoclasm, millenarianism, and the humanist concept of *adiaphora* fit into a pattern of larger significance.

It is natural to suppose that the fading of religious significance from common activities must have been a very gradual process and clearly visible only at a late stage. One of the surprises of this study will be how early this process began and how sudden and dramatic are parts of the story. Secularization often proves to have been a matter of conscious debate, promoted theologically and decided politically. The rapidity of the change was commented on by English and foreign writers at the time.

Beginning our considerations in the sixteenth century will strike many as rushing things. Most studies of a decline of religious belief have concentrated on the nineteenth century and viewed the subject as an aspect of industrialization and urbanization. French historian Lucien Febvre's *Le problème de l'incroyance au xvie siècle; La religion de Rabelais* is often cited as having shown that speculative atheism was impossible in the sixteenth century, by showing how thoroughly every aspect of thought was grounded in religious presuppositions. David Berman has argued how difficult the atheist position was psychologically even in the next century.[22] But there is some ambivalence here, for while Febvre was right to point out that one need not take literally the many accusations of atheism in that period, he might have concentrated more on those who made the accusation. Why were suspicions becoming so widespread at just that time? Was it a projection of unacknowledged doubts? Even if these defenders of the faith only meant by "atheism" a denial of a particular church or the use of colloquial expressions in Bible translation, could these things have pointed to the heart of religion for them?[23] Some cynically made the accusation of infidelity simply to destroy their rivals, but Rabelais' accusers seem genuinely horrified—as if they felt involved or unconsciously implicated in his "atheism." We will sense the same nervousness in contemporary attacks on Hobbes. So it is not too soon to look for signs of bad faith.

The chronological boundaries of the study are set by two dates of the first importance in the processes of secularization. Henry VIII's seizure of power over the Church and his secularization of its wealth and personnel (in the 1530s) is unquestionably the most dramatic episode in the process. By the reign of Queen Anne (1702–14), long before England industrialized, one encounters naturalistic and reductionistic explanations of the gods and of the religious sense itself. Obviously, religion has failed in its explanatory role when it is itself embraced in more inclusive terms—when one is satisfied that one has found "what is really behind religion." Frank Manuel's *The Eighteenth Century Confronts the Gods* describes several such theories, current by the early eighteenth century.[24] Manuel does not show that they were widely believed in English society, but even if they were only widely known, religion had become a more conscious choice and effort.

Viewed simply as institutional differentiation, some secularization had already taken place before the 1530s. England was very far from our picture of Old Kingdom Egypt. Just the creation of separate religious institutions is itself a big step toward setting religion off from the rest of life. For it is the paradox of secularization that the process begins by marking off an area of the sacred—

dramatizing the fact that the sacred is something out of the ordinary. The inverse of that process is a definition of the ordinary, the mundane or secular. The object, of course, is to increase the intensity of religious consciousness, but necessarily within a smaller circle. In the medieval period the area of the sacred had grown. The resacralization of numerous aspects of life has given rise to the common description of the medieval church as "worldly." But at that time it was quite possible to think of war as a religious activity involving God's "honor" and armored abbots. And it was logical to think of economic regulation as the proper concern of a church which was supposed to teach one how to treat one's neighbor. These were accepted as intrinsically religious activities; the Church did not give the impression of grabbing at power or bestowing an unwanted blessing.

Eventually, however, the medieval church felt it had to draw a line against the further sacralization of society if religion were to maintain its independent identity. As a result, the Church itself encouraged some secularization. For instance, there was a definite laicization of government in late-medieval England, with clergymen appearing less frequently as judges and administrators in the burgeoning royal government. Many of the factors that operated to destroy religious culture in the sixteenth century had appeared in the reign of Richard II (1377–99). There had been an antipapal campaign in the parliaments of the 1350s, culminating in the Statutes of Provisors and Praemunire which limited the Church's authority to chose its own leaders and to exercise legal jurisdiction (laws which Henry VIII would use). In the 1370s Parliament began demanding taxes from the Church.[25] And it was then that John Wyclif's proto-Protestantism gave the government a justification for an attack on the Church's wealth and temporal power in the name of a more spiritualized religion. The stage was set for a Reformation that did not happen.[26]

Henry VIII had precedents, therefore, but his conquest of the Church still stunned the English by its speed. In only four years (1532–36) he curtailed every aspect of clerical authority and substituted his own. The story has been told so often that we only need to be reminded that he constituted himself as the final court of appeal in all cases involving the Church, required that all laws used in the Church's courts receive his approval, abolished the study of church, or canon, law, eliminated the need for anyone's approval of his appointments in the Church, pocketed the taxes formerly sent to Rome, surveyed the whole wealth of the Church and began to nationalize it (which involved ending the monastic and mendicant forms of religious life), issued a statement defining heresy and religious truth, took responsibility for calling and presiding over the Church's governing assembly (Convocation), executed a cardinal, and encouraged an official translation of the sacred writings into the language of the laity.

All this did not transfer sanctity to Henry. He might discuss whether he should personally take over the ordination of priests, and he did serve a shortened form of the Mass. But 1536 saw the largest uprising of the century, the "Pilgrimage of Grace," against his exercise of a royal supremacy over the Church, among other things. Many priests predicted that Henry's changes would not outlive him, given their unpopularity, and even Thomas Cromwell, the king's main agent, was surprised that the government got away with its campaign against so much that was holy. The general revulsion against this desecration was such that Henry had to hire Protestant pens to argue the even-greater sacrilege of the papal regime.[27]

Henry's secularization of church authority was matched by a further secularization of the state. For example, he appointed fewer clerics to high government office. England's first lay chancellor in centuries (Thomas More in 1529) was shortly followed by its first lay Principal Secretary or "Secretary of State" (Thomas Cromwell in 1534). In 1711 a bishop of Bristol, John Robinson, became the last churchman to be appointed to the Privy Council (as Lord Privy Seal, an office filled by laymen since 1530). On the other hand, the laity was enabled to exercise ecclesiastical jurisdiction by a statute of 1545. The civil service saw an immediate increase in lay composition.[28] And while Henry did not abolish church courts, he did not put his weight behind the attempt to revise canon law to make it fit the new circumstances.[29] All this had an effect upon thought: the fear of excommunication was soon lessened to the point that by the 1620s an estimated one-sixth of the population of York were unrepentant excommunicants and their dependents.[30]

To follow events one more step, the life of parliaments was also changed by the subjugation of the Church. The House of Lords had a more secular appearance when the abbots disappeared (along with their monasteries), leaving the remaining churchmen (bishops) as a minority in that house. The House of Commons got a former royal chapel (St. Stephen's) as its first regular meeting place in 1549, just one of many buildings to be secularized.[31] More important, the experience of all the revolutionary legislation affected the thinking of members. On the eve of the Reformation, the legal authority Christopher Saint-German could still speak of statutes as subject to the law of reason and of God. But legislators soon recognized that their unprecedented activity implied—in G. R. Elton's words— that "the sanction of a statute rested not in its being consonant with some other superior law but in the authority behind it, in the sovereign will of the legislature."[32] The whole of our modern world is wrapped up in that notion of political autonomy. The exercise of this sovereignty would soon be followed by theories which grounded authority in popular consent rather than in God's will.

One cannot proceed with an account of secularization entirely in narrative fashion, of course. Later chapters will deal with basic categories of human activity and awareness, such as cultural anthropologists use in organizing their textbooks. These will insure a comprehensive treatment of the subject and will demonstrate the extent of the cultural change involved. One group of such categories will include language itself and the perceptions of time and of space. We shall also look at labor, art, and reflective thought and survey the categories of personhood, association, and power.

In the midst of these topical considerations it will sometimes be appropriate to revert to the political narrative, for the situation was subject to dramatic, often rapid, change. As leadership passed to a thoroughly Protestant regime under Edward VI (1547–53), then to a Catholic reaction under Mary (1553–58) and back to a lay-dominated Protestantism under Elizabeth (1558–1603) the sense of sacred or even settled institutions was eroded. Some have argued that a return to an earlier, unreformed religion was a possibility for England as late as the middle of Elizabeth's reign.[33] But when the unattractive James (1603–25) and the inept Charles (1625–49) encouraged Archbishop William Laud's attempts to restore religious institutions to their old position it generated an explosive reaction against the Stuart dynasty. Nor did Parliament and its army find a formula for the satisfactory settlement of a common religion.

The Restoration of the Stuart monarchy under Charles II (1660–85) brought back a church whose political position was much diminished. Religious regulations were decided by the civil authorities and enforced in the state courts.[34] The revolutionary philosophical issues of the day were not discussed primarily by the Church or in its universities but by a much wider public. When James II (1685–88) came to the throne that public took alarm at his religious policies and was relieved when his nephew William III (1689–1702) siezed command. The Revolution of 1688 meant, in effect, that the country would never again have to fear ecclesiastical government. A limited religious toleration could be granted because it was apparent that the unity of English society rested on a basis other than religious agreement. The ascendant Whig party was essentially the party of secularization, and religion began to be treated as a private matter.

While we should keep this history in mind, the order of chapters is meant to show a sequence that is not simply political. Following the reigns would make the story too ordinary, implying that the development was entirely in the control of the state. Instead, in an admittedly rough way, the sequence of topics is meant to represent their chronological succession, which may suggest lines of causation or influence. Beyond that, we have hoped to achieve a sense of anthropological unfamiliarity by backing away from the usual patterns of English historiography in this way, with only two chapters to treat the politics of secularization.

Nor should the story be told entirely in terms of the development of religious thought. Protestants had a positive program and were trying to seize the opportunity to deepen English spirituality. But much escaped their control in a movement which gained a momentum of its own.

Already we have noticed three recurring factors in preindustrial secularization: the aggrandizing nation-state, a Protestant spirituality which wanted to distinguish essentials from nonessentials and redrew the line between the sacred and the profane, and printing presses which could propagate these views. The remaining chapters will be full of these factors and their conjunction. Other matters such as urbanization, industrialization, and the growth of science come into the picture very late, if at all. Studies which have traced secularization through humanism, philosophical scepticism, modern science and Deism give a very different picture.[35] Not only do they ignore the structural changes which preceded these developments but they miss English society's visceral rejection of its religious culture. Most important, they slight the fact that the intellectual change was a response to secularization rather than the other way around. A concentration on urbanization and the Enlightenment is one reason that the study of secularization has been so puzzling; historians have looked for it several centuries after it happened, and when all that was left was the last phase—the decline of religious belief.

One way of viewing these changes is to see them as the development of the cultural grammar of Febvre's atheism. We may think of atheism as easy and natural, forgetting what a lot of explaining it requires. Where did the world come from and what was the thought behind it? How did we creatures come by our awesome intricacy? Where did freedom come from, and personality, and conscience? The beginnings of answers leap to our minds, of course; but they are complicated, controversial, and perhaps none of us could follow them out to the end. Even when accepted, on faith, they depend on the prior secularization of such categories as power, space, personhood, time.

By the early years of the eighteenth century some English thinkers were able to see the whole subject of religion from the outside, as it were. A recent study of hundreds of religious book titles indicates a shift from a personalistic understanding of religion to an objectified one by that time. Wilfred Cantwell Smith noticed that nothing like the term "Christianity" had appeared in a medieval theological title. The closest approximation was in the phrase "Christian faith," where the adjective denoted a moral attribute—a right faith. By the mid-sixteenth century, "Christianity" did appear on some Protestant catechisms as equivalent to Christian doctrine, thus denoting an intellectual category. At the same time, the term "religion" began to replace faith and in the seventeenth century became the favored term. But whereas faith had indicated a whole dimension of life and consciousness, religion now denoted an explanation of life or a set of propositions. The English began to speak of "religions" in the plural for the first time. It only remained to the eighteenth century to complete the transition from "religion" to an emphasis specifically on "Christianity"—as in "the truths of Christianity."[36]

In other words, by that time religion had achieved a certain independence from the rest of culture; it was no longer the basis of that culture. From a particular religious standpoint, this might be considered a gain. What was lost in breadth might be made up in depth. A considered faith may show greater stability than religious habit, and secularization is always compatible with cycles of religious revival. But the point is that religion would need such periodic revitalization as it became a movement within a nation's culture rather than the ground of that culture. We must remind ourselves that religion had not always involved faith of a modern kind; at one time it was as basic to thought as the structure of language and the sense of time and space.

2

The Secularization
of Space

An Englishman, Sir Isaac Newton, is remembered as a pioneer of modern thought for having postulated the uniform grid of space on which a rational age plotted all activity within the universe. This empty, neutral world was first set before the scholarly reader in 1687, in Newton's *Philosophiae Naturalis Principia Mathematica*.[1] Two hundred years earlier, such a featureless world would have seemed strange indeed. Space (and time) had nodes at which spiritual forces intersected with earthly life. Space was not uniform but differentiated, with certain spots at which one was more likely to meet God, just as there were certain times when God was more likely to be present. Naturally, the Church had become the custodian of such times and places. Not that it could make them sacred by its fiat, but it was unavoidable that sacred days and sacred shrines should be managed by God's ministers.

Why did Newton's transformation seem convincing to his contemporaries? How did the English lose their way in a well-marked cosmos and begin to wander a pathless world? Historians have sought to trace such changes of thought to the internal development of philosophy and the genius of such as Newton. But in part this transformation was the result of more mundane changes—most notably Henry VIII's seizure of the Church's lands and shrines. These were acts that would change the sense of geography and history, and even of space. The seizure of the monastery lands was what the English first meant when they began to speak of "secularization."

Bernard Manning reminds us of the concrete nature of medieval worship, in which place could be so important.

It did not satisfy the medieval conscience to repent of pride; one must do something; one must study skulls. In the same way it was not sufficient to reverence
God, one must reverence His house. . . . It was not so much an attitude of mind
as a series of acts. To take off one's hat, to creep to the cross, to provide lights and
decorations—it was by such means that the laymen showed his reverence. The
holiness of a church consisted not it its atmosphere nor in its associations, but in
a definite number of holy things which it contained. It was holy not because it
was the place where prayer was wont to be made, but because it contained certain
objects used in prayer. And as reverence consisted in a number of definite acts, so
irreverence consisted in the omission of them—not in a general attitude of
mind.[2]

Thus, the place in which a prayer was said could be as important as the words
involved or the thought behind it. For example, there was debate over whether
prayers were more potent in church, or in Rome, or perhaps Palestine.[3] By the
end of our period Protestants had established the doctrine that God was everywhere, and nowhere.

Manning may have exaggerated the unimportance of atmosphere in the old
worship. In describing the shrine of St. Mary of Walsingham, Erasmus has a
character note that "There's very little light: only what comes from tapers, which
have a most pleasing scent. All this is appropriate to religion." And yet he goes
on to remark on the material accessories which were commonly associated with
worship: "Yes, and if you peered inside, Menedemus, you would say it is the
abode of the saints, so dazzling is it with jewels, gold, and silver." When one
character observes "a small image displayed, unimpressive in size, material, and
workmanship, but of surpassing power," another remarks that "Size has little to
do with producing miracles."[4] Where so much is made of physical elements in
worship, however they operate, spatial location had to be important.

There were several ways in which land had come into God's possession.
Sometimes it had been marked out by a miracle, and thereafter maintained as a
shrine. Sometimes it was given to the Church in exchange for perpetual prayers,
like the prayers of the Cistercians of Ford Abbey which preserved the Courtenay
family through their many difficulties.[5] Churchyards were hallowed by the bones
of ancestors. And within the sacred space of churches there were differences, for
the medieval church building was broken up architecturally, arguing several degrees of holiness and requiring an etiquette of approach to God. Proper worship
was a counterpoint of movement and restraint. As we shall see, the Reformation
would sweep out the screens which had heightened this sense of mystery to make
auditoriums for the Word of Faith.[6]

The amount of England's land which had been given to God was quite
staggering—perhaps 40 percent of Kent, for example.[7] The most vulnerable, in
Henry's view, was the endowment of England's monasteries. Historians cannot
confidently estimate the extent of the lands which had been donated for their
maintenance. Most commonly they suggest a figure of about one-sixth of all the

land in the country, though estimates have run as low as one-twentieth.[8] But we must also count the lands belonging to friaries and to chantries—the endowments for priests to say masses for the souls of donors and their families. All of these lands were seized by the state. Added to this were the exchanges of lands belonging to bishops for manors belonging to the crown, so that the total amount of Church land that changed hands between 1536 and the end of the century probably reached something over a quarter of all the land in England.[9]

No aspect of secularization could have been more obvious and dramatic than this activity. It did not only affect the rural wastes of England and the Cistercians' lonely sheep. The urban townscape was affected even more; perhaps two-thirds of the ground in medieval London had been owned by the Church.[10] Friaries, which had very few rural manors to support their personnel, had concentrated in the towns they served, and their buildings were seized in 1538.[11] While there was no general disendowment of the bishops, the Tudors ejected them from their great London palaces. By 1560 all of those in the Strand between the City and Westminster had become townhouses for Elizabeth's nobility.[12] Space which had once been connected with God's service and servants now lost that association.

In March of 1536 Lord Lisle sat nervously in ambassadorial exile in Calais reading the gossip from London which was all about the imminent fall of the monasteries. He showed no regret, nor did his correspondents, over this loss to the Church. His only regret was that he might miss sharing the spoils, and his letters over the next few years are filled with matter-of-fact discussion of how to wheedle the king out of "some old abbey in mine old days."[13] Historians have looked in vain for evidence that the more conservative and Catholic of Henry's nobles were more backward in touching the Lord's inheritance.[14] They have concluded that land evoked very little sense of the sacred.

It may be that they are looking in the wrong place. This was the class, after all, that was least able to resist the temptation which Henry was putting in their way. The Act of Dissolution in 1536 translated the matter into the language they knew best, specifying the Church's "manors, lordships, granges, meses, lands, tenements, meadows, pastures, rents, reversions, services, woods, . . . annuities, rights, entries, conditions, commons, leets, courts, liberties, privileges, and franchises and other hereditaments whatsoever" (27 Henry VIII, c. 28). Those lower on the social scale knew that, whatever happened, they would not share in those hereditaments, and one might expect a different reaction from them.

Actually, there is evidence of bad conscience even in the parliament which despoiled the Church. That act began with a violent and scarcely credible attack on the smaller monasteries which were to be the government's first victims. It accused the abbots themselves of destroying the churches and consuming the ornaments, wasting "their goods and chattels to the high displeasure of Almighty God," whereas Parliament only meant to convert them "to better uses." Indeed, former governments had been careful to use church properties for related purposes, as when Cardinal Wolsey applied monastic endowments to the founding of his colleges. But in 1532 a precedent was set for profaning them to entirely secular purposes, when Henry took the large house of the Augustinian Canons at Aldgate, London, for his private use.[15]

Thomas Cromwell had ascertained that the royal courts would allow church lands to escheat to the crown if the monasteries failed in their duties or if their numbers dwindled to insignificance, just as other feudal grantees might fail in point of military service. But he and Parliament still felt the need of scandal to justify this secularization. Thus we see, and not for the last time, the importance of a *religious* justification for attacking an aspect of religious culture. The pretense of diversion of this wealth to other pious uses was forgotten once it had served its purpose, but hypocrisy was the government's tribute to public opinion. Meanwhile, the king usually gave new owners a fixed time in which to destroy the monastic buildings, for fear of a campaign to restore monasticism. This sometimes involved using gunpowder to blast the central piers, which was a memorable experience.[16]

Those who did not expect to profit by the Lord's loss often expressed dismay. There were precedents for tampering with consecrated wealth, stretching back over centuries, but contemporaries did not have the benefit of our historical knowledge. Likewise, they may not have noted declining trends in the monasteries' activities or spirituality, for any decline was not general. In fact, some of the monasteries were in the midst of building programs, so that David Knowles speculates that "some of those who worked as young men on the masonry of these edifices may well have earned good wages for pulling them down."[17] In any event, there was some outcry. Naturally, the records of a hostile government are not a good place to look for such protests, but there are plenty of fugitive accounts of the shock at rumors of the seizure of land and goods, of altar cloths used for bedspreads, copes for saddle blankets, and chalices for carousing.[18] Some of the protests involved women and were not always nonviolent: at Exeter in 1536 a group of them attacked the royal commissioners' workmen with shovels and pikes, breaking down the door to St. Nicholas Priory to get at them. One man, working at the destruction of the rood loft, had to jump from the church tower to escape them. If we pass such episodes off as amusing it is because we lack their horror at sacrilege. The government did not take this resistance lightly and considered how to procede with least publicity.[19]

Taking God's property was a test of the strength of Tudor government. To see sacred utensils used for profane purposes or to see roods burned to melt roof leads went to the heart of medieval religion, as much as did a theological refutation of transubstantiation. The stripping of bells and lead from churches must have seemed especially ironic to those who guessed that they would be recast as cannon and shot for Henry's wars. The Elizabethan antiquary John Stow mentions three churches in London that were used to store war materials and plunder from those wars.[20]

On the other hand, it is often remarked how willing even the lower orders were to buy the monasteries' doors, pans, pavement stones, locks, tiles and whatnot at the derisive public auctions, or even to loot the premises themselves. It seems to argue a long-standing disrespect toward monastic religion which was finally given vent. No doubt there was a section of the population which felt this alienation and was fertile ground for Protestantism. But in the view of J. J. Scarisbrick, the disrespect may have been the result of the government's sacrilege rather than its cause.[21] People worship power, and contemporaries may have seen religion more in terms of power than we do. Their government had shown superior power, breaking a religious spell which often had as much to do with fear as with love. The king's agents had proved that God did not intend to defend his own and that the devil would take the hindmost. Scarisbrick makes a similar argument with reference to the monks and nuns who initially were dismayed at leaving the contemplative life: they "were walking out of a past not because they had been pining to do so for years but because it had suddenly become mentally and psychologically possible to do so." In any event, the stories of spontaneous looting, ahead of the official wreckers, seem to come from 1538 and later, when the procedure had become familiar.[22] Then too, some of those involved only wanted to keep holy things out of the government's hands; there are numerous accounts of vestments, silver, altar stones and holy water soups being brought out of hiding when Mary restored the old worship.[23]

There was also a noticeable reluctance among the new owners to use former churches for profane uses. For example, only a handful of the many monastic churches abandoned in London and York at the Reformation were used for mundane purpose; the more common practice was to convert them to parish churches or else to pull them down altogether.[24] Lawrence Stone mentions "a few of the bolder spirits" who did convert monastic churches to secular uses but alludes to many more who were content to use only the domestic buildings. He concludes that "Most held back, owing mainly to a natural reluctance to indulge in heavy capital expenditure on property which, if things went badly, might have to be restored to the monks, and partly also to superstitious fear of committing sacrilege by wining, dining, and making love on once holy ground."[25]

To be sure, we should not imagine that consecration had always brought a proper hush over the rude worshippers of medieval times. The Gothic St. Paul's Cathedral of Henry's day was a temple in desperate need of cleansing. On a given day, a dozen scribes sat ready to draw up legal papers for the merchants and lawyers who came there in search of business. The unemployed stood by, hoping to be hired. Services in the choir were carried on with some difficulty when they had to compete with noise from this marketplace.[26] But the public's familiarity with God's things—bound up with community use—was unlike the government's actions, which converted them to private use.

There is evidence of feeling for the land taken from the monasteries as well.

Scarisbrick presents the institution of lay rectors (who owned church lands, collected the tithes and appointed the clergy) as "one of the most remarkable and shocking results of the Henrician Reformation."[27] Robert Aske, a leader of the Pilgrimage of Grace, seemed shocked at the laity renting out church lands "for lucre and advantage to themselves." And Archbishop John Whitgift—certainly no Catholic—would lecture Queen Elizabeth on the sin of taking lands dedicated to God, warning of the curse that could be expected on their use.[28] Until the end of the seventeenth century there were published accounts of the providential punishments visited on those who had seized God's property.[29]

Sometimes it was argued that the holiness of the monasteries derived from the sanctity of the men and women who were buried in them. An Archbishop of York pled for Hexham on the grounds that "many holy men sometimes bishops there be in that church, saints of name."[30] Royal progenitors sanctified certain locations, as the abbot of Faversham reminded Cromwell:

> Christ forbid that ever I should so heinously offend and commit against Almighty God and the king's highness and sovereign lord, that by my means and consent, so godly and ancient a foundation builded and dedicated in the honour of Saint Saviour of so noble and victorious a prince and one of the king's most noble progenitors, whose very body, together with the bodies of his dear and well-beloved queen and also the prince his son [King Stephen, Mathilda, and Eustace of Boulogne], there lyeth buried in honourable sepulture.[31]

Henry was not deterred by the associations which lands or buildings had with saints.

He turned directly to this point in 1538 when he determined to eliminate all the shrines of saints that enjoyed any attraction for pilgrims—that is, any commercial appeal. Their wealth might as well be his. Again, historians have sometimes supposed that the decline in devotion to shrines was far advanced by Henry's time, but in fact, the fifteenth century saw a larger number of cult formations than previous ones.[32] Stanford Lehmberg could detect no general decline in the offerings given to shrines in England's cathedrals in the fifty years before the Reformation.[33] Donations and reported miracles had fallen markedly at some of England's older shrines, but whether that argues a decline of attendance at those shrines is uncertain. Among the new cults was that of Henry VI, who was a candidate for canonization with over three hundred miracles to his credit. The quarrel over his bones would decide whether Windsor or Westminster would establish a shrine that might rival Becket's.[34] Henry VIII had worshipped at the shrines of St. Thomas of Canterbury and Our Lady of Walsingham a matter of months before ordering their treasures swept into his bag, showing the suddenness of his assault.[35]

Henry's attack on these shrines was perhaps his bravest act. He must have known that the murder of Archbishop Simon of Sudbury in the Peasant's Revolt and John Wyclif's mortal stroke were associated with the fact that they had belittled Becket.[36] And in attacking Canterbury's shrine Henry was insulting his fellow monarchs as well. For almost every king since Henry II had visited the shrine, and guides were happy to show not only the relics of Thomas and twelve other saints but also the jewels donated by kings of many countries.[37] It was a demonstration of how God's approval would bring worldly honor as well. Notwithstanding this, soon after St. Thomas was pronounced a traitor Henry's subjects noticed him wearing the most famous gem from the shrine, the "Regale of France," in a ring on his thumb. Twenty-six cartloads of loot rumbled off to Westminster, and the healing powers claimed for the well at Canterbury ceased immediately.[38]

Henry's bravado was strangely mixed with caution. Cromwell instructed his agents to remove shrine statues "as secretly as might be," for fear of popular wrath. When it was impossible to proceed in secrecy, Henry's commissioners turned the accusation of greed against the custodians, claiming that they were only using shrines to raise money from gullible pilgrims. One commissioner wrote back that he was careful to throw out all "the rotten bones that be called relics; which we may not omit, lest it should be thought we came more for the treasure than for the avoiding of the abomination of idolatry."[39]

In this atmosphere the discovery of a genuine fraud was a godsend. It fell to Geoffrey Chamber to send the tidings of the Rood of Boxley to Cromwell in February of 1538.

> This shall be to advertise the same that upon the defacing of the late monastery of Boxley, and plucking down of the images of the same, I found in the image of the Rood called the Rood of Grace, the which heretofore hath been held in great veneration of people, certain engines and old wire with old rotten sticks in the back of the same, that did cause the eyes of the same to move and stare in the head thereof like unto a living thing; and also the nether lip in likewise to move as though it should speak. . . . Further, when I had seen this strange sight, and considering that the inhabitants of the county of Kent had in times past a great devotion to the same, and to use continual pilgrimage thither, by the advice of others that were with me, [I] did convey the said image unto Maidstone this present Thursday, then being the market day, and in the chief of the market time, did show it openly unto all the people there being present, to see the false, crafty, and subtle handling thereof, to the dishonour of God, ard illusion of the said people, who I daresay, that if in case the said monastery were to be defaced again, the King's Grace not offended, they would either pluck it down to the ground, or else burn it, for they have the said matter in wondrous detestation, and hatred.[40]

Thereafter it was easier to counter the argument of government greed.

Pilgrimage to sacred localities did not die out just because shrines were levelled and wonder-working images broken up. For example, Edward VI's council found that it had to fence off the baths and wells at Buxton to keep pilgrims from continuing to seek miraculous cures there.[41] Devotion to these springs was per-haps older than Christianity, though by now it was associated with the Church; at least seventy-five wells in Wales were named for Mary.[42] These natural sites now had to compensate for the loss of saints' shrines. Sacred trees associated with local saints still had to be chopped down as late as Elizabeth's reign.[43]

Historians have either lamented all of this as making England less picturesque or have approved it as progress in religious sophistication. But we should not miss the point that it was the end of a polycentric if not polytheistic religion.[44] Medi-eval English men and women did not venerate a single Virgin Mary, who could be approached in spirit from anywhere on earth. Rather, there were various Marys who had to be worshipped at different shrines. Pilgrims argued over which one was more efficacious for a particular request. Individuals asked to be buried near certain paintings of Mary, willed money to particular images of Mary and some-times to several different ones. Likewise, worshippers addressed prayers to par-ticular roods and not generally to Christ's cross.[45] Oblations were made to certain popular roods like the one in Billingsgate Ward, which was found smashed one morning in 1538.[46] As Erasmus put it, people thought that "different things are bestowed in different places."[47]

Protestants treated this duplication as absurd, since they understood Christian-ity to be monotheistic. But Paul Tillich has suggested that this unqualified mono-theism would promote secularization. A monotheistic cult tends to reify a diffuse "divine power" into a being who is an object—of contemplation, discussion, perhaps rejection. God had been all this for theologians before, but now became an object even for simple believers.[48] The focus of faith was becoming a being, rather than the divine presence in the world.

Having seized the lands of the monastic clergy, Henry found a way to expro-priate the lands held by the non-monastic or "secular" clergy as well, or at least to loosen their grip on it. In 1536 he began requiring bishops to yield up the London palaces which were symbolic of their former political power, promising to compen-sate them with assets of equal value. By the end of his reign 187 ecclesiastical manors had been traded for others which were found to be noticeably inferior. His heirs Edward and Elizabeth continued this process, lowering the bishops to a level more commensurate with their reduced activities and status. The bishopric of Bath and Wells, for example, was reduced from twenty-four manors to only seven. The properties of dean's chapters and university colleges were subject to the same pressures.[49] Whether the estates lost any sanctity in this process may be doubted, but the bishops certainly lost local influence by these exchanges, at a time when land was power, wealth, and status.

After all of this activity, in the 1570s, Christopher Saxton produced a series of printed county maps which began a new age in England's secular self-awareness. Those maps went far beyond the older coastal or military surveys, in plotting out what had become a new country. The old landmarks—the paths of pilgrimage, the shrines that had tapped into grace and health, the monasteries that sheltered travellers and beggars—did not appear on these maps.[50] Saxton's work was made possible by the rise of professional surveying in the 1550s, which in turn was the result of the needs of a new crop of landowners—those holding the plunder from the Church. The public showed a remarkable aesthetic appreciation for England's secular topography. The gentry were so taken with the new perspective that they covered their walls with tapestry maps, complete with grid lines, and bought playing cards with the fifty-two English and Welsh counties on the backs.[51] For them, it would be a short step to Newton's abstract space—all made possible by the barter in church lands.

Disappearance of the sacred landmarks soon had an effect on the notion of time. Monastery ruins helped create an historical consciousness, a sense of a break with the past. Several authors, like Shakespeare, were touched by the sight of the "bare ruined choirs" which Henry left. John Webster expressed the sense of secular change most strikingly, in *The Duchess of Malfi* (1613?):

> I do love these ancient ruins:
> We never tread upon them but we set
> Our foot upon some reverend history.
> And questionless, here in this open court,
> Which now lies naked to the injuries
> Of stormy weather, some men lie interr'd
> Lov'd the church so well, and gave so largely to't
> They thought it should have canopy'd their bones
> Till doomsday; but all things have their end:
> Churches and cities, which have diseases like to men,
> Must have like death that we have. (V, iii, 9–19)

Secularization cannot be described more clearly than that. Such an awareness of the past as irrevocably gone is a major characteristic of secularity, the concentration on the present age (or *saeculum*), the temporal rather than the eternal. Abbey ruins were the most obvious reminders of the passing of an entire age.[52]

The most dramatic opposition to this secularization of land was the Pilgrimage of Grace (1536), which was the greatest domestic threat that any Tudor government faced. Historians debate the causes of this episode, and it is possible to emphasize political and economic factors over religious outrage. The government itself preferred an economic interpretation, since that would cast blame on local owners rather than central authorities.[53] But the timing of the risings indicates that the religious issue was more immediate and may at least have been the catalyst.[54] The first item among the York Articles, for instance, was "the suppression of so many religiouse howses." Whether or not that was the rebels' deepest grievance, they apparently thought it was the least controversial, the one that would most easily unite their disparate forces. It may be more important to know that the dissolution was their best propaganda point than to know their basic motive. In the next list of articles, from Pontefract, they added other religious grievances: the lay supremacy over the Church, the countenance of foreign heresies, diversion of church taxes, attacks on the right of sanctuary and on clerical immunity.[55]

When the rebel leader, Robert Aske, was interrogated he began with the suppression of the monasteries, while showing how the Church was involved with economic, political, and social life more generally.

> To the statut of subpressions, he dyd gruge ayenst the same and so did al the holl [north] contrey, because the abbeys in the north parts gaf great almons to pour men and laudable servyd God; in which partes of lait dais they had but smal comforth by gostly [spiritual] teching. And by occasion of the said suppression, the devyn service of almightie God is much minished, greate nomber of messes unsaid, and the blissed consecracion of the sacrement now not used and showed in thos places, to the distreas of the faith and sperituall comforth to man soull, the temple of God russed and pulled down, the ornamentes and releques of the church of God unreverent used, the townes [tombs?] and sepuleres of honorable and noble men pulled down and sold, non hospitalite now in thos places kept, but the fermers for the most parte lettes and taverns out the fermes of the same houses to other fermers, for lucre and advauntage to them selfes. And the profites of thies abbeys yerley goith out of the contrey [county] to the Kinges highnes, so that in short space little money, by occasion of the said yerly rentes, tents, and furst frutes, should be left in the said country, in consideracion of the absens of the Kinges highness in those partes, want of his lawes, and the frequentacion of merchandisse. Also diverse and many of the said abbeys wer in the montaigns and desert places wher the people be rud of condyccions and not well taught the law of God; and when the said abbeys stud, the said peuple not only had worldly refreshing in their bodies but also sperituall refuge both by gostly liffing of them and also by speritual informacion, and preching; and many ther tenaunds wer ther feed servanunds to them and serving men, wel socored by abbeys; and now not only these tenauntes and servauntes wantes refresshing ther, both of meat, cloth, and wages, and knoweth not now wher to have any liffing, but also strangers and baggers of corn. . . . Also the abbeys was on of the bewties of this realme to al men and strangers passing threw the same; also al gentilmen much socored in their nedes with money [loans?], their yong sons ther socored, and in nonries ther doughters brought up in virtuee; and also ther evidenses [legal documents] and mony left to the uses of infantes in abbeys handes, alwas sure ther; and such abbeys as wer ner the danger of see banks, great mayntenours of see wals and dykes, mayntenours and bilders of briges and heghwais, such other thinges for the comyn welth.[56]

In light of the seriousness of this rising, Parliament never passed a second act of dissolution to deal with the larger monasteries. Rather, it was found that the courts would accept the voluntary surrender of these perpetual corporations by the present occupants. The law which passed in 1540 (31 Henry VIII, c. 13) was only to assure prospective owners that their title would be legal.[57] Nor was there ever a law abolishing monastic orders; having praised the larger monasteries in the earlier act—by contrast with the supposed delinquency of the small houses—the government could not reverse itself so speedily. In the end a few abbots had to be executed for the "treason" of not surrendering their abbeys; treason had been found to be a legal ground for forfeiting abbey property as well as lay fiefs.[58]

Long after these disturbances thoughtful persons continued to doubt the crown's right to deal thus with ecclesiastical property, as seen in the popular publications of the historian Sir Henry Spelman. His grandfather, Sir John Spelman, was one of the judges at the trials of Cardinal John Fisher and Sir Thomas More and had been rewarded with some of the monastic spoils. The grandson experienced such difficulties with this tainted inheritance that he became convinced that God's curse still attached to it, restored the lands to the Church of England, and published his thoughts on the issue in *De non temerandis Ecclesiis; Churches not to be Violated* (1613). In arguing the sanctity of temples, Spelman used examples from pagan history and appealed to natural law as well as Scripture.[59] Apparently even pagans had been taught not to profane the things of God.

Pagans were easier to convince than Puritans, who had read Christ's words, that God was indifferent to the locale of worship and sought those who would worship Him in spirit. They liked to assert that Jeremiah worshipped God in a dungeon and Job on a dunghill. And in their eagerness that the word *ecclesia* be understood to mean the congregation of the faithful, the most radical of them spoke disparagingly of church buildings as "steeple houses."[60] John Knox even suggested that all medieval churches might have to be destroyed because of superstitious associations. As he put it, sometimes the only way to get rid of rooks is to knock down their nests.[61] So Spelman had to argue indirectly from the Puritans' sabbatarianism, since without consecrated buildings "the place appointed to the public sanctification thereof" would be lacking.[62]

It was a weak argument, and Spelman soon turned to something more telling—the providential history of sacrilege. From a lifetime of historical study, he had culled examples of God's judgments on trespassers. In 1646, when Parliament was considering a nationalization of cathedral property (the deans' and chapters' lands), his son Clement used those examples in a republication of the earlier work. There were grisly stories of the mishaps of greedy monarchs from William the Conqueror onward; three of William's children, for instance, had died in the New Forest, in which William had razed dozens of churches. His son, the notorious William Rufus, was felled on the very spot where a church had stood. Quicksand had swallowed King John's loot from Peterborough and Croyland abbeys. The string of such unmistakable judgments came down to Henry VIII's time, when Wolsey and all six of his agents in diverting the wealth of convents to his colleges had come to bad ends. It did not matter to the Protestant

Spelman that Wolsey's support of education could be contrasted with a superstitious monasticism; God's revenge was as inexorable as a natural law. Henry VIII's line had died out with his three children. And Thomas Cromwell and the duke of Somerset, though pious Protestants, had defaced churches and died under laws that they themselves had sponsored. In short, Spelman thought he had practical proof that *"a statute directly against the Law of God, is void."* This unsecular assertion was, he claimed, a common principle of the law books.[63]

In Spelman's view, the whole history of sixteenth-century England was overshadowed by the nation's sacrilegious offense. Rebellions, diplomatic reverses, military defeat and famine had all come in its wake. So long as the monasteries stood, he claimed, England had no need of poorhouses or poor rates. The tax burden was not lessened by seizing them, and none of the promised social benefits had materialized. Henry had not profited from his theft, but died with the disgrace of a coinage made of copper, tin, even leather, and ended with a *smaller* royal desmesne. The Civil Wars, of course, were the ultimate national disaster and therefore argued some "general and National sin."[64]

Spelman's original work caused sufficient stir that two more editions were published in 1616, and *An Apology of the Treatise De non temerandis Ecclesiis* appeared in 1646. Clement Spelman's much-expanded edition of the original treatise (also in 1646) needed reprinting in 1668, 1676, and 1704. Seven editions within a century represent a degree of popularity very uncommon for works which were neither fictional nor devotional—probably more than four thousand copies for the 16,000 gentry households to which the work was directed.[65] Later editions claimed that the original work had convinced a few of the gentry to restore lands to the Church.[66] Indeed, the subject was so explosive that the posthumous publication of Spelman's *History and Fate of Sacrilege* was delayed until 1698 for fear that "the Publication of it should give Offense to the Nobility and Gentry." Presumably, by that date there was no longer much chance that it would achieve its purpose of increasing "the Terror of Evil Doers."[67]

The unrecognized irony of Spelman's work was in the novel way that he marshalled his evidence. For the study was a pioneering effort in statistical history, representing a mode of thought not usually thought congenial to a religious or even a humanistic mentality. Spelman taught his readers to be scientific even in tracing God's Providence. Some of his statements go unsupported: "within Twentie years next after the Dissolution, more of our Nobility and their Children have been attainted, and dyed under the sword of Justice, then did from the Conquest to the Dissolution, being almost five hundred years." But others bore the precise figures: of 260 recipients of monastery lands "in one part of England," fewer than sixty had sons to inherit from them.[68] Within a twelve-mile radius in his own county of Norfolk only two of about twenty monastic estates were still in the families of their original purchasers, while the rest had turned over three, four, even six times. By contrast, the twenty-four non-monastic estates in the area continued in their pre-Reformation families.[69] Such scholarship could only encourage the kind of secularization which replaces "Thus saith the Lord" with "Studies show . . . . "

Spelman admitted that horror over Henry's profanation was evaporating in the seventeenth century. The first generation after the dissolution, he wrote, was afraid to use the buildings which fell into its hands. Later generations had to be told why they were having such bad luck, why buildings made of church stone tended to fall down.[70] They had to be told why church bells, now scorned because of earlier superstitious use in exorcism, had a habit of sinking in the harbor as they were shipped abroad, taking ships down with them.[71] Spelman's sense of England's decline may be seen more widely in the popular myth of the monks as more generous landlords. While historians cannot find evidence that monasteries differed from lay landlords, the view had a long currency. Perhaps the fact that the dissolution came before the worst of the sixteenth-century inflation encouraged this nostalgia for a "merrie England" of yore.[72]

Reformation changes in the use of space within churches might well strike us as a sacralization of those buildings, rather than a secularization. Churches had formerly been used for many activities that now had to find new homes: feasting, dancing, councils, courts, elections, shelter for travellers, schools, and the "incubation" of those awaiting cures or visions.[73] But while this fits our notions of a growing "spirituality" of religion, the activities which were displaced were losing their connection with religion as it had been known.

Sanctuary was the most notorious of these. Sanctuary for crime or debt was a special provocation to the state. In a rougher age it had been a notable triumph of the Church to be allowed to shelter offenders until they could be delivered to the proper authorities or abjure the realm, or even to house them permanently in a kind of monastic imprisonment. This right was granted in deference to the saints whose relics graced the particular church, and it was supposed to have a "penitentiary" aspect. More than three hundred individuals fled to sanctuary in Durham cathedral between 1464 and 1524.[74] Political refugees sought out churches during the Wars of the Roses. Their rights were generally respected by enemies who may have feared that they would need similar protection one day.[75]

Sanctuary had sometimes been violated in the Middle Ages, most notably in the case of Thomas Becket. But Henry II had paid dearly for that offense, having to give up plans to do away with the right of sanctuary and other aspects of the Church's jurisdiction. Monarchs as late as Henry VII had felt constrained to apologize publicly for occasional violations, promising that they did not constitute a precedent. In the case of Perkin Warbeck, Henry restrained himself from such violation, not wanting to appear less pious than Richard III, who had long honored the sanctuary of Westminster Abbey in the case of young Richard of York and his mother.[76]

But sanctuary was coming to seem a greater offense to the more orderly state of the sixteenth century. St. Martin le Grand in London had become a refuge for unrepentant debtors and swindlers, so that any association with penance or mercy seemed strained. Even before the Reformation, judges had whittled away at the right, on the grounds that it ought to derive from some royal grant.[77] Henry VIII and Cromwell marked sanctuary for elimination as they were ending other independent jurisdictions in England, and a series of laws of 1529–40 saw sanctuary virtually disappear. King Edward's regent, Protector Somerset, generously reinstated some of the older rights, but St. Martin's itself was pulled down at that time (to make room for a tavern). By Mary's reign there was no question of a right of sanctuary in criminal processes, so that the remaining issue concerned debt. Such civil matters did not greatly concern the state, and thus the statutes necessary to end the last vestiges of sanctuary waited until 1723.[78] We must assume, however, that this connection of space with God's mercy had faded much earlier.

The decline of the Church's visual presence in England was rapid after 1530. John Stow's contemporary survey of Elizabethan London is very largely a discussion of the commerce in churches and abbeys. This seems to have been a matter of sadness to him, as he wryly reports instances such as the area around Clarke's Well, once famous for mystery plays and now used for wrestling exhibitions.[79] The number of churches in England declined dramatically, especially relative to the size of the population. This was especially true in cities, where churches had dominated the environment even more than in the countryside. Stow could list 125 churches in a London of something like 150,000 souls. A survey of London in 1738 when the population was close to 650,000 lists 134 Anglican churches and 98 Dissenting chapels available for public, English-language services.[80] That translates into a rise from a very crowded 1,200 souls per church to a wholly unrealistic 2,800.

Ironically, a consideration of accommodation for worshippers should have been growing in importance. To the medieval mind it was irrelevant that England was oversupplied with churches. Churches honored God just by their presence and were built as good works, with little regard to need. In discussing cathedrals, Stanford Lehmberg notes that "Cathedral services were sung mainly for the glory of God, not the edification of man." There was some debate over whether the laity was even welcome at cathedral services.[81] Church dimensions had been dictated more by the requirements of occasional processions than by the size of a regular congregation.

The Reformation raised the utilitarian issue of accommodation that we assume without question. Consequently, at first the redundant churches were allowed to fall down by the hundreds. In his study of philanthropy, W. K. Jordan recorded the building or rebuilding of 123 churches in the ten counties he studied over the period 1480–1660. Incidentally, and less systematically, he noted 306 parish churches which were destroyed or abandoned in the same period. Since most of the former number were merely rebuildings, it appears that the net loss was substantial.[82] It would be in Sir Christopher Wren's time, after 150 years of Reformation, that the nation belatedly recognized its need.

At that point, a redesign of churches showed the irrelevance of spatial considerations to new ideas of worship. Medieval religion involved space and movement within space, most notably in the form of pilgrimage and procession. Historians tend to treat these merely as colorful elaborations of worship rather than an essential part of one's approach to the holy. But they were a counterpart to the fencing off of sacred spaces within churches. The debate that Lehmberg noted regarding the use of cathedrals had concerned the desire of city fathers to insist on a place in sacred procession. Something very different was going on by 1562, when Canterbury Cathedral purchased an hourglass for its pulpit. By that time some cathedrals were providing as many as 170 sermons and lectures a year, for worshippers who came to listen rather than perform.[83]

When churches again began to be built, by Wren and his disciples, they embodied a new understanding of space and worship. Care had once been taken to design interiors in which God would be approached at a proper pace by priests and penitents. Forbidden areas were what the laity expected in the presence of their Maker. The new churches looked different; they were auditoriums, in which the space was to be filled with the preacher's voice. Sightlines were cleared so that one could see, and be seen. Pews dividing social classes replaced the screens that had separated priests and worshippers. Communion elements might be passed among the congregation.

When Archbishop Laud saw Puritans sitting while the things of God were delivered to them, it was too much to bear. But he found that government could not undo what it had done. Legislation and extortion and crowbars had transformed sacred space into a wasteland. The profanation of monastic buildings and ecclesiastical manors, the destruction of shrines and churches, were the earliest and most rapid forms of secularization. Popular reaction was formidable but short-lived, for the nation seemed to learn very quickly that there was a world of difference between the polycentrism of the old worship and a transcendent monotheism. And if Newton were not directly inspired to project the grid of this secular space into God's own heaven, less sophisticated persons found themselves receptive to this sense of things.

3

The Secularization
of Time and Play

Historians have had to abandon their assumption of the uniformity of time when dealing with early modern societies. We learn, rather, to think of our ancestors as living—or just existing—from one holiday festival to the next. Whatever else the "work ethic" may mean, it has made us think of the hours spent at work as more real than holidays. This has taken a revolution in thinking, and the revolution had happened in England by 1739. That was the year that a puzzled Thomas Gray described his experience in Italy: "Carnival lasts only from Christmas to Lent; one half of the remaining part of the year is passed in remembering the last, the other in expecting the future Carnival."[1] Like Gray, we are offended at the thought of peasants gorging and swilling at certain times instead of spreading their meager provisions and pleasures more evenly through the year. But it was not just that they lacked the means of preserving food: holiday, with its excess and entertainment, arrested work time much as eternity suspends the temporal. Inebriation was a foretaste of heaven.

"Time" is not something given in nature but is defined by cultures. Generally speaking, there are two approaches to the subject—time seen as repetition and time as irreversible direction.[2] The former is commonly associated with religion, the latter with a secular perspective. The temporal as development gives its name (secularis) to "secularization," while a concentration on its opposite, the timeless (aeternus), seems essential to most religions. Time comes late in the order of creation; eternity is the primordial state. Experience of the holy often involves a stillness which suspends time. Ritual reenactment is a way of recapturing the eternal, working against the current of historical direction.

There is even some time reversal in religious redemption, when lost time or action is redeemed.

Christianity is unusual in its historical sense, seeing God's plan unfolding in time, through stages or "dispensations." Different forms of Christianity find different points of balance between sacramental or mystical invocations of the eternal and faith in an unfolding Providence. But in general it tolerates a greater tension between the eternal and the temporal than is characteristic of most religious cultures. The risk is that this tension might dissolve in an entire immersion in the mundane, neglecting any sense of spiritual depth.

The medieval mentality had compromised Christianity's historical sense. For example, it found correspondences between historical epochs and the "ages of man" or the days of creation. Such correspondences created a static religious outlook rather than an expectant and historical faith.[3] Protestantism shifted the emphasis toward a directed history, from the sacramentalism of a religious culture toward a pilgrim's faith. Protestants even redefined the sacraments, as reminders—and therefore historical—rather than reenactments. The time sense could not have been more different.

Before the Reformation, holy days set the pattern of time and were when the community felt most alive. Good Friday and Easter marked the annual recreation of God's good world; St. Stephen's Day was the time for letting horses' blood.[4] There was a time and season for everything, and the Church knew when it was. This was a part of medieval religion that meant more to the populace than to the clerical elite. From the thirteenth century, at least, the clergy had complained that holy days had multiplied without regard for true, spiritual observance. Catholic reformers, such as Erasmus and More, wanted a reduction of holidays, which they thought were bringing religion into disrepute.[5] Like Protestants, they ranked the ethical and the expressive elements of religion differently than did the public, and showed a preference for work time over play.

But whatever More's objections to the pagan survivals and Bacchanalian associations of saints' days, he objected even more strenuously to William Tyndale's dismissal of the whole notion of a sacred time. In their famous debate, the Protestant Tyndale went so far as to say that any day of the week could serve as the "Lord's Day." He would accept a ten-day week and two Sabbaths! After all, the only reason for such an observance was to have a time to teach religion and duty. Or, England could do without holy days altogether "yf the people myght be taught wythout yt." After all, Jesus' reported impatience with the law of the Sabbath showed that its sacred character had never been intrinsic but was only a convention. More treated such teaching as the height of impiety, an "abhomynable blasphemy" of "the deuyls ape."[6]

The government sided with Tyndale. A petition of the House of Commons in 1532 asked Henry to reduce the number of holy days (especially during harvest) and to curb the wantonness of their celebration. There is nothing suspicious in this association of piety and thrift. Surely God would not want crops to spoil and people to go hungry for the sake of religious observances with so poor a pedigree. But Henry's bishops dragged their feet. They agreed that it was a shame if holidays were accompanied by gross offenses, but some of the saints honored during harvest were too holy to be slighted in such a way. They argued that these holidays were "incorporated in the law," not recognizing that laws governing religion were now matter for debate.[7]

Henry's more Protestant bishops, Hugh Latimer, Thomas Cranmer, and Nicholas Ridley, endorsed the view that the choice of which days to set aside for worship was a matter of indifference, none having an intrinsically holy character.[8] And in 1539 a revision of the liturgy saw the number of saints invoked in public worship fall from fifty-eight to thirty-eight. The first part of the liturgy to appear in English—the *Litany* of 1544—mentioned the saints only as a group.[9] When the Council began regulating saints' days in 1541 they treated this as an administrative reform, not bothering to invoke the royal supremacy. Things were moved about quite freely; a proclamation of 22 July 1541 changed St. Mark's Day from a fast to a feast.

The government did observe some limits while scrambling the sacred calendar. Edward's parliament declared that "all dayes and tyɪ ɪes consydered arr Godds creatures [creations] and all of lyke holiness" (5 & 6 Edw. VI, c. 3). In other words, since holy days were not designated in Scripture they could be chosen arbitrarily by the "rulers and ministers" whom God had set over the Church. But in fact the twenty-seven holidays which the act did allow (besides Sundays) were chosen from among the traditional holy days; Parliament did not take it upon itself to create *de novo*. And to show that habits died hard, Parliament continued to use the Church's calendar in its statutes, stipulating that one was to take effect "from the feast of Easter next coming" and another to last until the nativity of St. John the Baptist, or that a fiscal year was to end on Michaelmas.[10] One official, Richard Morison, suggested an annual holiday in celebration of Henry's triumph over the pope, with bonfires, parades, feasts, and prayers—like Passover in its commemoration of deliverance from bondage. He thought it would give people a good chance to mock monks, nuns, and friars, instead of celebrating Robin Hood and the forces of lawlessness. The proposal died for lack of a second.[11]

But the public tried to incorporate reformation within its calendar of play. By 1539 some village festivals included follies attacking the pope.[12] At first glance this seems like the old rituals of inversion, when religious things were mocked at certain times which were themselves sacred. The difference is that the new antireligious observances did not mark a momentary inversion but were to represent the constant sentiments of society. So there was a shift toward the more linear treatment of time despite traditionalism.

Mary's Catholic restoration tried to create an authentically religious holy day on November 30, in commemoration of the reestablishment of papal supremacy in 1554. But this "Feast of Reconciliation" sank into oblivion with the queen's death.[13] Puritans were likewise unsuccessful in promoting certain times and seasons in their enthusiasm for an irregular rhythm of fasts. Works such as Thomas Becon's *A Fruitful Treatise of Fasting* (1552) apparently stimulated a scattering of public fasts in localities distressed by famine, fire, drought, or plague. And in 1581 Paul Wentworth proposed a national fast in view of England's perilous circumstances—the Catholic invasion of Ireland, Spain's resurgence, the plight of the Netherlands, and the infiltration of Jesuit plotters. His motion passed the House of Commons, but Elizabeth, ever jealous of her authority in religion, summoned the Speaker to indicate her displeasure. James I was found to have no objection to parliamentary fasts, however, and in his son's reign the practice of opening each session of Parliament with a fast became established practice. It was entirely natural, therefore, that the Long Parliament would begin with a motion for a general fast, and all through the wars Royalists and Roundheads deployed fasts against each other.[14]

Puritans did have some success in bringing the country with them in a new Sabbatarianism. This would mark a sacred rhythm in the week, even as it was being lost in the year. In time, tradition would hallow the English Sunday. John Milton is credited with the wry observation that preaching and sitting still on Sunday had become the religion of England.[15] Already in the 1630s English tourists in Holland registered shock at the lack of respect shown to that day by their Protestant coreligionists. France, of course, was worse.[16] It is this shock—like the shock at blasphemy—that suggests a sacralization. But it was not universal in English society; a truly Puritan Sabbath observance divided the country rather than creating a new cultural unity. It became one of those peculiarities which pushed Puritans to the margins of society.

To the extent that Sunday observance did catch on, it also had something to do with economic factors. England's economic development required a greater regularity in its work schedule than the Church's calendar had allowed.[17] The inverse of a hallowed Sabbath was a profane work week. In their discussions of Sabbath observance Puritans often took occasion to preach the duty of work on the other six days.[18] This does not mean that their eye was only on the maximizing of profits; it was the "play element of culture" that they opposed.[19] Puritanism was an experiment in seriousness, breaking free of indulgences which now seemed childish. Philip Stubbes expressed it simply: "Any exercise which withdraweth us from godlines, either upon the sabaoth, or any other day els, is wicked and to be forbiden."[20] So the new Protestant rhythm was pitted against any notion of inversion or play.

Religious festivals had given the English their main occasions for play. Play is by definition the opposite of economic activity, being any practice that is obviously, even ostentatiously, noninstrumental. Medieval religion had mildly encouraged play and the comic since these were reminders of the transience of this world and its mundane concerns. The more strenuous Protestants saw no need to relax a sense of duty. They did not recognize that work without the relief of play would lose its relative character and absolutize itself. Thus, ironically, work became an essentially profane activity.

The play involved in ritual inversion was often blasphemous, as the Puritans pointed out, but the medieval Church had allowed it and even presided over it, trusting that it suited a paradoxical human nature. Even a priest such as John Lydgate, who was horrified at the thought of translating the liturgy into English, could write a parody of the Mass and address it to Cupid.[21] But Protestants did not see any useful purpose served by the ritual profanation of sacred names and things. As Peter Burke remarks, "The theologians could not see the difference between a mock baptism and a mockery of baptism."[22] Stubbes viewed the holiday tradition of designating Lords of Misrule as nothing less than devil worship.[23]

As Puritans gained their point, the only way to assert the rights of doubt or comic inversion was to maintain an unbelief fully as serious as the Puritans' belief. So England lost the knack of handling profanity within a religious context. All profanity and blasphemy then took place in "real time" rather than in ritual or play, and therefore presented a greater threat to religion.

The Puritans' success against holidays was remarkable, given the fact that they were opposing some of life's greatest pleasures. Christmas itself required a resuscitation after their efforts. Christmas had once been a focus for all kinds of play. It was the main occasion for children's participation in the community, through a variety of activities between St. Nicholas' Day (December 6) and Holy Innocents' (December 28). Some villages held their football game on Christmas, and gambling (a notably noneconomic activity) reached its height at that time. Theatrical activity was most active then, including Christmas masques at court.[24] But Puritan opposition could not be ignored. It invited caricature, as when Ben Jonson in *The Alchemist* (1610) has the puritanical Ananias correct someone who had spoken of Christmas: "Christ-tide, I pray you." As another pamphleteer analyzed the theological objections to Christmas: "Plum broth [pudding] was Popish, and mincepie—oh, that was sheer idolatry!"[25] A religion that enjoys the security of humility can afford to laugh at itself; one that makes an issue of humor will only be laughed at by others.

Some of the Puritans' opponents became just as grimly purposeful in their attitudes. Archbishop Laud could not simply laugh off their opposition, and an insistence on holidays became part of his dogged campaign to revive religious culture. He also attacked the more rigorous proponents of Sabbatarianism, seeing it as an issue of episcopal authority.[26] Numerous books, plays and satires were published on the subject of holiday celebration during the 1640s, creating cultural conflict. Local scuffles spoiled holiday celebrations, showing conflict at a lower, emotional level. Finally, it appeared that the Puritans would have the last, harsh laugh when it was rumored that Charles I's trial would start on Christmas Day.[27]

With Puritans in power, time was managed politically and viewed historically. In August of 1642 Parliament established a monthly fast for the last Wednesday of each month, dedicated to prayer for the situation in Ireland. As this situation did not improve, the fast became a regular observance. (This was the law that brought the regime directly up against Christmas, which fell on the last Wednesday of 1644.[28]) Parliament's fasts commemorated some historical event or expressed a concern over the nation's future. Thus they encouraged an historical sense and directed attention to a providential plan, a "Deuteronomic" view of history which implied that England was the new instrument of God's will.[29]

National fasts were meant to draw society into a sense of this historic mission. The campaign would involve seeing all of time as religious and not just certain points during the year. But efforts to sacralize all of time must necessarily fail. Counting every day as holy means that none is really special; total sacralization can seem the same as secularization. Moreover, by 1649 Parliament admitted the failure of its fasts to capture the imagination of the country: Wednesday fasts were "in most places of this Commonwealth wholly neglected." The regime was tempted to abolish the fast in order to avoid profane attacks upon it, but decided instead to authorize an additional fast day to repent the violations of the old one. Puritans never learned how to promote their solemn fasts or their even more "solemn thanksgivings."[30]

Still, as Dennis Brailsford has shown, the anti-Puritan Restoration could no more bring back the old spirit of community celebration than the Puritans could enforce a new religious consciousness of time. Sports and play revived, but without any authentic religious associations.[31] And while the Puritans had promoted both the uniformity of time seen in the modern work-week and the religious rhythm of the "English Sunday," the shifting balance can be seen in the lowly almanac. Those of the sixteenth century had included lists of good and evil (or lucky and unlucky) days, which were said to have been revealed by an angel to Joseph, or perhaps Job. These lists disappeared in the following century, on the grounds that "their Maker made them [i.e., days] all alike."[32] It is a Puritan sentiment.

While the observance of a sacred time was under debate the English state saw an opportunity to nationalize time. Just as religious holidays were declining, national holidays were declared and achieved some measure of popularity. The practice of festival—the suspension of time in order to celebrate society's deeper existence—was sponsored by the state in a wholly secular context. Like holy days, these national holidays were meant to heighten the individual's spiritual participation, but in the nation's history rather than in eternal verities.

Queen Elizabeth's Accession Day (November 17) was the first to generate such spontaneous enthusiasm among the public as to be maintained even after the monarch's death. The nation's choice was significant. Elizabeth seems to have been Protestant especially in the negative sense of that term, so it should not surprise us that her accession day should have been primarily an anti-Catholic observance. The first records of its celebration date from the Rising of the Northern Earls and Elizabeth's excommunication in 1569–70. Bonfires and fireworks were lit in defiance of Pope Pius V and England's recusants. Bell ringing, which had been frowned on for its associations with popish conjuring (especially in warding off storms), was revived for this nationalistic celebration—showing that even bells could be secularized.

Catholics and Puritans alike complained that the celebrations exalted Elizabeth to the position of a goddess or the Virgin Mary, and historians suspect that this was entirely deliberate on the part of her council. Tournaments and courtly entertainments were performed within "an eschatological framework in which she assumes the dimensions of a ruler of the Last Days, whose virtues alone hold back the reign of Antichrist."[33] Catholics were disturbed that antiphons were sung to the queen in that day's service, and that St. Hugh of Lincoln had lost his place in the calendar to make room for this sacrilegious celebration. They had also heard that an antiphon for September 7, which had traditionally honored the Virgin, had been rewritten to celebrate Elizabeth instead. The government commissioned Thomas Holland, Oxford's Professor of Theology, to refute such allegations. He assured readers that the antiphons of November 17 were of a "meere Eucharistical" nature—expressing thanks but not worship. As for Hugh of Lincoln, Holland indicated that the less said about that supposititious saint the better.[34]

In 1602 John Howson had to follow this up by repelling attacks from Puritans who feared the rise of new superstitions in place of the old. Howson thought he could satisfy Calvinists by treating the matter of holy days as God's election of certain days to a state of grace. In his view, the measure of divinity which seemed to surround monarchs should surely justify days in their honor. Certainly there could be no question in the case of Elizabeth, whose gift of healing was attested by three or four hundred cures every year. She seemed also to have the gift of prophecy—"as I may call it"—in her undoubted political prescience. Beyond that, she was the obvious recipient of providential care. All in all, Elizabeth appeared to be in the same relation to God as the Old Testament monarchs, who were entrusted with "power absolute without limitation, accountable only to God for their actions."[35]

This kind of talk would get later monarchs into trouble, precisely because it was a sacralization of their office. But it was perfectly safe to use Elizabeth as the focus of a national cult once she was dead. For then she came to symbolize the nation's independence and its defiance of a sacred but foreign power. Accordingly, Elizabeth's Accession Day remained more popular than the accession days for living monarchs.[36]

But James I got a special day too, in commemoration of his escape from the Gunpowder Plot of 5 November 1605 (Guy Fawkes Day). Celebrations were authorized by the secular power (3 Jac. I, c. 1) making it England's first official national holiday. Such bogus holy days did not secularize time in the sense of making it uniform, but they transfered this practice from church to state. As part of the negative ideology of no-popery nationalism, Guy Fawkes Day would catch the popular imagination.

After the Civil Wars the nation had another whipping boy, in the Puritan rebel. So Parliament added two more holidays to the calendar in 1661, a fast to honor Charles I's martyrdom (January 30) and a feast on the anniversary of Charles II's restoration (May 29). Thus the first two secular holidays had an anti-Catholic and the second two an anti-Puritan emphasis. This might suggest the persistence of a religious tone in social celebration if their essentially negative character were not so apparent. They do not symbolize the nation's new religion so much as its antireligion, its exasperation with both papist and presbyterian pretensions.

Anti-Catholic days caught on more enthusiastically than anti-Puritan ones. By 1673, when the Restoration hysteria had died down and Dissenters seemed tame by comparison with Louis XIV's sinister forces, a tradition of pope-burning parades began. Some of the color of the old religious holidays was revived to celebrate England's delivery from papal intrigue. Participants dressed up as Catholic clergy and the high point was igniting effigies of the pope and the devil that might cost £2,500 and have live cats inside—who "squawled most hideously as soon as they felt the fire." In London, crowds estimated at 200,000 turned out to enjoy the floats, fireworks, skits, bonfires and toasts.[37] Such celebrations expressed a social rather than official ethos, since the pro-Catholic Stuarts could hardly offer a lead in the revels. In fact, Charles II looked for opportunities to suppress them.[38] The Stuarts tried to revive older, more religious usages, such as scheduling their coronations on St. George's Day (April 23).[39]

A sacred character could not be transferred to new observances by fiat, however, as Parliament realized. The preambles to its holiday resolutions take pains to say that Parliament was only recognizing the sacred character of the nation's epic moments. The law requiring observance of Gunpowder Day, for instance, observed that England's deliverance was "miraculous." That is, God had marked out the day, in the same way that saints' days had been identified. The law authorizing observance of Charles II's restoration remarked on its coincidence with his birthday. This gave the day a symbolic significance, in that the kingdom was "new borne and raised from the dead on this most joyful day" (12 Car. II, c. 14). To the charge that this holiday was established on merely human authority, Parliament retorted that it was a day that "the Lord himselfe hath made and crowned with soe many publique Blessings," so that it was perfectly natural to celebrate with religious services. The martyrdom of Charles I for his church presented something more obviously like the old holy days. The fast in his memory drew parallels with Good Friday, encouraging all subjects to implore God that the guilt of his "Sacred and Innocent Blood" might not "be visited upon us or our posterity" (12 Car. II, c. 30).

Despite such analogies, it was impossible to invent a truly religious holiday at this late date. The remarkable parallels of his execution with Christ's, the political and ecclesiastical significance of the episode, and the attendant miracles might have established his case in the Middle Ages. But the Church of England tried in vain to keep a celebration of the day alive or to canonize the royal martyr. The publication of sermons preached on January 30 petered out in 1795. Parliament interred its own commemoration service in 1811, long after its natural demise.[40]

Nor was it possible to maintain indefinitely a truly religious sense of the nation's history in the style of John Foxe. We must defer discussion of England's apocalyptic nationalism until later chapters on social relations (nationalism) and scholarship (historiography). But J. G. A. Pocock has indicated the ambiguity of this kind of national sacralization. An apocalyptic perspective puts the nation in the place of the sacraments: "against the real presence [of Christ in the Mass] as the true vehicle of Christian redemption . . . England was shown as the embodiment of this truth throughout history." And yet

> . . .apocalyptic, which sacralizes secular time, must always in an opposite sense secularize the sacred, by drawing the processes of salvation into that time which is known as *saeculum*. The apocalyptic and millennial tones which distinguish English Puritanism from adjacent forms of Calvinism are therefore, in some degree, the product of English secular and institutional nationalism.[41]

Whether or not this nativist millenarianism is evidence of secularization, it was outlived by a nationalism which could only be termed religious on a broad, functional definition.

Beyond all considerations of Protestant or political impulses, an undifferentiated and secular time was encouraged simply by technological developments. In the period of the Restoration England was fast becoming a leader in clock and watch manufacturing. She began the sixteenth century lagging far behind Catholic Flanders and southern Germany; by the late seventeenth century London was the clock- and watch-making capital of the world.[42]

It is generally agreed that religious institutions were Europe's first constituency for tools of time measurement. Monastic piety moved in a daily round of offices, and punctuality demonstrated the monks' devotion. This encouraged medieval Europe to overtake China's lead in clock making and calendar reform. But in the view of David Landes, it was economic change that brought a real revolution in this area. Monastic clocks, after all, rang unequal units—the canonical hours—which varied with the length of daylight. "The future of the infant clock industry lay with the bourgeoisie," Landes maintains, in a classic instance of secularization by transfer.

> As commerce developed and industry expanded, the complexity of life and work required an ever larger array of time signals. These were given, as in the monasteries by bells: the urban commune in this sense was the heir and imitator of the religious community. . . . When mechanical clocks appeared on the scene, the cities of western and Mediterranean Europe could afford to build them as complements to or successors to the cathedrals—a symbol of a new secular dignity and power. . . . The church clung to old ways and, so doing, yielded the rhythm of life and work to the lay authorities and the bourgeosie. Equal hours announced the victory of a new cultural and economic order.[43]

Town clocks became almost "totemic" in their importance. They were "the secular analogue to the religious relics that had long been the most potent attraction to pilgrims and travellers."

Though town clocks were more prominent in Italy, England took the lead in the manufacture of more personalized timepieces. The influx of Protestant clock makers fleeing religious persecution gave England a dominance that lasted well into the eighteenth century. By 1680 alarm or "repeater" watches, which could ring the nearest five minutes, became widespread. By 1700 minute hands had made their appearance, for those who were truly time-haunted.[44]

Even watches are not as striking a sign of the uniform, undifferentiated sense of time as was the spread of newspapers, especially in the 1690s. Periodical publications or "journals" (from the Latin *diurnalis*, for daily) created a new tempo for events and for thought. The concept of the "news"—a daily budget of information which one must absorb in order to be socially involved—has been a major solvent of any sense of eternal concerns. For, from the beginning, journalists could scarcely admit that nothing important had happened since their last issue; they strove to give a new urgency to the mundane. Religion could be newsworthy, of course, but only religious change. Since 1700, the newspaper has been the preeminent means of maintaining a constant interest in change—in the temporal rather than the eternal.

Eighteenth-century visitors to England remarked on the fact that the Church was hardly involved in the sports, festivities and amusements for which the populace lived.[45] E. P. Thompson observes that by then merchants were doing more than the Church to promote holidays.[46] In short, the times and seasons did not direct one's mind toward religion as they had once done.

Just as an undifferentiated space secularized sight, so an undifferentiated time helped secularize thought. Secular rationality is said to depend upon the dominance of this time perspective. Causal thinking "consists of linking present choices to consequences more or less remote in time by the use of recipes that map a route from one to the other." This describes the secular mode—a concentration on linking oneself to one's goals by proximate steps. Some have supposed that the main incentive to such thinking was the promised rewards of a market economy.[47] In England's case, the state and Protestantism were at least catalysts in this change. Insofar as Protestantism concerned itself with antistructural release it was envisioned either in the remote past (Eden) or the distant future (heaven), so there were no times in this life when the absolute validity of rationality could be qualified or overturned.[48]

At one time English religion had emphasized the static or the recurrent aspects of worship. Then, for a century or more, England was conscious of acting a sacred history, as opposed to reenacting it. The Restoration dealt a heavy blow to that notion. Work time, national holidays, the selling of time in the form of legal usury, the measurement of time in minutes and daily editions, all helped dispel sacred rhythms and sacred history. Words were coined to express the new consciousness of time and of change. "Primitive," "decade," "progressive," "epoch," "century," "contemporary," "antiquated," all date from this period.[49] The term "new" became prevalent in book titles in the seventeenth century, as authors expressed a secular restlessness.[50] In short, change was becoming the only constant in England's life.

4

The Secularization
of Language

Nothing makes Shakespeare seem more dated than his constant recourse to swearing, cursing, calling the powers of heaven to witness—a hundred times or more in the course of a play. Characters cannot get through a speech without cluttering it with at least an "i'faith" or "ud's pity." We race through this as so much filler because we have no sense of the holiness which forms its background; with the decline of the holy there has been a corresponding decline of "profanity." By the 1690s already, swearing was in sufficient disrepute that the Societies for the Reformation of Manners actually hoped that they might be able to drive profanity out of public life altogether. The fact that swearers were not eligible for poor relief gave these societies some leverage. They were encouraged by legislation going back to 1606 that forbade profane oaths on the stage.[1] Granted, the societies were ridiculed at the time, but that they existed at all would have seemed incredible just a century earlier. The notion that swearing was antireligious in and of itself would have been just as surprising.

Secularization of language goes to the heart of the subject of religious decline. The languages we use are as basic as our habits of perception, and the changes dealt with in this chapter created a vocabulary which could express real unbelief. Again, in considering secularization with respect to cursing, swearing, state oaths, glossolalia, literacy, language theory, and statistics, we will constantly be aware of two familiar factors, state power and Protestant piety.

Language was among the first things to be secularized as a part of Henry's reconstitution of the Church. Latin, of course, had become sacralized by long association with religion. Since the English had their own language, the Church held a virtual monopoly over Latin and could decide what statements made sense and which were nonsense in official religious discourse. In the fifteenth century, Reginald Pecock, bishop of Chichester, had gotten into trouble for using English in refuting the Wycliffite heretics, for the church hierarchy foresaw the consequences of discussing such matters in a language belonging to the people.[2] To be sure, Pecock had warned his readers that they could not expect to judge by their own wits or by a scriptural literalism. He objected to popular preaching since its appeal was always due to oversimplification. But even to address a general audience had gone too far toward encouraging it to become involved in religious debate.[3] The issue was not just whether English was adequate to the expression of theology; one of these Lollards pointed out that there was more heresy written in Latin than in English. The issue was elite control. With the example of Wyclif before it the Church had ruled (in 1407) that the very fact of translating Scripture or theology into English constituted heresy.[4]

This was the sort of prohibition that excited Henry's jealousy, as he sought to extend a lay authority over religion. As early as May of 1530 he surprised his bishops by telling them that he planned to have the New Testament "faithfully and purely translated into the English tongue to the intent that he might have it in his hands ready to be given to his people as he might see their manners and behaviour meet, apt and convenient to receive the same."[5] Whether or not this was in violation of the Church's canons, the royal supremacy later allowed him to carry out this promise. In 1538 Cromwell sent a circular letter to the bishops directing that an English Bible be made available in every parish church and the laity encouraged to read it.[6]

Would this prove to initiate a sacralization of English, or a secularization of discourse? Rudolph Otto, in his classic description of "the numinous," held that it is almost a requirement of liturgies and scriptures that they contain archaic and obscure elements if they are to convey any sense of the holy. The "wholly other" character of divine service suggests a "language of the gods."[7] Thomas Harding, professor of Hebrew at Oxford, recognized all this back in the 1560s and warned that the lower orders would not be as deferential toward Scripture if they heard it in their own language. It would lose its aura of mystery and its incantatory power if taken in a merely literal sense.[8] Harding understood, as we are slow to do, that a growing familiarity with Scripture would erode religion in England. He knew that the English Bible would give reformers a basis from which to attack the most heartfelt religious habits and beliefs of the English, on the grounds that they were unwarranted and superstitious. One might argue that this would be a salutary change, a purification of English Christianity. But our subject is not just Christianity, which was only a part of medieval religion.

A sense of mystery in religious language had always been part of English worship, whether in the sound of Latin or of archaic spells. But there was now a change in the balance between the rational element in religion—which had been entrusted only to scholars before—and the spiritual and expressive aspects of religion. Worshipping God with all one's mind was to become as important as worshipping God with all one's heart and soul. It was part of the development of a personal and conscious faith.

When William Tyndale published his English New Testament in 1525, some old priests assumed that anything called a "New" Testament must be modern and heretical.[9] And certainly Tyndale did intend his translation to be subversive. One can see this in his choice of a very plain English diction as against more Latinate alternatives. Translating *ecclesia* as "congregation" rather than "church" is perfectly accurate, historically. But it was a cunning choice, in avoiding all the connotations that had gathered around the term "church" in the course of 1500 years. Using "repent" instead of "do penance" emphasized a more spiritualized, interiorized piety that would be harder for the Church to control. Translating *presbyteros* as "elder" rather than "priest" dissipated a whole system of ritual propitiation.[10]

Sir John Cheke, tutor to Edward VI, went even further. He strained for effect when he snubbed Renaissance Latinity to use "crossed" for crucified, "hundreder" for centurion, "freshman" for proselyte, and "moond" for lunatic.[11] This overfamiliarity did not catch on. But Tyndale's more elevated diction, as followed in the Authorized Version of 1611, would eventually be hallowed in English culture.

In the 1530s the issue between conservatives and reformers was not just that English was too crude and undeveloped to carry the meaning of Scripture. Conservative humanists had admitted that the original language and style of Scripture were rough. Thomas Becon even suggested that the condition of English made it a perfect match for the crude original Greek.[12] The issue was the Church's control. In 1532 Sir Thomas More took public issue with Tyndale's insistence on scriptural authority. The Church was before Scripture and had produced and validated it, More pointed out. Beneath Scripture was God's unwritten word—church tradition—"that artycle taught and byleued[,] as the chyrche wythout any doute or questyon byleueth."[13] In other words, More felt that religious culture and the religious establishment were threatened by a literal application of specific texts of Scripture.

More showed no awareness that there might also be contradictions and inconsistencies within religious culture, but took its unity for granted. A greater historical sense would have suggested that the Church was as ambiguous as Scripture. As for that, More thought it was a point in his favor that his oral "Scripture"—meaning Church tradition—was always open to new directions. For God continually provided "new prophetes in sundry partes of hys catholyke chyrche, holy doctours, and preachers, and faythfull men, and good lyuers, for whome bothe quycke and dede he doth shewe myracles in hys catholyke chyrche."[14] This seems disingenuous in a work whose constant theme is that none of the recent prophetic voices could be right to question settled tradition.

More's sense of things was better than his arguments. He realized that print and a concentration on an English text, would make the Church's authority a constant issue. Translation, publication, and literacy together would put cultural authority in secular hands. In the final analysis truth was not the issue so much as peace. Community solidarity, ever the goal of religious culture, was easier to achieve in an oral culture, or in a scribal one in which the texts are protected by certified experts. By 1542 we see rearguard action in support of this position, when conservative bishop Stephen Gardiner submitted a list of about a hundred Latinisms which he hoped to see in any subsequent revisions of the authorized English Bible. They would, presumably, ring right in ears attuned to ecclesiastical pronouncements and remind auditors of the old, expert authority.

Even Henry VIII became nervous about allowing Bible reading when he saw it breaking down patterns of authority. A proclamation of April 1539 complained that:

> his majesty's intent and hope was that they that would read the Scripture, would with meekness and wish to accomplish the effect of it, read it, and not to maintain erroneous opinions and preach, nor for to use the reading or preaching of it in sundry times and places and after such fashions and feats as it is not convenient to be suffered.

In short, the English Bible was not to be used for "prophetic" purposes, to challenge the existing order.

Things had already gone beyond this, however. Simply to have the Bible bound as a single book was a momentous cultural change. Always before, Scripture had appeared in parts, divided according to the uses which the Church had found for it. The state, printing houses, and Protestantism now conspired to issue this ultimate authority as a self-contained whole, sometimes without the benefit of marginal notes or other directions for its use. By 1550 even Protestants such as Thomas Becon regreted the use that self-educated radicals had found for God's words. Others, however, were gratified by the insolence of these common people when they were arraigned before the popish bishops.[15] For these rebels were inspired by the English Bible to attack England's religious culture, whether or not they could read it for themselves.

Before Henry had begun to worry about the threat which the English Bible presented to his authority, he was using English in other areas of religion to extend his power. The first doctrinal statement of his reformed church, the Ten Articles (1536), was issued in English, as was his more conservative revision in the Act of Six Articles (1539). From 1536 on, royal injunctions went out to the clergy in English. Addressing the clergy thus, when many of them could have coped with Latin instructions, invited the laity to read over their shoulders. In 1544 the first inroads were made into the divine liturgy itself, in an English litany. Edward VI's councillors saw only gain in this new direction, which made English men and women more aware of their faith. A proclamation of 31 July 1547 even directed that graces said at dinner be in English. Overshadowing all of this was the momentous decision to put the whole of the Church's liturgy into everyday speech.

The Book of Common Prayer of 1549 changed English religion from a matter of practice to a matter of thought. Suddenly worshippers were forced to think about what they were doing and what they believed. The Prayer Book Rebellion of that summer in Devon and Cornwall showed the revulsion that many felt toward the English liturgy and Bible. Clearly the rebels did not view this change as the sacralization of the vernacular. Rather, they were disgusted at hearing their religion on unclean lips, as it were. While they had a variety of motives, the rebels emphasized their demand for the Latin Mass. The English Bible was to be banned, for "otherwise the clergy could not confound the heretics." A proper respect for the things of God required that many things be protected against overfamiliarity, as by the continued use of Latin. Communion should be offered only once a year (at Easter) and in bread only. The host should be reserved and worshipped as before, and the use of ashes, palms, and holy water restored to complete the tactile associations that were important to the older culture.[16]

These rebels did not represent all English opinion, however. In that same year of 1549 Robert Kett's rebels in Norfolk voiced other religious grievances. They demanded a preaching clergy who would teach poor children the catechism and primer. This is virtually opposite to the demand of their West Country counterparts. They thrilled to the sound of religion in a form which could be grasped by the mind.

It may seem perverse to count this desire for religious instruction among the forces promoting secularization. But the growing availability of vernacular Scripture would have that result. With the advent of printing, the flow of Bibles could not be stemmed. By 1543, when Henry was having second thoughts, there had been thirteen editions of the Bible and at least twenty-five more of the New Testament. By 1640 there may have been about 630,000 Bibles and 400,000 Testaments produced, in a country of perhaps 1,250,000 families.[17] One might view this as a purification of Christianity, but by purification we mean the elimination of much that had been part of English religion. An enthusiasm for Scripture doubtless caused an efflorescence of interest in religion, which would last for a century. Putting the Bible into the hands of a literate public would certainly encourage discussion of religion, but that is not the same as promoting religion. In fact we will see that by 1700 such discussion was raising questions not only about Christianity but about religion more generally.

Initially, Reformers supposed that only good could come of wider discussion. But the introduction of English and therefore of "common sense" into religious discussion would eventually mean the loss of religious authority. The clergy could never establish itself as sole experts in the use of English, even within their own sphere, as they had with Latin. In terms of our analysis, the translation of religion into English is an instance of the transfer of religious functions into lay hands, with a consequent loss of the "distance" conducive to the numinous experience. The rapid decline of respect for the Restoration church, after a century of high religious interest, may show how familiarity had bred indifference and even contempt. Still, as argued in chapter 12, while the English Bible laid waste to much that had been honored as religion, it also became the focus of an emerging faith.

In 1554 John Standish, a priest of Queen Mary's Catholic restoration, pathetically described the damage that the English Scriptures had already done to religion as he knew it. He expected his readers to agree that those who seemed most eager for English translations had shown themselves no friends of religion. He could not see that they were representatives of any religious position at all, describing them as froward, perverse, lewd, and wicked. Standish concluded that they were using Scripture to discredit religion.[18]

Recent events had driven Standish to maintain the view that Scripture is deliberately obscure, since mystery and awe are of the very essence of piety: "It is most decent to hide the holye and unsearcheable veritie of the heavenly sprites in the mystical speakings of scripture with secret coveringes and most holy signes." Jesus and the apostles had warned that their words would be obscure, in order to hide the truth from those who would only mock it. Indeed, the "mystery" of Scripture is its most impressive feature, and not its teachings! Standish is carried away with his argument when he asserts that Jesus never meant for his teaching to be written down, expecting the Gospel always to be a matter of oral proclamation.[19] One suspects that Standish had forgotten that he only intended to argue against vernacular *translation*, as he went on to reject any written Scripture.

On the other hand, Standish naively accepted the self-evident necessity of any and all religious customs that he found threatened by Scripture. At least he knew that the "rude and ignorant" commons needed them. For an elite, he seriously suggested that the secret method of cabalism was the best model of religious discourse. Jewish mystics had learned to look through the lifeless words of their Scriptures to the sacred and inexpressible reality beyond. Vernacular Bibles, by contrast, had increased stubbornness and licentiousness and impiety, even among servants. The English liturgy distracted worshippers who came to church to pray. If this plague were to persist, Standish predicted the end of religion and the Church as he knew it.[20] He was not wrong.

Standish knew the power of words, being part of a generation that believed that language could even effect changes in nature. Curses, charms and spells as well as the Church's liturgy were respected and feared. They were used by scholars of the occult and Protestant reformers as well as by village ːsewomen. For example, the revised and more Protestant *Book of Common Prayer* of 1552 included "A Comminacion Againste Synners" which was a litany of curses, invoking woes upon impenitent sinners.

The tide was soon running against this feeling for words, however. By the early seventeenth century, the Anglican poet George Herbert complained that blessing and anathematizing were both neglected by his fellow priests. From being overvalued before the Reformation, they were falling into disuse; "We are fallen . . . from superstition to coldness and atheism."[21] At a higher level, Renaissance scholarship and the advent of printing had initially encouraged and spread a fascination with occult usages. But in 1614 a damaging blow was struck at this philosophy with the proof of a disappointingly late origin of the "Hermetic" writings. It was by a leading Protestant scholar, Isaac Casaubon, patronized by the state in the person of James I.[22]

Keith Thomas's surprise, in studying the decline of a mystic faith in words, was that it was caused more by Protestantism than by science. Protestant writers associated "magical" philosophies and technologies with the Catholic Church and disparaged them at a time when scientists were still maintaining open minds. In turn, Catholics taunted them for being jealous of powers of spiritual exorcism which they did not command. But Protestants had adopted the view that words, even God's Word, addressed the understanding and the spirit and not mundane reality.[23] In short, words were to create a reasoned faith.

It was for this reason that Protestants generally rejected the revival of the New Testament practice of speaking in tongues. Given its apostolic origins, it seems arbitrary for them to oppose the sectarians who stumbled on this gift of the Spirit. Protestant horror at glossolalia seems similar to that of Catholics at hearing God speak in English—a fear of the laity's uncontrolled access to a source of supernatural power. To justify their abhorence Protestant leaders argued that the age of miracles and ecstatic prophecy had ceased with a completed Scripture.[24] Scripture gave Protestant leaders the same security that traditionalists had looked for in the Church's authority. They preferred to use Scriptural language rather than glossolalia, not because it was more religious but because it was less so.

Oaths, of course, had been a pervasive religious expression within English culture. The decline of oaths, which called heaven to witness one's actions, involves the secularization of the person and society, and will be treated at greater length in chapter 10. Briefly, it may be said that oaths and vows were elements in the ancient code of honor. In Shakespeare's time one swore in order to establish and maintain a reputation for honor. By oaths one set up marks to shoot at, asking not only bystanders but even God to judge one's accomplishments. Merchants used oaths in vouching for their wares. Even the poor might have to swear to their innocence, hazarding their only possession—an immortal soul. This sense of honor was now being eclipsed by a value system based on charity—which requires thinking of others rather than of one's own reputation. The latter is a more specifically Christian value system than the other, which goes back to origins which were aristocratic and pagan. Calling a value system based in honor "pagan" does not deny that it was religious. It was, however, alien to a triumphant Protestantism.

Any reduction in the religious use of vows or oaths would be a secular trend in that there was no Protestant activity which could quite correspond. Such oaths as survived were almost sure to be profane. Meanwhile, the government began to multiply political oaths, as we shall see, and to extort them as a matter of civic duty. This was a profanation of another sort, and even Protestants felt uneasy at this development. By the Affirmation Act of 1696 a Protestant government allowed Quakers to avoid oaths since, ironically, Quakers still viewed them as a religious act.[25] A further irony is in the fact that by the seventeenth century, wherever a new state oath touched on religion, it specified only what one must *not* believe—either the pope's authority (Oath of Allegiance, 3 Jac. I, c. 4), transubstantiation (Test Act, 25 Car. II, c. 2), invocation of Mary or saints, and the Mass (second Test Act, 30 Car. II, s. 2, c. 1). The main job of sacred oaths, it seemed, was in proscribing a religion.

A growing self-consciousness concerning religious discourse found a parallel in the Renaissance curiosity about rhetorical theory and the nature of language. Students of seventeenth-century literature describe a variety of plain styles which arose in that period—anti-Ciceronian, utilitarian, rationalistic, and Puritan. Naturally, Puritan preachers promoted a rhetoric which avoided a prideful display, wanting to call attention to their message rather than to their manner.[26] To be sure, the Puritans had an expressive language of devotion derived from the Psalms—the "language of Zion," which their critics loved to mimic. But since their religious position was new, they had to try harder to explain their faith than religious conformists had done. For that reason the Puritans adopted and developed an expository style.

By the Restoration, even their Anglican rivals agreed with them that the "market" should become the arbiter of style, recognizing that there was indeed a market in religion.[27] Before that time the clergy would not have felt such a need to convince the public. Popular indifference had not represented a threat when the Church had no religious competition and enjoyed unqualified support from the state. Now Anglicans as well as Puritans recognized the need to base religion in public opinion, rather than in cultural or political institutions.[28] This in itself does not show a decline of religion, but only that it lacked the former cultural supports and social consensus.

The secularization of language is seen even more clearly in the efforts of natural philosophers to create an idiom more suited to their activites. The new science was describing a new reality, and philosophical terms long associated with theological speculation began to be seen as unsuitable. The Royal Society of London for Improving Natural Knowledge (chartered in 1662) is notable for its attempts to formulate a natural language. The hope was that such a language— mathematical in its precision, with words being the exact equivalents for things— would become the universal substitute for Latin.[29] While these proposals did not win acceptance, some members were developing the numerical and statistical expressions which have indeed become something like a universal language.

Even in the use of numbers as a language there had to be a shift from the "numbers esoteric" of the Renaissance to the "numbers banal" of the seventeenth century. Numerology had long been used for religious expression, but occult numbers could never represent the scientists' view of reality. One may date the acceptance of a statistical language to the Royal Society's recognition of John Graunt's *Natural and political observations . . . upon the Bills of Mortality* (1662).[30] It represented a new enthusiasm for recording precise data and placed England in advance of the rest of Europe.[31] John Nef has remarked that the century between 1550 and 1650 saw "many indications that exact time, exact quantities, exact distances were coming to have a greatly increased interest for men and women in connection with private and public life."[32] "God's language" was found to be in nature, rather than in books, and in time this would seem to limit philosophy to positivistic statements.[33] All this activity led to the rise of theories of the human origin of language, as against the earlier view that language was as much a part of God's creation as things were. Once again, English scholars, from Bacon to Hobbes and Locke, were leaders in this speculation.[34]

Finally, print literacy contributed to the demystification of language. At the same time, literacy helped dissolve cultural consensus by encouraging a questioning and individualistic spirit. As Jack Goody has explained it, literate societies

cannot discard, absorb, or transmute the past in the same way [as illiterate ones]. Instead, their members are faced with permanently recorded versions of the past and its beliefs; and, because the past is thus set apart from the present, historical enquiry becomes possible. This in turn encourages scepticism.[35]

Recent attempts to measure the early modern rise of literacy may introduce a false precision, especially when estimated by the ability to sign one's name. But the movement of literacy, if not its level, is probably accurately reflected in those figures. In 1640 something like 30 percent of all men and 10 percent of women in England could sign for themselves. By 1714 that had risen to about 45 percent for men and 25 percent for women, and by 1750 the figures are more like 60 percent and 40 percent. Only Puritan New England and Calvinist Scotland are thought to have surpassed England in this period, with the Reformed areas of the Netherlands close behind. Catholic France, on the other hand, lagged fifty to seventy-five years behind England. Aggregate figures mask differences between rural and urban populations and between different classes and occupational groups. Occupational differences remind us of the importance of economic factors in promoting literacy and book production. But all students of the subject acknowledge the role of Protestantism in this development, with its promotion of Bible reading as a religious act.[36]

Had this rise in literacy been in Latin the effects on religious culture might have been different. But with the eclipse of the Latin Bible, the Latin liturgy, glossolalia, and the cabalistic search for Adam's lexicon, religion had to fall back on a language designed for the mundane activities of life.

A spread of literacy promoted an objectification of religion that one can trace in the dictionaries of the time. In 1538 the humanist Thomas Elyot defined religion as a personal attribute rather than an abstract subject: "a reuerende drede, doubte leste he shall offende. Also a conscience, or as a man mought say, a scruple of conscience." Faith he defined, not as assent to doctrines, but as "belefe, truste, promise. It is a stablenes and truthe in promyses and couenauntes."[37] Thus, religion was not reified as something objective, but was a manner of being. As late as 1611 Randle Cotgrave agreed that religion was an aspect of personality: "holinesse, pietie, godlinesse, the worship of God, or of things held sacred; a reuerend, and conscientious affection unto them, or feare of offending them."[38] John Florio, in the same year, likewise saw religion as "holiness, devotion, scruple of conscience, a reverent and awefull feare, or true worshipping of God or holy things."[39] Florio's inclusion of "true" indicates his assumption that religion must be true; false belief would not qualify as religion. Thus "true," Christian, and religious were synonymous.

A century later things had changed. In 1658 Edward Phillips defined religion primarily as "The Worship of a Deity," though he goes on to list "Piety, Godliness, Devotion." And the object of religion became abstract; any "deity" would do to certify a religion.[40] Abel Boyer's definition of faith (1700) came close to making it a system of belief: "Belief, or Doctrine, or Fidelity."[41] With Phillips also, faith amounted to "Belief, Credit, Trust, . . . a real Belief of the Truth of the Gospel." By 1735 Thomas Dyche made faith "the belief or assent that the mind gives to a proposition."[42] Thus religion was changing from devotion to deliberation.

This is, of course, the change which Lucien Febvre looked for in vain in Rabelais' France. Only such an objectification of religion would allow the possibility of atheism. And according to the *Oxford English Dictionary*, many new words were available to describe new doubts. Some of the terms already existed in a Latin form, but English equivalents brought the public into the discussion. "Atheist" is first recorded in an English work in 1568, followed by "atheism" (1587), "sceptic" (1587), "atheistical" (1603), "deist" (1612), "rationalist" (1626), "sceptical" (1639), "scepticism" (1646), and "deism" (1682). A hardening of the line between natural and supernatural realms is indicated by the appearance of the terms "supernatural" (1526), "naturalist" (as opposed to "religious," 1608), "occult" (i.e., magical science, 1633), and "naturalism" (1641). The "godless" (1528), "libertines" (1563) and the "credulous" (1576) had earned themselves names early on; more surprising is that by the seventeenth century names were needed for the shades of belief: "conformity" (in religion, 1622), "conformist" (1651), "supernaturalist" (1650), "theist" (1662), and "theism" (1678). New words were also needed to describe related intellectual activities: "investigate," "dubious," "discovery," "distinguish," "critic," "criticism," "analyze," "consciousness," "scrutinize," and finally "self-consciousness" (1690).[43]

England had come a long way since 1531, when an observer described the Latin cursing of a heretic with bell, book, and candle in Exeter Cathedral: "What a shout and noise was there, what terrible fear; what holding up of hands to Heaven: that curse was so terrible." Only thirty years later, excommunication could be treated with derision.[44]

On the other hand, the English would eventually develop their language into a vehicle of religious consciousness. The "Jacobethan" language of the Authorized Translation of 1611 seemed more and more archaic as Restoration literature became increasingly conversational. This helped sacralize the words of Scripture by setting them off from ordinary diction. According to C. S. Lewis, the language of the "King James Version" reached the height of its reputation in the late eighteenth century, when the Bible was "appreciated" for its "literary power." This is, of course, a very different thing from its religious use, and Lewis believed that it marked the end of the Bible's real spiritual power in English culture generally.[45]

In 1500 religion had a language of its own, or perhaps several languages—of devotion, consecration, penitence, hagiography and occult wisdom, and also of malediction. All of this began to fade in the milder light of common sense. Religion forced its way into consciousness when it had to be expressed in everyday terms. To be sure, this would create a new religious enthusiasm, which lasted at least a century. But it also brought doubts. Doubts had existed before, but only indistinctly. By 1700 it was faith that had a job to sustain itself in a vocabulary drawn from elsewhere.

5

The Politics of
Secularization (1529–1603)

One would expect a change which reached so deep as the basic sense of space or time to be subtle, gradual, and unconscious. But what we have seen has been rapid. It has involved deliberate, political decisions and has developed according to a conscious rationale. A narrative of this religious revolution will show more of the intentions of the parties involved and of the reactions to change.

Until recently, historians tried to account for the rapidity of changes in the Reformation by asserting the decrepitude of late-medieval religious practices. Some treated them as hollow and formal, and therefore easily swept away by the conviction of Reformers. Others treated those practices as too fervent and sensuous, characterized by a morbidity which was too exaggerated to last. Historians often betrayed their disapproval of a piety that "ran the risk of confusing the spiritual and the temporal," or they alluded to the presence of fear, as if this were unworthy of religion. Recently, however, revisionist historians have emphasized the continuing popular support for the Church in the early sixteenth century, showing that the endowing of chantries, decorating of churches, production of expensive rood lofts and images, gild activities, ordination rates, and the elaboration of ritual were all evident and often growing in England, at least outside the southeastern counties.[1]

As stated earlier, we need not concern ourselves with a judgment of how "healthy" these religious expressions were. Fear is an appropriately religious emotion, and sensuality is not necessarily a mark of religious decadence. Nor should our notions of the proper division between the spiritual and the temporal be a standard; a fusion of the two is what we would expect of a more religious culture. Also, it is to be expected that some aspects of religious culture would develope while others declined.[2]

The principal argument for a pre-Reformation religious decline in England is simply the speed with which the Reformation changes were established. When the habits of centuries can disappear in a single generation there is suspicion that the whole edifice of religious culture was eaten from within or so overripe that it fell of its own weight. Should not a religion that served vital functions have stood its ground more strongly?

Two considerations should be kept in mind; for one thing, the religion of late medieval England was quite diverse. Not only does Christianity embody paradoxes at its core, but it was mixed with other elements, both ancient and innovative. It has yet to be shown that together they formed a coherent whole. Second, what we call the superstitious elements of medieval religion had tended to grow and multiply beyond strict necessity. Superstition has no natural enemies. As J. H. M. Beattie puts it, "mythical agencies, unlike scientific ones, tend to proliferate."[3] That is, while science looks for new ways to analyze and test and reduce reality, myth and ritual seek ways to express, dramatize, and elaborate reality. In terms of Beattie's dichotomy, theology falls within the category of science. Protestants were often quite theological, forever seeking out the warrant for a practice. By contrast, their image-worshipping neighbors may have felt little need of a unifying cosmology. Their "superstitions" did not necessarily involve or compromise each other and were nearly impervious to disproof, enjoying a self-validating character. On the other hand, the old believers did not always put up much resistance to change. We will notice both violent rejection of sacrilege, which is more to be expected, but also an apathetic acceptance of change.

It is astonishing to think that a single individual could be responsible for changing the character of English culture, but Henry VIII exercised that kind of power. His subjects must have wondered about his intentions toward religion as they saw the inconsistency of his actions. In the midst of the campaign to dissolve the monasteries he took time to found some of his own. He endowed masses for his own soul even after having confiscated chantries on behalf of others.[4] The enthusiasm he showed for chastity and celibacy in his *Defense of the Seven Sacraments* and the Act of Six Articles made an odd contrast with his own matrimonial adventures. But Henry displayed a real gusto in religious observance when he needed to silence the doubts of others, as during the campaign to pass the Six Articles in May of 1539:

> On Holy Thursday his Grace went a procession about the Court at Westminster in the Whitehall; and my Lord Cobham bare the sword before the King's Grace, with all other nobles a great multitude. And the high altar in the chapel was garnished with all the apostles upon the altar, and mass by note, and the organs playing, with as much honour to God as might be devised to be done. And they that be in the King's chapel shewed me, and so did Killigrew also, that upon Good

Friday last past the King's Grace crept to the Cross from the chapel door upward, devoutly, and so served the priest to mass that same day, his own person, kneeling on his Grace his knees. . . . Also . . . there was one hanged for eating flesh upon a Friday, against the King's commandment. . . . And his Grace every Sunday doth receive holy bread and holy water and doth daily use all other laudable ceremonies, and in all London no man upon pain of death to speak against them.[5]

But it would not have been wise to jump to conclusions about Henry's intentions on the basis of scenes like these.

There were other Englishmen, however, who would provide a consistent rationale for purifying religion and restricting it to its "proper sphere." The essential distinction for the promotion of secularization was the notion of *adiaphora*, or "things indifferent." Humanist and Protestant opinion postulated a three-part division between the essentials of religion, "ceremonies," and superstitions. Essentials were those things necessary to salvation. Ceremonies might aid one's devotion but were in themselves "indifferent." Superstitions misled the worshipper into idolatry or error. Most Reformers judged that only a few things were essential to salvation, but they recognized that it was often helpful to frame them with practices (ceremonies) that were recognized as optional. When the latter took on an importance in their own right (as superstitions), however, they usurped the place of God and deserved divine wrath.

Protestantism was an effort to pare religion to its essentials, using Scripture as guide. As historical scholarship awakened in Europe, scholars became aware that many things that were accepted as part of their religious duty were never envisioned by Jesus or his Apostles. The Church usually took apostolic usage as its test of doctrine and practice, but over the centuries many practices had been sacralized without clear apostolic sanction. "Sacramentals" were instituted with a similar power to convey grace as the sacraments themselves. Papal decretals were declared to have the same force as if Christ had issued them. Reformers complained that there was a lack of proportion or moral discrimination when people were more concerned about sprinkling holy water than about charity to the poor, or when priests worried more about missing a rubric in a rite than about whoring after someone's wife.[6]

The first English writer who identified the Church's mistake as this lack of judgment in religious observance was Thomas Starkey. His *Exhortation to Unity and Obedience* (1535) popularized an idea of *adiaphora* (inessentials) that had appeared in Erasmus' writings and in Philipp Melanchthon's *Loci Communes Theologici* (dedicated to Henry VIII).[7] Since Starkey was in Henry's service, it is not surprising that this distinction of essentials/*adiaphora* assumed an official character and found its way into many of the government's statements on religion. The first royal injunctions in 1536 began by distinguishing between things necessary to salvation and other matters "convenient to be kept and used for a decent and a politic order."[8] The distinction became foundational to England's national church.

This made a contrast with earlier notions. In 1532 the Church had given a rather vague answer to Parliament's criticism of the proliferation of saints' days, and especially of those that interfered with harvest. The clergy protested that the six holy days that fell in August and September were all of "great antiquity, and incorporated in the law, and of them [i.e., refer to saints] that be so high in the favour of God, by whose intercession and means we may the better obtain His favour towards us in His benefits, which is specially to be regarded in the harvest time."[9] The same fog could have covered anything the Church had found "useful." But on 11 March 1538, after the ecclesiastical revolution, a proclamation plainly declared that Lent was "a mere positive law of the church" and not a "necessity" and could therefore be altered by "the public authority of kings." Within religion, then, there were things that were done because of God's clear command, and things that one did because one was an English subject and wanted to observe the order of the realm.

The English peasant probably made little distinction between the center and periphery of religion. Either a thing was sacred or not. If it was of no use to one's luck or salvation it could hardly be a part of religion, even though it might promote social harmony. It must have seemed odd to hear the proclamation of 16 November 1538 which required everyone to continue to observe the customs of holy water, holy bread, candle, creeping to the cross, purification of mothers, processions, kneeling, and offering days until the government would direct otherwise, though they were "not to repose any trust of salvation in them." When the old church had ordered such usages there had been some spiritual urgency about the matter. The new state admitted to being arbitrary, ordering certain "customs" for the sake of social decorum.

Starkey anticipated an objection here. He argued that a *res media* (an indifferent or optional observance) could become a *res necessarie* by the simple fact of the government's commanding it. That followed from Scripture's order to obey earthly authorities. Protestants divided on this point. There were those who only rejected things definitely forbidden by Scripture, things which the old church had justified but which were clearly idolatrous. Others were less liberal, but were inclined to accept any custom which was "not repugnant" to Scripture. Later ages would associate this moderate position with "Anglicanism."[10] Some took the position that any practice would have to demonstrate its "positive accord" with Scripture to be allowed in the Church's practice—the "Puritan" position. Even more extreme, there were sectarians who would allow nothing that was not directly commanded by Scripture. This had been the position of the Lollards.[11]

In England the battles were fought between the two middle positions. Moderates, such as Archbishop Cranmer and Bishop Ridley, differed from early "Puritans" like Bishop John Hooper and John Knox on the effect of cultural usage.

Puritans thought that some practices which might be squared with Scripture had been so compromised by association with a corrupt church that it was no longer possible to allow them. In 1550 Hooper and Ridley debated whether this were the case with clerical vestments, Hooper claiming that in the minds of the people such "Aaronic" garb implied the existence of a sacrificial priesthood and rite. Ridley only thought it created a decorum which was proper to any worship. Apologists for the old church, Bishop John Fisher and Sir Thomas More, maintained that the Church could not have erred so greatly that any traditional religious customs would be objectionable. They feared that a general social, moral, and religious breakdown would follow a questioning of customary practice.

Thus, what we are calling "religious culture" became a direct issue.[12] Some Protestants took the view that the Church had been so thoroughly subverted by cultural innovation that it was now the most anti-Christian force in the world—Antichrist, in fact. For them, there was an urgency in dismantling false worship. Others in the first generation of Protestants, however, tended to think that time was on their side. Having experienced the gospel of free grace as a liberation, they could not imagine new generations submitting to the old bondage of religious legalism. So they temporized with some practices for the sake of public order, expecting time to erode the Catholic position.[13] There were only a few sectarians in the first century of reform who were determined on "Reformation without Tarrying for Any," which meant separating themselves from the religious community of the realm.

In the light of these debates Edward VI's government declared its position in a section of the 1549 *Book of Common Prayer* called "Of Ceremonies, Why Some Be Abolished and Some Retayned." The very term "ceremonies" suggested the neutral, indifferent character of "mere outward forms." The burden of the argument was that, since there must be a common order in religion, the state must decide which customs would promote the greatest unity and edification. The authorities knew they would not please everybody:

> whereas in this our tyme, the myndes of menne bee so diverse, that some thynke it a greate matter of conscience to departe from a peece of the leaste of theyr Ceremonies (they bee so addicted to their olde customes), and agayne on the other syde, some bee so newe fangle that they woulde innovate all thyng, and so doe despyse the olde that nothynge canne lyke them, but that is newe: It was thought expediente not so muche to have respecte howe to please and satisfie eyther of these partyes, as howe to please God, and profitte them bothe.

Addressing the old believers, the author emphasized that "Christes Gospell is not a Ceremonial lawe (as muche of Moses lawe was), but it is a relygion to serve God, not in bondage of the figure or shadowe: but in the freedom of spirit." To reformers, he wrote that

wythoute some Ceremonies it is not possible to kepe anye ordre or quete
dyscyplyne in the churche . . . [and] in suche a case they oughte rather to have
reverence unto them for theyr antyquitye, yf they wyll declare themselves to
bee more studious of unitie and concorde, then of innovations and newe-
fanglenesse, whiche (as muche as maye bee wyth the trewe settying foorthe of
Christes religion) is always to bee eschewed.

The government thus disparaged an addiction to old rites on the one hand and
a restless spirit of innovation on the other. Cultural relativism is fully acknowledged in the statement that "every countreye should use such ceremonies, as thei
shal thynke beste to the settying foorth of goddes honor, and glorye: and to the
reducying of the people to a most perfecte and Godly living."

Obviously, those in charge of England's church had an attenuated sense of the
holy. The phenomenological distinction of sacred and profane is a division of the
forbidden, the uncanny, the awe inspiring, from the ordinary and the useful. It is
true that the medieval church had made a distinction between levels of holiness.
True adoration (*latria*) was due to some manifestations and simple devotion
(*dulia*) to others, allowing adoration of the Host but only devotion to images, for
instance. Protestants claimed that simple folk were not able to make the distinction. After all, devotion and adoration were both part of religion; neither was
optional. *Adiaphora*, by contrast, were not a part of one's religion in the sense of
giving access to supernatural power. They were the husk of religion and more a
part of one's political duty, showing a proper, obedient spirit. But they were most
of what was left of divine service. Thus the state and its Protestant allies developed a rationale for secularization.

The Mass was, of course, a particular provocation to the Reformers. If the
Mass were really a renewed sacrifice of Christ, as real as the original Crucifixion,
then the communicant was present at the center of all eternity. The Church
would be justified in allowing true adoration of the bread which hosted the body
of Christ. The holiness of the rite was such that a lesser communion in "holy
bread" was allowed for the scrupulous.[14] For Protestants, however, Christ had
sacrificed himself once for all time, so that they tended toward the view that
Communion was little more than a commemoration. There was an important
difference in the sense of time involved: a mass changed the spiritual world by
creating grace, whereas Holy Communion stimulated a historical memory. The
Mass gave immediate access to grace, whereas communion looked forward to a
fulfillment of religious joy hereafter. So Protestants tended to exist between the
Scriptural past and the apocalyptic future. Their present was a secular age in
which God's presence was only apparent to the eye of faith.

This was made explicit in the statute of Edward's first year which dissolved
the chantries. These were endowments to support priests to say perpetual
masses for specified souls. The act (1 Edw. VI, c. 14) denied that the Mass was a
sacrificial satisfaction for sin: such a notion was due to "the ignorance of their

very true and perfect salvation through the death of Jesus Christ, and by devising and phantasing vain opinions of purgatory and masses satisfactory, to be done for them which be departed." The government was successful in creating an outpouring of hostility toward the "godmakers," if that was its intent. More than thirty tracts and many scurrilous ballads and bills were posted against the Mass in the next year (1548) alone.[15] In fact, the very first statute of Edward's reign and three quick proclamations had to try to forbid disputes on the matter, undoing some of the damage.[16] Meanwhile, the government stalled until it could formulate its own position on the Sacrament.[17]

A church which did not know what it believed was something new in history. And the English church was in the strange position of defining its doctrine by contrast with earlier beliefs. Mostly, it knew what it was against, and everything that these Protestants "protested" was an anchor of popular religion: candles, palms, ashes, holy bread and water, creeping to the cross, ritual gestures of the priest, frequent washing of his fingers and kissing of the altar, mumbling of the holy words and shifting of books, lifting of the paten and chalice and breathing on them, ringing of sacring bells.[18] Were these the "trappings" of religion or the thing itself? Protestants thought that if they attracted any devotion (or adoration) they would have to go. Thus it was precisely the most "religious" elements of culture (those most likely to secure God's blessings) that required destruction.

With images and relics, Edward's council was perfectly sure of its position. These had not been an optional part of religion before; Lollards had been forced to worship images, to prove their orthodoxy. Indeed, Margaret Aston's study of iconoclasm suggests that "The eradication of idolatry amounted to the very rationale of the reformed Church of England." She thinks that historians have not noticed its centrality to the Reformation because it was so entirely successful.[19] The fact that we think image worship to have been somewhat peripheral—a mere "expression" of devotion—shows how successful Protestantism was in destroying even the memory of a religion.

For Protestants, iconoclasm itself was a religious act, a heroic reenactment of the deeds of King Josiah or of Jesus's attack on the Temple. Like fire, iconoclasm was cleansing as well as destructive. Vulnerable roadside crosses were the first to go, as early as 1529.[20] Henry's government tried to moderate the iconoclastic impulse; its injunctions of 1536 mildly reminded subjects that it was better to give to the poor than to shrines, better to be at work than on pilgrimage. Saints, it said, were only examples, and images were only reminders of holiness—not talismans. The injunctions of 1538 directed parochial clergy to remove only those images that attracted any devotion or offerings or pilgrimage.[21] By definition, this meant all images which had any religious potency. Preachers were constantly admonished to explain the proper and improper use of images to their parishioners.[22] Nothing could have undermined a naive and hearty devotion more thoroughly than continually being made to think about the propriety of one's religious practices.

Reason and compromise proved impossible in this area. Of course churches and abbeys were pillaged and burnt in the Middle Ages—as recently as the Wars of the Roses. But these were calculated insults to a particular locality, affronts to local saints in a polytheistic diplomacy. The new iconoclasm was an attempt to sweep away all miracle-working objects, to show that none of them could protect themselves. Glastonbury thorn was hacked down, St. Cuthbert's banner burnt, along with images of Mary from the great shrines at Walsingham and Ipswich. In a particularly ugly case, the image of Derfel Gadarn from Wales was burnt in the execution fire of Friar John Forest.[23] So the greatest idols in the land were humbled. It would have been natural to feel cheated if one had made oblations to them over the years with only ambiguous results and now to witness their impotence.

Of course, there are contrary accounts of resistance to the image smashing. On 17 November 1547 the government tried to remove the great rood and the major images in St. Paul's at night so as to avoid unpleasantness, and yet two men were killed in the fracas and others wounded.[24] A hundred years later, it still required armed guards to protect workmen assigned to remove the stained glass image of Thomas Becket in Canterbury Cathedral.[25]

Just as much emotion was shown on the other side. Some have remarked that Protestant iconoclasm was more inspiring than its theology.[26] Does the outpouring of hostility indicate a long frustration with an oppressive religion, and a faith so fragile that it was on the verge of collapse? Even contemporaries puzzled over this question. Citizens of York made bequests to chantries right up to the eve of the Reformation but then scrambled to buy up the redundant churches in the city.[27] A contemporary recalled that as a boy he had been shocked at such a spectacle:

> Persons were content to spoil them [the monasteries], that seemed not two days before to allow their Religion, and do great Worship and Reverence at their Mattins, Masses and other Service, and all other their doings: which is a strange thing to weigh; that they that could this day think it to be the House of God, and the next day the House of the Devil: or else they would not have been so ready to have spoiled it. . . . For the better Proof of this my Saying, I demanded of my Father, thirty years after the Suppression, which had bought part of the Timber of the Church, and all the Timber in the Steeple, with the Bell Frame, with other his Partners therein (in the which steeple hung viii, yea ix Bells, whereof the least but one, could not be bought at this Day for xx pounds, which Bells I did see hang there myself, more than a year after the Suppression) whether he thought well of the Religious Persons and of the Religion then used? And he told me Yea: For said He, I did see no Cause to the contrary: Well, said I, then how came it to pass you was so ready to distroy and spoil the thing that you thought well of? What should I do, said He: might I not as well as other have some Profit of the

Spoil of the Abbey? For I did see all would away; and therefore I did as others did. Thus you may see that as well they that thought well of the Religion then used, as they which thought otherwise, could agree well enough, and too well, to spoil them. Such a devil is Covetousness and Mammon! And such is the Providence of God to punish Sinners in making themselves Instruments to punish themselves, and all their Posterity, from Generation to Generation! For no doubt there hath been Millions of Millions that have repented the Thing since; but all too late.[28]

Others reacted quite differently, gathering up the bones which the king's agents threw out of the shrines, transporting relics to the English exiles in Louvain, and preserving the relics of Henry's persecutions, like the arm of Prior Houghton who was executed for treason.[29] Some who despoiled the Church were only expressing the traditional view that church plate, for example, was emergency wealth for use in community crises, to be replaced later. That is, things were taken by people who only thought they had a better right to them than the government, at least. Much was hurriedly sold by churchwardens so that the proceeds would actually be used for religious purposes—church repairs, prayer books, and charities—forestalling a government that had less religious ends in mind.[30]

J. J. Scarisbrick has expressed doubts that the spoliation means that English men and women had been pining to shake off their old faith. After all, the Church had protected them with charms, blessed their passage through life's tight spots, given them relief in periodic rites of social reversal, promoted local pride, guarded marriage, propitiated the gods. Protestantism, by contrast, was more remote and bookish and represented a loss of local control. He doubts that it could have been established without the muscle of Tudor government.[31] The notion that Catholic practice was imposed on a grumbling populace was only the sense that later historians could make of things, the evidence for Catholic survivals being hidden from them as it was from the government. Robert Whiting, from his study of Devon and Cornwall, likewise concludes that royal visitors were only obeyed out of a mixture of loyalty and fear, with much resentment.[32]

Perhaps the key to understanding the rapid change of heart is that contemporaries thought of religion more in terms of power than we do. They had seen the state's power and they had seen the impotence of the relics and images. The latter had been insulted and yet the sky had not fallen. Perhaps the Protestants were right, that God had never approved of the traditional practices. Maybe God was on the side of the Reformers and that was why they were in power.

As with the Mass, Edward VI's government ended any uncertainty over images. On 21 February 1548 the Council ordered the removal of all images and not just those that had been "abused" by worship. It complained that distinctions in this regard were too subtle for common folk, who wanted to kiss, lick, kneel, crawl, or offer incense, candles, oats, wool, cheese, or cake to their favorites.[33] By a proclamation of 31 July 1547 preachers were directed to explain that the old practices had never been efficacious:

> Offering of money, candles, or tapers to relics or images, or kissing and licking of the same, praying upon beads, or such like superstition, have not only no promise or reward in Scripture for doing of them, but contrarywise, great threats and maledictions of God, for that they be things tending to idolatry and superstition, which of all other offenses God almighty doth most detest and abhor, for that the same diminish His honor and glory.

Sprinkling holy water on one's bed, on images and other "dead things" seemed worth prohibiting, along with carrying holy bread about, making palm crosses during Palm Sunday services, exorcising with the holy candle, dressing of images, and the keeping of shrines at home.

This was less a reformation than a wholesale demolition. The blessing of candles at Candlemas, of ashes on Ash Wednesday, creeping to the cross on Good Friday, bells on All Saints' Day were forbidden. By 1550 altars, images, and roods were gone, even in the provinces. Other rites disappeared without commandment—Corpus Christi processions with the Host, the Easter sepulchre, hallowing the font on Easter Eve. By contrast, the Protestants' contribution to the visual sense in worship was the austere whitewashed interior, with Bible texts where scenes of judgment had been.[34] It is hard to imagine that this really substituted for the life which went out of churches when the candles were all extinguished.

Taking a lead from the government, the public was quick to stop offering its goods to further God's honor. W. K. Jordan's massive study of philanthropy in ten counties gives dramatic evidence on this point and indeed he concluded that his study of English philanthropy was actually a study of secularization. Jordan's failure to take inflation into account does not affect the evidence of the declining percentage of philanthropy which was directed toward religious uses. Before 1540 over half (53.5 percent) of all bequests were made to support religion. In Edward's time that figure fell to 4.8 percent, recovering only to 7.2 percent in the more stable circumstances of Elizabeth's reign. Money given for education or for redistribution to the poor now went to lay administrators rather than the Church, in instances of differentiation and transfer. Table 5.1 gives the adjusted levels of religious giving and the share of philanthropy that went to religious purposes.[35] The dramatic recovery of giving to the Church in the 1620s was, of course, due to pressure from Charles I and Laud. As we shall see, this was resented and the reaction sharp.

One might argue that donors still intended religious benefits from their charity, but there is some doubt as to that even in such an area as education. Before 1530 three times more money was given to the universities than to

TABLE 5.1. Religious and Secular Philanthropy, 1480–1660,
from Jordan's Sample of Ten English Counties

Year	Religious gifts in constant pounds	Religious gifts as a percentage of total gifts
1480–90	£29,907	60.6%
1491–1500	61,478	70.8
1501–10	81,836	56.9
1511–20	40,840	49.9
1521–30	35,501	43.4
1531–40	26,598	44.4
1541–50	11,344	28.0
1551–60	5,354	8.7
1561–70	4,589	12.2
1571–80	2,534	6.6
1581–90	1,968	5.1
1591–1600	1,790	5.9
1601–10	4,192	8.3
1611–20	9,107	9.8
1621–30	15,699	16.8
1631–40	23,600	33.5
1641–50	4,440	11.6
1651–60	5,204	11.6

grammar schools, when the religious tenor of university instruction was far more pronounced than at the grammar-school level. From 1530 to 1600 grammar schools received twice as much as the universities. This was at a time when the grammar-school curriculum was becoming, if anything, even more secular under the influence of a new classicism.

Jordan believed that the secularization of philanthropy was noticeable by 1510. This would indicate a declining faith in the institutional church even before the state broke its power and before Protestantism had presented a more spiritualized view of religion.[36] But the chronology of this development is not that clear. As a percentage of total philanthropy, religious giving rose from 60.6 percent in the 1480s to 70.8 percent in the 1490s, before dropping back to 44.4 percent by the 1530s. It was only when Henry's intentions became clear that giving to the Church fell suddenly, to 28 percent in the 1540s. Under Protestant monarchs it collapsed.

The influence of an unsympathetic state (as opposed to waning belief) is shown even more specifically in a fall in the endowment of masses (which Jordan terms "prayers"). Between 1480 and 1530 this category had accounted for 51 percent of all religious giving. But as religious giving plummeted, the endowment of prayers and chantries fell even faster, to 44 percent of religious giving in the 1540s, 19 percent in the 1550s and 0.6 percent in the 1560s. Jordan believed that the whole system of endowed prayers was in "disrepute long before the Reformation." But his figures show that, even after adjusting for inflation, such giving rose from 1480 to the 1520s (except for the dip in all categories of philanthropy in the 1510s), indicating that the political change came before the mental one.[37]

The attack on endowed prayers for souls in purgatory was a major blow to the old religious economy. Even Thomas Starkey warned of how destructive this would be to all religious culture:

> Under the color of driving away man's tradition and popishness . . . [the reformers] had almost set your people at such liberty from all old customs and ceremonies that they began . . . little to esteem other virtues or honesty. And with the despising of purgatory, they began little to regard hell, heaven, or any other hereafter to be had in another life. For when the knot of obedience, wherein your people had lived many a day, was once broken and plucked away, then the multitude, which ever by their own nature are prone, and ever have been, to all pleasure and liberty, began to slip from all ancient customs and ceremonies.[38]

Henry was not deterred. In 1536 his Ten Articles for religion declared belief in purgatory to be an *adiaphoron*. And although Henry's subsequent formulations of doctrine edged back toward Catholicism, purgatory was the one belief which continued to fade, disappearing from the teaching of his church by the time of the *King's Book* of 1543.[39] If one can judge by the fact that Henry endowed masses for his own soul just as he left this life, it does not appear that he was convinced of the error of this doctrine. More likely, the wealth of chantry endowments had tempted him. He did not justify their seizure in doctrinal terms. In 1545 (by 37 Henry VIII, c. 4) he simply used the fact that apprehensive trustees were diverting those funds to social projects to justify his own confiscations.

Edward's advisors did see the issue in theological terms and made a clean sweep by a statute of 1547 (1 Edw. VI, c. 14). The preamble to this confiscation dismissed the "phantising vain opinions of purgatory and masses satisfactory." The government's determination to destroy every last college, stipendary priest, obit, anniversary, or light was clearly a matter of principle, since the amount recovered was often less than the cost of recovery. For example, administrators had to deal with four old cows that maintained a poor Somerset priest, and secularized "a stock of bees" which supported a candle on the altar of a church in Gloucester. They were scrupulous in seizing only those parts of gild endowments which were related to "superstitious uses."[40]

The one religious activity for which giving rose during the Reformation was sermons. Endowment of lectureships and sermons began soon after endowment of prayers declined, rising from 4 percent of all religious philanthropy in the 1570s to 29 percent in the 1580s, levelling off at 21 percent for the balance of

Jordan's period. Interest in raising the standard of preaching obviously represents a desire to spread religion, or at least the discussion of religion. In fact, such lectureships had a divisive effect within English culture, for it is with only slight exaggeration that Jordan titles this category "Puritan lectureships." As with religious publishing, we cannot count this activity as conducive to the settlement of a religious culture. A mass is a religious act in itself; lectures might be only a consideration of religion. Indeed, Puritan lecturers were often striving to break up an earlier religious mentality.[41]

In 1549 the English liturgy was ready, replacing the Mass with something superficially similar. There was public objection to every aspect of the new service—to the use of common, loaf bread instead of wafers, to giving bread into the communicant's hand rather than mouth, to the replacement of altars with portable Communion tables. Any one of these practices would jar those who looked upon the Host as the holiest thing in the world and who wanted it guarded against profanation. Instead, the new Book announced that Christ's body was only in heaven.[42]

The Western or "Prayer Book" Rising of 1549 reveals the thinking of many. The West Country had missed the Pilgrimage of Grace, so it seized this new occasion to march behind the banner of the five wounds of Christ, behind pyx and censers, and to have priests formulate their grievances.[43] Religion ought to mean, the rebels declared, that the Church was guided by "the general counsall and holy decrees of our forfathers," including the Act of Six Articles. They wanted only the priest to take the sacrament except at the customary Easter Communion, though they wanted the Host to be suspended over the altar to be "worshypped." They wanted the Mass to be said in Latin and not in English, which had made the new service seem "lyke a Christmas game." (Of course, parodies of the Mass had been known in the Middle Ages, but then people had known what was real and what was play. It was disconcerting not to be sure.) When communicating, the rebels desired only bread, but wanted holy bread and holy water to be administered every Sunday. They insisted on palms, ashes, images, and "all other auncient olde Ceremonyes used heretofore, by our mother the holy Church." Prayers for souls in purgatory were to be revived. Heretics were to be executed. And by way of a compromise, they wanted half of the Church's lands in anyone's possession to be returned to support two resurrected abbeys in each county, to "pray for the Kyng and the common wealth."[44]

Sympathetic riots spread to Berkshire, Oxfordshire, Buckinghamshire, Northamptonshire, and perhaps Sussex and Yorkshire. But they failed, and the episode ended with the hanging of a priest from his steeple, loaded with his vestments, bells, beads, holy-water bucket and "such other like popish trash."[45] The state lost no opportunity to show its contempt for the instruments of a defeated faith.

When Edward's government died with him in 1553 and the news of Queen Mary's accession reached Exeter the Protestant bishop, Miles Coverdale, was in the middle of a sermon. Most of his congregation got up and left him stranded in his cathedral pulpit.[46] They knew there would be a change in religious policy. But religious culture could not be mended any more than Humpty Dumpty could be put back on the wall. It was not for lack of trying. Mary tried a restoration rather than a reform of the old worship along Tridentine lines.[47] Historians lament her lack of creativity and the failure to "revivify the old religion by means of fresh minds and ideals."[48] This is the twentieth century speaking, on the assumption that a change in religion could be anything other than an admission of failure. The leader of her church, Cardinal Reginald Pole, purposely avoided a campaign of Counter-Reformation preaching to win England back. He hoped to revive a childlike trust in the Church and constantly used the imagery of childhood innocence. Persecution seemed the appropriate discipline for the simple-minded people he thought the English were. Processions and commemorative services took the place of debates, and the government hoped for years of quiet to nurse England back to spiritual health.[49]

Many Catholics were less patient, and used as much violence in restoring the Mass (even before the government's direction) as Protestants had used in destroying it. Sacred relics reappeared, and there were new English martyrs to remember, thanks to Henry.[50] Mary's first injunctions ended the use of English and ordered the restoration of holy days and fasts, with all other "laudable and honest ceremonies which were wont to be used, frequented, and observed in the Church." So rood screens were rebuilt and images replaced, altars and crosses restored. Mary's inquisitors quizzed suspects to see if they believed in the necessity of holy water and holy bread, ashes, palms, confession, purgatory, prayers for the dead, candles at Candlemas, sepulchres for Holy Week, processions, creeping to the cross, kissing the pax, for these were no longer "things indifferent." The scriptural texts on church walls were whitewashed over in their turn—as a distraction and a provocation.[51] One might look for some discrimination among these elements which would indicate that some were thought more central than others. But the whole apparatus seemed necessary.

Mary did compromise, however, in the matter of the Church's former lands. And Cardinal Pole did not stand on the Church's rights in this matter since this would place "in the utmost peril the cause of the faith and of the unity of the Church." Of course, he did not expect this to be the end of the matter; future generations would surely offer a landed endowment to the Church to match the one that was lost.[52] Mary herself set an example, restoring six monasteries from the property still in her hands. But at that point England discovered the irreversible damage done to the old religious culture. Only about a hundred monks and nuns returned, out of perhaps 1,500 ex-religious still living. Historian David Knowles concluded that "while twenty years of religious turmoil and secularization had not extinguished the sense of vocation in a few individuals, the conception of the religious life as an occupation for a young man in the neighborhood of a monastery had gone forever." That is to say, "monasticism as an integral part of society" had passed.[53] It was a severe disappointment that "no single lay owner of monastic land felt moved to imitate the Queen's generosity."[54] One can also see evidence of decline in the disappointing scale of the rood lofts and screens in comparison with those from Henry's early years.[55]

In retrospect, it seems inevitable that Mary should fail to undo decades of secularization by purely reactionary policies. In the words of D. M. Loades, England was already "a secular community still thinking, largely to its own confusion, in religious terms."[56] For instance, Mary was forced to act as supreme head of the Church of England despite herself. Her policies were enforced by justices of the peace rather than by church courts, and the desecrating statutes of previous reigns were all repealed by the same secular authority that had passed them. Eventually Mary even adopted the means of her enemies in sponsoring a Catholic translation of the New Testament, a Catholic catechism and homilies to underpin her people's faith. She never recognized Protestantism as a religious position—viewing it only as an excuse for faction—but its approach to religion began to affect her own.[57]

In one respect, Mary's reign carried secularization further than ever: she made the old religion seem foreign. As Claire Cross puts it, "because of her passionate loyalty to the Pope, and to her Spanish husband, Mary unintentionally had made Catholicism appear to some of her subjects as a foreign form of religion, which it had never done before."[58] Protestants also had to answer the charge that their doctrine came from Germany or Switzerland. Neither side could present its religion as an English birthright, as a culture must be. It was a sign of the times that while Sir Thomas Wyatt personally viewed his rebellion against Mary (1553) as a religious struggle, he downplayed that aspect in order to appeal to a wider, more secular nationalism.[59] This makes a contrast with the religious tone of the rising of four years before.

Mary's restoration of religious culture might have been more successful if her reign had been as long as her sister's. Other European nations managed to maintain Catholic observance in the face of severe challenges. Elizabeth's religious policies were not universally popular; there was local opposition to removing roods and images, as in Edward's time. The government was often simply not obeyed in parishes that kept their altars, processional banners, churchyard crosses, and shrines.[60] But on the whole, Elizabeth found it easier to restore the settlement of her brother's reign, shakey as it had been, than Mary had in bringing back even older usages.

To be sure, Elizabeth insisted on more of the old cult than Puritans wanted. For example, she restored the clerical vestments that implied a sacerdotal priesthood. She would have liked to restore crucifixes but found she could not proceed beyond keeping one in her own chapel. Even that was such a notorious affront that it was actually stolen several times. Rood screens were retained (though not the roods) to remind worshippers of the holiness of the things and places behind them.[61]

But even Catholic historians have shown little sympathy for the more "superstitious" of the recusants left stranded at Mary's death. We do not understand the outrage of those who had rosaries snatched away by their vicars, knowing that this would not mean the end of religion as we know it.[62] But those rosaries had allowed the devout to concentrate on traditional prayers amidst the distractions of an alien liturgy. We may think that it was high time that royal commissioners removed the votive paraphernalia that the people had restored under Queen Mary. But without our sense of what religion should mean, contemporaries often objected violently. Court records are full of the complaints of those who were denied the comforts of holy water, bells, prayers for the dead, and wafers rather than ordinary bread.[63] We should probably try to imagine these as central elements in a religion long lost, just as we must try to recapture the shock of seeing the royal arms displayed everywhere Christ's rood had once stood.

Elizabeth was like her sister in realizing that theological debate was not the way to settle "religion" on England. Her first injunctions observed that:

> In all alterations, and specially in rites and ceremonies, there happen discourds amongst the people, and thereupon slanderous words and railings, whereby charity, the knot of all Christian society, is loosed; the queen's majesty being most desirous of all other earthly things, that her people should live in charity both towards God and man, and therein abound in good works, wills and straitly commands all manner her subjects to forbear all vain and contentious disputations in matters of religion.

Accordingly, Elizabeth outlined a scheme for censoring publications, "because there is a great abuse in the printers of books, which for covetousness chiefly regard not what they print, so [long as] they may have gain."[64] Ironically, what passed her censors would be as unsettling to religious culture as the "unfruitful, vain, and infamous books" she had in mind. This is true wherever religion becomes a thing to think about, rather than a way of thinking.

Finally, one must ask what the essentials of religion were for Protestants, that they distinguished from superstitions and from "things indifferent." What gave them access to supernatural powers if not that range of customary activities and culture? In chapter 12 we will consider their religious initiatives. For now we may simply recall the common observation that Protestants were people of the book. Their devotion to the written or printed word is everywhere apparent. As the Church's homily for Rogation Week put it, "In the holy Scriptures find wee Christ, in Christ finde wee God."[65] Accordingly, sermons took on a new sanctity. Vernacular psalms and prayers became central to worship, rather than ritual gestures or incantation. Godly conversation, laced with "the language of Zion," became central to charity and to fellowship, in place of church ales.

Or one can ask, instead, what was the greatest sacrilege for Protestants. Here again, one finds that verbal blasphemy was a greater horror than anything one could do to the Communion elements, for example. In 1597 Thomas Beard, who is famous as Oliver Cromwell's Puritan schoolmaster, published his view of the sacrilege of his times. Among all the things he might have mentioned, his examples involve words. Beard had collected instances of judgments on cursing and blasphemy, on perjury, on adding anything to God's worship, on the misuse of Scripture in dramatic performances. Playing the part of Christ had actually brought death or madness to several actors. He also registered his delight in the fixity of print and of God's Word. It provided an anchor for humanity's wayward imagination and affections, "seeing that God hath set downe a certaine forme of doctrine and instruction, according to which hee would have us to serve him."[66]

J. J. Scarisbrick has summed up the change that came over English religion in terms that will now be familiar:

> The Reformation simplified everything. It effected a shift from a religion of symbol and allegory, ceremony and formal gesture to one that was plain and direct: a shift from the visual to the aural, from ritual to literal exposition, from the numinous and mysterious to the everyday. It moved from the high colours of statue, window and painted walls to whitewash; from ornate vestments and altar frontal to plain tablecloth and surplice; from a religion that, with baptismal salt on lips, anointings and frankincense—as well as image, word and chant—sought out all the senses, to one that concentrated on the word and innerliness. There was a shift from a religion that often went out of doors on pilgrimage and procession to an indoor one.[67]

The fact that Protestantism mediated this reduction—translated religion into a new idiom—may have made secularization less traumatic than in France, for example, where power was used without religious persuasion.

For Beard, religion was expressed in verbal symbols. Words awaken faith. In time, a vernacular culture would again hallow an area of English life. The words of the catechism, of the marriage ceremony and the liturgy, of certain hymns and the authorized translation of Scripture, would be sanctified by use. But in the meantime the mysteries of medieval religion had been resolved into questions. Questions awaken debate. And though the debate might be on religion, it marked the end of a religious innocence.

6

The Secularization of Technology and Work

Any discussion of the secularization of work will reveal certain assumptions. It would be well to mention them at once so that they may be tested, but also so that they can direct us to the evidence, which is slim for this most important topic. While work filled up most people's lives, it seems to have been the last thing they wanted to write about. The hints which we find must be magnified to get a sense of their importance.

Obviously the economic decline of the Church at Henry's reformation—as landlord, patron of the arts of worship, sponsor of crafts and of agricultural festivals—reduced the presence of religion in work. We would also expect work to lose its religious associations as it ceased to be agrarian and became "industrial." Rural life is lived close to God's nature and is obviously dependent on forces outside human control; towns are a human creation and reflect our image and purposes. We know that agriculture had become overlaid with magico-religious practices, whereas the crafts of townspeople might not be affected that way. For these reasons we will expect to see work take on a more secular character.

On the other hand, we have been taught that medieval peasants and theologians looked upon work as a divine curse, whereas Protestantism is supposed to have given work a positive religious valence. Protestants may have generalized the Benedictine approval of labor, which had remained a minority position through the Middle Ages. If every useful occupation became a religious vocation, then all labor could be a means of grace. So this might be one area of life which was sacralized by the Reformation.

Once again, we may usefully begin by contrasting two ideal types. First is a view of the world as lying under enchantment. Humanity must wrest a living from a nature which is partly under the control of contrary forces—fairies, witches, the devil himself. One would need some magic to counteract such forces and detoxify nature, giving ordinary technology a chance of success. Keith Thomas believes that Christianity had originally spread through Europe as a superior form of magic and that its connection with magic had been close ever since. He contends that through the Middle Ages there was no consistent line between the Church's magic and the impious magic which it condemned.[1] Other scholars also notice that Christian expressions are common in their charm texts, indicating that religion and magic existed on a continuum.[2]

In the other view humanity confronts a nature which is already neutral, ready for its command. There is no need to invoke supernatural aid to overcome some spell which lies over nature. The only problem is in ourselves—our persistence in labor and our knowledge of efficient causes. Thomas traced the replacement of magic by just such a work orientation as part of his theme of the triumph of a more sophisticated religion over magic.[3] Under the more consistent monotheism of Protestantism, the area of the sacred narrowed. By implication, humanity had mainly itself to contend with and not a recalcitrant world of spirits.

Some anthropologists have viewed magic itself as a secular technology, and have doubted that practitioners think of it as involving supernatural powers. Whether or not that was the case for the Trobriand Islanders of Malinowski's time, English men and women in 1500 obviously crossed back and forth over the line between magic and religion very easily. It is possible that their healing and tilling charms were part of Saxon religion and had adopted Christian terms to avoid the prohibitions on paganism.[4] But Thomas's examples of magical practice regularly involve Christian symbols and thus would have been associated with the supernatural forces of religion. Magical spells often used the sacred languages of Latin, Greek, Hebrew, and Aramaic, or corruptions of these. Detection of criminals or lost objects commonly involved the use of Bibles or Christian phrases. "Mosaical rods" were used to find treasure.[5] "Cunning" men and women identified the cause of maladies as supernatural and sold what Thomas can only call "christian charms." Meanwhile, Christian monks and priests were popularly thought to engage in occult, alchemical, and magical activity, and sometimes are known to have done so. So despite the Church's frequent opposition to a rival magic, there is no question of a consistent distinction in the mind of the time.[6]

Another modern difficulty in thinking about our subject is in supposing that the devil is a secular figure, and that invoking him is a secular activity. The devil and God are equally spirits, and dealings with either can be considered "religious." Indeed the Homily for Rogation Week, composed around 1550, complains that for many people the devil was the god of work. The homilist scolds his audience:

If wee stand in necessitie of corporall health, whither goe the common people, but to charmes, witchcraftes and other delusions of the Devill? If wee knewe that GOD were the author of this gift, wee would only use his meanes appoynted, and bide his leysure, till hee thought it good for us to have it given. If the Merchaunt and worldly occupier knew that GOD is the giver of riches, hee would content himselfe with so much as by just meanes approved of GOD, hee could get to his living, and would be no richer than trueth would suffer him, hee would never procure his gaine and aske his goods at the Devils hand.[7]

Perhaps this language already seemed a little quaint and the preacher intended a little humor. It may only have been a pleasantly metaphorical assault on those who "increase them selves by usurie, by extortion, by perjury, by stealth, by deceits and crafts." But a wealth of stories, from all over Europe, suggests that he was not far from the mark.

After all, who was it that approached the characters of so many English folk tales and morality plays, promising them success in business—and a spiritual compact?[8] Fortunes were to be made in the devil's service, apparently. These stories surely go back in some form to pre-Reformation times. But viewing the devil as "the god of this world" had biblical precedent even for Protestants; there are statements to this effect throughout the New Testament.[9] Most familiar was the story of Christ's temptation in the wilderness, in which Satan offers him "all the kingdoms of the world."[10] So even Protestants knew that humanity needed help to make its way through an enemy's territory.

The homilist had opposed a more secular attitude as well, that success could come without God's or the devil's help: "Such good things which wee call goods of fortune, as richesse, authoritie, promotion, and honour some men may thinke, that they should come of our industry and diligence, of our labour and travaile, rather than supernaturally." They should consider, was it by man's brain that he had subdued

the great strong beasts and fishes, farre passing the strength of man, how fierce soever they be . . . ? Nay rather this invention came by the goodnesse of God, which inspired mans understanding to have his purpose of every creature. . . . It could not be verily (good Christian people) that man of his own wit upholden, should invent so many and diverse devises in all crafts and science, except the goodnesse of Almighty GOD had been present with men, and had stirred their wits and studies of purpose to know the natures and disposition of all his creatures, to serve us sufficiently in our needes and necessities.[11]

Similarly, by the seventeenth century the stories of fortunate apprentices commonly ignored the devil as benefactor and concentrated on the effect of diligence and thrift.[12]

The medieval church's official view of work was not identical to folk beliefs. Theologians treated work partly as punishment on a rebellious humanity and partly as penance to restore a proper relationship with God. As discipline, work was considered a good thing, even though painful. It was with this understanding that monks joined in, and not from a "work ethic" in which they found their identity in their labor. They did not believe in the dignity of labor but entered into it as an exercise in humility. They also contrived to leave the harder work to lay brothers. Contemplation, not work, was humanity's highest activity, for it transcended this world and entered God's own realm.[13]

Nevertheless, there was still some recognition for work. Peasants could see themselves memorialized in cathedral glass and carving, working away at the Ark or the Tower of Babel or at their ordinary, life-sustaining labors. Even so, they were often portrayed as misshapen by their efforts.[14] Medieval writers at least agreed that work was better than idleness, and less prone to temptation than was commerce.[15] Still, it ranked below contemplation in the view of the clergy, and was self-evidently below the more spirited pastimes of the aristocracy. So it would have been surprising if peasants and artisans imagined that their labor had any religious significance.

What, in fact, were the peasants doing while theologians refined their views? Along with the material technology of the day, they were invoking supernatural powers—our initial definition of religion. No doubt this was in varying degrees depending on the region, the occupation, even the individual. It may stretch our definition of culture to include activities that were largely secretive, if peasants refused to share their secrets of the unseen world. But it often showed some connection to religion and even to Christianity.

When the English husbandman prepared for Plough Monday by lighting candles, it was on the altar in the parish church.[16] He blessed his trees on Epiphany, his corn on Palm Sunday, and read the Gospels to the corn and hay and springs periodically, to lay evil spirits. It seemed natural to use prayers when engaged in such basic activities as planting and grafting.[17] There were spells for fertilizing and seafaring, often associated with specific saints, just as the various barnyard animals had specific protectors, such as St. Legearde (for geese) and St. Leonard (for ducks).[18] In some places, at least, rents were paid on Christmas, Easter, and Martinmas,[19] and every job fell on the appropriate saint's day:

> Cut your thistles before St. John,
> You will have two instead of one.[20]

Laborers about to lift a burden might say "In the name of God, that is, In the power of God."[21]

Housework could also go wrong without the proper attention to unseen powers, so there were spells for brewing and baking. The little rhyme which helped in churning

> Come, butter, come,
> Come, butter, come,
> Peter stands at the gate,
> Waiting for a buttered cake,
> Come, butter, come

was typical in its small but suggestive religious reference (from Acts 12).[22]

There may have been some uneasiness of conscience in these matters, despite the Christian references. Puritans had no doubt that such things as the Rogation Day perambulation were mere superstition, sneering at that practice as "charming the fields."[23] Even the old priests were horrified at some of the usages, as when parishioners sneaked the Communion host home to scatter bits of it to save their bees or to kill their caterpillers.[24] It was usual to lock covers on baptismal fonts to keep the water from being taken for magical purposes.[25] So there was a conscience against magic that may be responsible for the meager appearance of charms in the historical record. For example, John Fitzherbert, in his *Booke of Husbandrie* (1523), mentions God's blessing frequently but does not allude to charms.

However common rural magic may have been, Keith Thomas points out that such behavior was not restricted to agricultural labor. The building trades had long sought divine help. When the four piers were sunk for the tower gate on London Bridge (in 1426) each of them had "Ihesus" inscribed on them. John Stow had heard that the Tower of London's "turrets and walls do rise from a deep foundation, the mortar thereof being tempered with the blood of beasts," suggesting sacrifice. Even such manufactures as metal working and weaving had their magical precautions.[26] And, in comparison with the housewife crossing her dough before kneading, the craft gilds' religious apparatus seems rather elaborate.[27]

One of the first tasks of any business or craft was to decide on a patron among the saints. Gild regulations always included bows toward piety. The Grocers of London, despite the fear of spoilage, decided to sell nothing on Sunday or Holy Days. The Porters also agreed not to work on Sundays, except in Lent when there would be fish to unload for fasting customers. The Cutlers worried about their members who worked into the holidays "to the grete displeasure of Allmyghty god," and forbade work after three in the afternoon on the eve of a festival, "for the pleasure of god." Bakers imprinted crosses or holy names on bread loaves, and Scriveners swore on the Gospels to afix honest dates on letters and deeds.[28]

The Reformation eroded these resolutions. The clerks of the Clothworkers of London abruptly stopped inscribing "Jhus Amor" at the top of each page of the company minutes. They also promptly purchased monastery buildings for conversion to industrial use, installing fulling mills and looms.[29] The Merchant Taylors of London ceased to celebrate St. John the Baptist's feast day, removed his statue from their hall and melted down all the company plate that bore religious emblems. They did set up a Bible in the hall in 1578, but all that remained of company devotion were prayers before their quarterly meetings.[30]

Just as significant was the loss of business which went with the change in religious style. The Wax Chandlers, who had sold fifteen hundred candles to Henry III for a single festival in St. Paul's, were devastated by the Protestant attack on votive lights and lavish funerals. Perhaps the decline of the company explains why their chapel in St. Paul's was soon turned into a wine cellar.[31] The Gild of Organ Builders disbanded in 1531; and the Mistery of Painters, which had once proudly ordered the use of fine gold in all painted work in churches, found that no such work was required any longer.[32] Nor was the labor of masons, glaziers, goldsmiths, and tailors who had specialized in creating the equipment of worship. Thus, much work that was once directly devoted to God's glory was simply no longer done.

The greatest blow to the crafts' religiosity was the government's attack on their system of charity and intercession. Occupational identification had once been a means of grace. For in the medieval economy, to work in gold was to be goldsmith and a member of a brotherhood of goldsmiths. Foremost among one's duties as a member of the London company was attendance at twenty-five obits yearly—anniversary masses in commemoration of former members. Just as the Church included the company of the faithful departed, so each company communed with its former members in this way. To be sure, by 1521 the Goldsmiths had found that so many days, even with the "potations" provided by some wills, had grown burdensome. They hit upon the idea of combining "wet" and "dry" observances, making the time spent shorter but sweeter.[33] But companies had no wish to do away with obits entirely, for the gild was as much a religious congregation as the parish church. To be a Goldsmith was partly a religious designation, like being a Dominican.

All trade and craft gilds had either originated as religious confraternities or had later adopted religious ceremonials and functions. The Shrewsbury Drapers made no mention at all of economic functions in their first charter but concentrated on the chantries that served their members.[34] The London Clothworkers' first ordinance concerned the maintenance of thirteen lights before the image of Mary in Christ Church monastery for the souls of their members.[35] A major project of the Merchant Taylors was arranging for several monasteries to include their members in the prayers of the monks. An illuminated list of these fringe benefits hung in the company's chapel in St. Paul's.[36] The Cappers of Coventry at least made a point of sitting together during divine service.[37] The poorest gilds might show their spiritual solidarity in brutally simple ways, as when the Waterbearers' Fraternity protected its members by use of "the great curse."[38]

Thus, work created a network of spiritual support. For example, the alms of such gilds were not disinterested charities. The Goldsmiths stipulated that the almsmen they supported must attend Mass twice a week in order to pray for their company benefactors. Everything down to the coal given to the poor was supposed to be repaid by prayers for the souls of the company's members. In return, the fines which companies imposed—for unbrotherly competition—were usually designated for use as alms.[39] Thus they created a loop which included member's offense, company's judgment, penance (fine), charity, almsman's intercession, and member's reinstatement.

The religious character of occupational groups ended with the Reformation, along with that reciprocity between rich and poor. By the Chantries Act of 1549 the government seized any corporate endowments which had supported obits, lights, and all other purely religious observances, leaving only the endowments for charities.[40] So corporate philanthropies had less point now that there were no spiritual benefits accruing to the donors. The historian of the Shrewsbury Drapers noticed that as their charities ceased to be associated with prayers of intercession they ceased to grow. Corpus Christi Day, which had been the proud occasion for the gilds to perform their religious plays, was there renamed "Shrewsbury Show."[41]

The government's attack on agricultural habits was less direct. Plough Monday was abolished in 1548 along with other holy days, many of which had agricultural significance. In 1559 Elizabeth ordered her clergy to "teach and declare unto their parishioners, that they may with a safe and quiet conscience, after their common prayer in the time of harvest, labour upon the holy and festival days, and save that thing which God hath sent." Speaking for the Almighty, the Church warned that "if for any scrupulosity or grudge of conscience, men should superstitiously abstain from working upon those days, that then they should grievously offend and displease God."[42] God's wishes in these matters now seemed more reasonable.

One of humanity's greatest tasks is healing, and medical practice was very slow to give up its religious or magical associations. Professional physicians already had a reputation for religious scepticism, whether deserved or not. But much of healing was of the unofficial variety, and a recent study concludes that as late as 1600,

> The world in which most traditional healers acted was not divided into distinct material and spiritual parts. Minds, spirits, appearances, objects, all mingled with one another in ways that some well-educated contemporaries termed "superstitious."[43]

Healing and childbirth seems to have been the area of technology which was most closely related to the use of charms and religion, just as hospitals may be the most active prayer centers in the modern world. At least an episcopal visitation article or question of 1559 singles it out:

Whether you know of any that do use charms, sorcery, enchantments, invocations, circles, witchcrafts, soothsayings, or any like crafts or imaginations invented by the Devil and specially in time of women's travail.[44]

The anxiety surrounding illness and birth was probably one reason that an act of 1512 allowed bishops to help examine and license physicians, surgeons, and midwives (3 Henry VIII, c. 11). The preamble mentions sorcery, and doubtless unauthorized religious practices would be a special temptation here.

Donald Caton dates what he calls "the secularization of pain" much later than our period. He has shown that the technological treatment of pain was controversial as late as the nineteenth century.[45] It is perhaps what one should expect, given the life-and-death stakes involved. Older ways of understanding and dealing with pain and cures were held tenaciously. After all, contemporaries did not share our assurance that these had never worked. They *had* worked—usually. Sometimes, anyway. And if they sometimes failed, the more naturalistic science of the physicians had not given surer results. So in the seventeenth century, back trouble was still treated by pronouncing

> Christ rode over the bridge,
> Christ rode under the bridge,
> Vain to vain, strain to strain,
> I hope God will take it back again.

Bleeding, with its obvious theological associations, was fought by the following:

> Thro' the blood of Adam's sin,
> Was taken the blood of Christ.
> By that same blood I do thee charge,
> That the blood of (name) run no more at large.[46]

Keith Thomas has wondered why the old healing methods would decline at all, when haughty physicians could offer no more relief than the nearest witch. To the extent that they did, one factor in the decline must have been medical publication. The medical handbooks which increased along with literacy were on the side of Protestant disenchantment. It could not be said of them, as of the astrological publications of that time, that these books actually spread and strengthened a doomed lore against "modernizing" forces. Paul Slack noticed that the plague remedies that abound in fifteenth-century manuscripts—like saying the Paternoster, Ave, and Creed while signing the cross over eye, armpit, and thigh—just don't appear in sixteenth-century publications. In short, this was a time when a wise person used everything available, praying a blessing on the medicine the doctor had prescribed.[47]

Technological advance clearly played a part in secularizing some kinds of labor. What we call "industrial" activities do not usually involve the live forces of God's creation. Increasingly, men and women worked on the products of other people's efforts, as more of the work force moved from primary to secondary processes. They would see their labors in the context of those efforts, so that prayers would be less to the point. Religion would remain relevant to this labor only in the sense of creating a proper attitude and fostering the interior virtues of patience, honesty, resignation. But by concentrating on work attitudes, Protestants actually accelerated the profanation of their technology.

Two of the classic Protestant texts of the mid-seventeenth century, Richard Allestree's *The Whole Duty of Man* (1657) and Richard Baxter's *Christian Directory* (1673), give a sense of how such a profanation was proceeding. The former, is usually viewed as the most characteristic statement of Anglican social attitudes. What is remarkable is that Allestree completely ignores the most common experience of his humble audience. One of the seventeen chapters is on trade, and countered the opportunities for deceit in economic relations, but there is nothing on such vital economic concerns as coping with the weather; curing livestock; encouraging fertility; repelling fire, or blight, or plague. Baxter's work distilled the casuistical divinity of several generations of Puritans, and was the main source for Max Weber's thesis on the Protestant ethic as it regarded labor. Baxter does insist on taking delight in one's labor:

> Do not carnally murmer at it, because it is wearisome to the flesh, nor imagine that God accepteth the less of thy work or thee: but cheerfully follow it, and make it the matter of thy pleasure and joy that thou are still in thy heavenly Master's service, though it be about the lowest things.[48]

In other words, work should not be seen as a cure or a discipline, in the Catholic manner, but as a form of worship. So far, it sounds like the most ordinary activities of life could be sacralized. Baxter cites St. Paul on doing one's work as unto God and not to please others. "This interest of God in your lowest, and hardest, and servilest labour, doth make it honourable, and should make it sweet," he observes.[49]

But Baxter had not faced up to his real attitude, which comes out when he warns readers to "Drown not your hearts in worldly business or delights; for these breed a loathing, and adverseness, and weariness of holy things."[50] Thus he approves of diligence in work, but only so long as one is concentrating on one's attitude. One needs to think about the worker constantly; to think about the work is worldliness. This comes out more clearly when Baxter suggests that one should choose a calling which will not engage the mind, so that one can concentrate on spiritual matters. So by the end of this classic statement of the work ethic he has not progressed beyond his initial comment, which was to "Be very watchful redeemers of your time, and make conscience of every hour and minute."[51] In effect, work is measured not by the powers exercised or the service rendered or the thing produced, but by the diligence shown in the time God has given. Proper attitudes toward working are a part of one's interior religion, but the culture of work—one's technology—is not.

Baxter was not out of touch with his audience. At about the same time, a Puritan woodworker was recording in his diary the need to fill his day with honest toil. Nehemiah Wallington made it sound like a perfectly arbitrary discipline: if one had to work, at least show God that you can do it uncomplainingly and honestly. He did not mention work among the "religious duties" in his lists of resolutions. And it was no longer really possible for Wallington to make something for God out of wood. The Christian worker was building character. Paul Seaver remarks that for Wallington "religious principle and social reality [his worldly calling] existed together in some considerable tension."[52] That is, Wallington did not live in a religious culture which had harmonized the two.

Baxter's contemporary, John Flavell, announced his intention to spiritualize work in popular books entitled *Husbandry Spiritualized* (1669) and *Navigation Spiritualized* (1682). But in fact he was only interested in finding the allegorical meaning of these occupations. Flavell knew husbandry and seafaring, not from observation, but from having read about them in the Bible. His job was to elaborate the lessons that are hinted at there. At best, the many copies of these works (ten editions by 1700) could only have distracted farmers and sailors from their tedious labors.

Work was not a means of grace for Protestants, though it might be a mark of grace. Labor could be regulated by religion, but it was no longer a part of religion. This might strike us as a higher view of the matter than that of medieval peasants, who hoped they could insure their harvest by a deal with God or the devil. But we cannot call it a more "religious" view than that which invoked spiritual power against "the prince of this world."

The change was momentous. The religious mind of the Middle Ages had viewed contemplation as the highest activity and work as a painful discipline or a necessary evil. In the new age, humanity would show its superiority to the rest of creation not by contemplating it but by changing it.[53] No wonder society became so absorbed in work that it became an end in itself. The contemplation of creation paled before the possibility of becoming the creator.

7

The Secularization
of Art

It is a notorious fact that the English Reformation destroyed more religious art than it produced. Protestant spiritualization of religion reflected the view that there was more danger than possible benefit in giving physical form to the holy. Thus a Puritan iconoclasm would leave England poorer in sacred art, while artists and artisans turned their talents to more secular subjects. A survey of architecture, painting, sculpture, music, and literature and of the venues created for each of these arts will show just how rapid was the change.

Henry VIII's seizure of church buildings began this process even before we can speak of the influence of Protestantism. Not only was monastic architecture destroyed or profaned for other uses, but the government's evident hostility froze the impulse toward church building in general. W. K. Jordan's ten counties show a decline from £17,823 given for church building in the first decade of the sixteenth century, to £2,753 by the 1550s, and a low of £570 in the 1580s.[1] Taking inflation into account, that represents a fall of 99 percent.[2] Often there were not even funds for the repair of dilapidated churches; a sixteenth-century survey of rural Buckinghamshire lists 107 of 116 churches as in serious disrepair.[3] Meanwhile, Henry engaged in extensive palace building, setting a style for his aristocracy. Of course this activity left few resources for the employment of artisans in giving glory to God.[4]

Traditionally, religious art did not simply represent the sacred, but built on or enshrined things known to be sacred in themselves. A medieval church chose a site that was already marked out as sacred—by a vision, healing, or martyrdom. Failing that, one might create holy ground by transporting sacred relics to the site. This became a requirement in Western Christendom by order of the Council of Nicaea in 787, directing that saints' relics be used in the consecration of all altars and churches.[5] It was not necessary to stop with the minimum require-ment, of course. Relics were installed in the steeple of St. Paul's Cathedral, for instance, to ward off lightning.[6] Beyond this sacred presence, the arrangement of churches reflected a religious orientation. Churches all resembled a hallowed original by approximating the Temple plan in Scripture. This was taken to be a prefiguration of heaven, so that worshippers were introduced to their true, super-natural home. Since it was to be a place fit for God, economizing could hardly be justified. Accordingly, churches were decorated by painting, carving, altar cloths and banners, colored glass, vestments, incense, and music, so far as resources would permit.

Protestants, by contrast, remembered Jesus' claim that he would himself replace the Temple of Jerusalem. And they remembered St. Paul's comment that believers collectively formed the temple which is the body of Christ.[7] It followed that a house of worship should be a congregational meeting place, more in the tradition of the synagogue—a house of prayer and teaching—than of a temple, a place of sacrifice. As such, there was no point in the careful gradations of sanctity of Catholic churches in which a nave housed the congregation, a chancel the choir, and a sanctuary the interceding priest, with changes in elevation marking these divisions. Protestants were especially opposed to the screen which confined the laity to the nave, and the rail which blocked access to the sanctuary. When holy things had been thought of as more physical and with a greater sense of "dread," the laity had been glad to keep a certain distance.

England's churches could not easily be changed to eliminate the sense of procession into God's presence and of divine mystery. For one thing, there was little call for new buildings in most of the country. That was because the Middle Ages had overbuilt; church construction had been a meritorious act, and had not been limited by regard to "need." Norwich had about fifty churches for a popula-tion of something between 8,000 and 12,000, housing an average of only two hundred worshippers.[8] As a result, there was only a conflict about the remodeling of churches.

In 1550 John Hooper, bishop of Gloucester and often called England's first Puritan, suggested blocking off chancels in order to eliminate any area reserved to the clergy. That happened in some churches, so that all worship was transferred to the nave. Hooper argued that the idea of a fixed "altar" was alien to Christian-ity, and convinced Bishop Ridley to begin changing practice in the diocese of London to reflect this conviction.[9] It became Elizabethan practice to bring a moveable table to the front (west) of the chancel or even into the nave during the celebration of Communion.[10] The casual quality of this worship was a shock to old believers and was no doubt meant to be so.

Of course, many of the changes apparent by Elizabethan times were wrench-ing, as Horton Davies points out:

Elizabethan churches were simple and bare compared with their appearance in the Middle Ages. The stained glass windows had not entirely disappeared, although the representations of the Deity and the saints had been removed and increasingly clear glass was replacing coloured panes. The rood-lofts, with their carved and painted figures of the Christ, the Virgin and St. John, had been pulled down, and the painting of the doom on the tympanum had been whitewashed over. So also were all of the wall paintings of scenes in the life of the Virgin, or of St. Christopher bearing the Christ child. The pillars of the nave had had wooden or stone brackets with saints standing in the niches; all were torn out. What was to replace all this aesthetic richness? . . . painted wooden boards bearing the Royal Arms, the Lord's Prayer, the Creed, and the Tables of the Ten Commandments, affixed by royal commandment, and the sculptured tombs placed there by rising families.[11]

The underlying pattern was of a religion of the Word, replacing that of the image.

Stuart monarchs took more interest in church building, using their few opportunities to introduce continental styles. Rather incongruously, this meant Greek temples; Inigo Jones's Queen's Chapel (1623) and St. Paul's, Covent Garden (1630) are the most prominent examples of paganism enlisted in the service of the Church. Some architects continued designing Gothic churches even after secular architecture had gone over to the new styles, adopting a deliberate archaism for its sacred associations.[12] But the incongruity felt in adopting Greek styles was soon overcome, as baroque architects convinced themselves that the classical "orders" went back ultimately to Solomon's Temple. When Jones began dressing up the Gothic St. Paul's Cathedral in a classical facade, it was thought appropriate to the reign of a king (James) who had been compared to Constantine.[13]

In 1666 the Great Fire of London gave Protestants a chance to build churches which would be more suited to England's new faith. These were meeting houses rather than temples, meant to encourage a more rational worship. Sir Christopher Wren himself described them as "a convenient auditory" in which "everyone should hear the Service and both hear and see the Preacher." His elevation of the Word is everywhere in evidence. In line with Stuart conservatism there were altars and altar rails, but they were not in a separate apse or chancel and were quite dwarfed by the elaborately carved pulpits.[14] Where medieval styles had evoked mystery, Wren's churches were marked by clarity, with no room for exploration, little feeling for the struggle of light and darkness.[15]

In 1689, when the Act of Toleration allowed Dissenters to build their own chapels, the implications of Protestant worship became even more obvious. Decades of meeting furtively in barns, homes, or rented halls had given Dissenters time to think what they needed. Within ten years 2,400 chapels were raised on a fairly standard, unornamented pattern. Seats surrounded a central table with a pulpit rising behind it. If the building were rectangular, the pulpit would be placed along the long wall rather than axially, to maintain the closest contact between speaker and audience. As in so many things, Quakers reached a logical conclusion by meeting in boxes without pulpit or table. There they could wait for God's spirit to move or quiet them, without aid from human priests, ministers, or architects.[16]

These developments in ecclesiastical architecture mainly describe London, where the Fire had offered an opportunity for innovation. Elsewhere in the country the dead hand of England's architectural past retarded such change. As well designed as medieval churches were for the kind of worship they housed, their presence may have subtly slowed the growth of Protestantism. Indeed, Horton Davies believes that Anglicans have those churches to thank, in part, for the compromising character of their ritual tradition.[17]

The furnishing of these churches called for some conscious decisions, however. Even medieval clerics had complained of popular excesses, as when in 1356 Ralph Fitzralph, archbishop of Armagh, complained that statues had achieved an independent sanctity. St. Mary of Walsingham was not represented by the statue there; she *was* the statue—which took on the powers of a relic. In the popular mind "she" was a rival of St. Mary of Lincoln, St. Mary of Leicester, and so forth.[18] When Henry menaced such shrines, their supporters offered arguments for considering this art to be sacred. For instance, Sir Thomas More argued that natural objects reflect a spiritual world and that art was therefore the most natural language for the expression of the creator's mind. Pressed by Tyndale, More denied that churches had to choose between using their wealth for the decking of images and for relieving the poor; they could do both. He asserted that the commandment against graven images must have referred only to false gods. And he denied that there was any difference between images and verbal expressions, implying that they could be "true" in the same sense. Never did More indicate that the nation should graduate from the school of illiteracy, where images were the books of the poor. For him, representing a religious culture, the goal was not enlightening the mind but stirring the spirit, and images did this best.[19]

More did acknowledge a distinction between sacred objects and religious art. The former were holy in themselves and did not only promote religious reflection. He was not far from the position of a moderate reformer, such as Thomas Starkey, who was willing to treat religious art as a matter "indifferent"—to be allowed or not depending on its proper use.[20] But moderates were more likely to agree with reformers that since God is a spirit, worshippers should not need signs or pictures. In line with a more theological religion, the concern grew that misunderstanding art was more likely than mistaking ordinary words—in reading and preaching.

There was an even more radical position. Bishop Hooper showed how a truly spiritual faith transcended art and sacred objects to find a danger even in mental images. He pointed out that the sin of idolatry was in the mind, not in the object. Worshippers can hardly avoid trying to imprison God in mental images, which are only a slight refinement on the statues in their churches and likewise falsify spiritual truth. One may see here the germ of Francis Bacon's "Idols of the Mind," attacked in *Novum Organum* (1620).[21] It suggests a link between a puritanical spirituality and scientific abstraction.

Henry VIII's government tried to compromise the issue of religious art, treating images as *adiaphora* and trying to regulate usage. Henry's first injunctions to the clergy (1536) ordered them not to "extol any images, relics, or miracles for any superstition or lucre, nor allure the people by any enticements to the pilgrimage of any saint . . . seeing that all goodness, health, and grace ought to be both asked and looked for only of God." But Edward's Council refused to recognize any distinction between images which had been worshipped and those that had not and in 1548 simply ordered all of them removed.[22] This was not, however, to extend to spoiling the aristocratic tombs in churches, which would needlessly undermine social authority.[23]

Command was followed by explanation in the Homily Against Idolatry. It was many times longer than any of the others—sixty-six pages against an average of eleven—perhaps indicating the central position that images played in popular devotion. It might have been shorter, except that the author was still groping to understand his own position. He did remember that while alive the saints had forbidden men and women to worship them, as had angels in their appearances on earth. The early martyrs had prefered to die than to "kneele, or offer up one crumbe of incense before an image." Obviously they did not view such images as "things indifferent." Thus, Pope Gregory the Great had been unwise in his famous comment "that images bee the Lay-mens Bookes, and that pictures are the Scriptures of idiotes and simple persons." The truth was that these lying images had made Christians into "idiots and stark fooles."[24]

History proved to the homilist that human beings were naturally susceptible to idolatry. Explaining this susceptibility led him into an analogy with fornication, since religious and carnal uncleanness were both primarily visual. The glitter of the gilding and decking of images was what proved seductive; the cure was a return to rusticity. The Church Fathers had recommended wicker baskets for communion bread and glasses for communion wine, and the plainest of vestments for the clergy.[25] In short, they shared the Reformer's more spiritual faith.

Churchwardens who read the signs of the times unloaded the offending furnishings on the best terms they could get. Three or four shiploads of images were exported to France in 1550, according to a report to Edward's council.[26] Fancy plate and vestments also escaped the country, including the Syon Cope.[27] Many parishes hid their church furnishings—hedging against a restoration—and a number of churchwarden's accounts show them finally being sold in the middle of Elizabeth's reign, when that hope had faded.[28]

Some insight into the Catholic view of this art can be gained from Queen Mary's orders for restoring images. To show that representation was not the point, she insisted that images and crosses be replaced by actual carvings and not mere paintings of the same.[29] Clearly, rounded figures create a reality that pictorial representation cannot convey. Only Protestants thought it was enough to be reminded of another world; Catholics sought to bring that world into their midst by the use of holy objects.

When Mary died the production of "sacred objects" ceased. From now on art might treat biblical subjects, but it could not be the object of worship. Artisans who had produced the silver plate and reliquaries, the frescoes, altarcloths, and images now had to produce for a secular market. Without church patronage, the painters of glass turned to heraldry. Manuscript illuminators became portrait miniaturists. Church decorating adopted secular motifs, as when carved pew ends changed from religious symbols to fauna and flora.[30] And a survey of art during Elizabeth's and James's reigns concludes that in that whole period "there is no known religious picture that can be ascribed to an English painter or the 'English period' of a foreign painter"—an astonishing fact. The author attributes this to the privatization of religion and the greater assertion of state power. Meanwhile, other genres developed: classical allegory (including "semi-pornography"), treatments of everyday life, landscape painting.[31] Portrait art flourished, including conjectural portrayals of ancient statesmen which embodied a philosophical didacticism, but hardly a religious purpose.[32]

Those who craved religious art had to import it from the continent. The Protestant earl of Leicester had several Italian and Dutch paintings on biblical subjects in his collection. Usually this kind of collecting was the mark of Catholic nostalgia; the earl of Arundel's devotion to Renaissance religious art, for example, was a faded reminder of his family's Catholicism. In one historian's view, "the Earl's devotion to collecting was a substitute for religion."[33] In the eighteenth century William Hogarth was still sneering at the connoisseurs who brought "shiploads of dead Christs, Madonnas and Holy Families" from Europe.[34] Whether or not these still had the power to focus one's devotion, there was no one to produce them in England.

The one art form that was popular with continental Protestants was the single-sheet print. In Germany, where such prints had long been treated as real art, great numbers of them were produced as a medium for spreading the new religious views. In England, however, after some biblical wood-engravings by French immigrant printers in the 1560s, religious themes were replaced by classical and allegorical subjects in prints and wall paintings. The prints that were produced avoided an iconic treatment for a narrative approach.[35] Otherwise, the English mostly contented themselves with defacing the pictures on indulgences and in copies of *The Golden Legend*.[36]

There had been woodcut book illustrations in England before the Reformation. Edward Hodnett's catalog of such prints shows that almost half of those were on religious subjects. But as he observes, "Henry VIII's ban on the old religious books nullified the usefulness after 1535 of half of the supply of blocks on the shelves of printers." Protestants did not seize the initiative by producing a counter-art of their own, despite the success of the illustrations in Foxe's *Acts and Monuments*. So Hodnett dates a general decline of English book illustrations from the 1530s, since secular themes did not inspire as much illustration as religion had done.[37] In 1635 the first of fifteen editions of Francis Quarles' *Emblemes* appeared, creating something of a fad. Emblem books combined verses, epigrams, and illustrations of a devotional or doctrinal nature on each page. Quarles was, however, a prominent Laudian, and the popularity of this genre suffered somewhat in consequence.[38]

The last area of the visual arts to be secularized was tomb sculpture, showing how hard it is to secularize death. Indeed, such sculptures invaded churches in even greater numbers after the saints' images were banished.[39] But it is often noted that the new tombs are less religious in spirit than medieval ones. The latter had sought to involve the viewer in prayers for the departed soul, whereas Renaissance tombs seem more intent on informing observers of the accomplishments of the deceased. This was expressed at the time in Webster's *The Duchess of Malfi*:

> Princes' images on their tombs
> Do not lie, as they were wont, seeming to pray
> Up to heaven, but with their hands under their cheeks,
> As if they died of the tooth-ache; they are not carved
> With their eyes fixed upon the stars, but as
> Their minds were wholly bent upon the world,
> The self-same way they seem to turn their faces.
> (IV, ii, 156–162)

It fits the stereotype of Renaissance worldliness.

As for the tombs of England's heroes, a new category of shrine came to replace the repudiated saints. Westminster Abbey began its career as a hall of fame for secular figures shortly after Becket's shrine was removed from Canterbury. At the accession of Elizabeth there were perhaps thirty royal and ecclesiastical tombs within the church, crowded into the east end. In 1556 the erection of a monument to Chaucer began the tradition of monuments to statesmen, soldiers and sailors, scientists, artists, writers. It is ironic that the first secular notable to be so honored is best known for memorializing a pilgrimage to Becket's shrine. Tombs of magnates and their wives began to fill up the now useless side altars.[40]

Churches and monasteries had been the museums of medieval England, when people wanted to see wonder-working relics and images. At Canterbury they could gape at the point of a sword broken in the assault on Becket, his hair shirt and drawers and staff, a neckcloth and silk pallium, as well as some of the clay out of which God made Adam and a part of the table of the Last Supper.[41] A new age had different interests. The seventeenth century was the time of the virtuoso's "cabinet" or curio collection—of odd shells, fossils, coins, birds, and objects of historical or mechanical interest. There were even commercial ventures along this line, most notably the natural history museum opened by John Tredescant in London in the 1630s. Called the "Ark," to recall Noah's zoological collection, it was the first to achieve a national reputation. In the 1740s something like an art gallery was created in the London Foundling Hospital. There one could see some religious art, including Hogarth's biblical paintings, amid historical scenes and works in other genres.[42] Seeing these shows did not amount to a religious experience, however, as when relics were presented to be kissed.

Some religious motifs were preserved in English art at the expense of being transferred to the royal court. Elizabeth, the Virgin Queen, was surrounded by symbols once used for the Virgin Mary, appropriating the rose, star, moon, phoenix, ermine, and pearl. Thus Protestants tried to adapt traditional iconography rather than destroy it, making their own use of such themes as the adoration of the Magi and the coronation of the Virgin. Other religions besides Christianity contributed to the sacralization of her image, offering the symbolism of Astraea-Virgo, familiar in Latin literature as the imperial virgin, "empress of the world, guardian of religion, patroness of peace, restorer of virtue." In Francis Yates's view, Elizabeth used all this more for its religious overtones than for nationalist ones, nervous as she was after her excommunication in 1570: "The lengths to which the cult of Elizabeth went are a measure of the sense of isolation which had at all costs to find a symbol strong enough to provide a feeling of spiritual security in face of the break with the rest of Christendom."[43] Still, all this can be taken as secularization by the process of transfer, given the fact that Elizabeth's spiritual character remained only metaphorical.

The secularization of music presents a more equivocal development, since professional musicianship and congregational participation led in different directions. Protestant and Catholic reformers agreed that late-medieval musical settings of the liturgy—the major form of musical composition—had already become too florid and self-involved to be an an aid to worship. The Council of Trent decided on a simplification of liturgical music in the interests of greater devotionalism, but only after England had ceased to be affected by that church's decisions.[44] In England, such music was not reformed so much as abandoned. With the closing of the monasteries about fifty choirs disappeared, and in the dissolution of the chantries a number of collegiate churches lost theirs as well. Only about thirty-two cathedrals and churches in England and Wales retained trained choristers, while another eleven choirs at the universities and royal chapels ("peculiars") were not so accessible to the public.[45]

More damaging was the fact that there was less and less for these choirs to sing. The problem was that the number of places in the liturgy at which singing was appropriate fell from eight in the first *Book of Common Prayer* to only one (the Gloria) in the 1552 revision. Also, with the change from Latin to English the old compositions were worthless since they did not fit the new texts.[46] Gifted composers, such as Thomas Tallis, William Byrd, Thomas Morley, and Orlando Gibbons, continued to compose musical services, experimenting with a more expressive and subjective style. There is some question whether this would have been conducive to worship or a debilitating humanization, for liturgical music is supposed to illuminate the text and not reveal the composer's feelings about it. In any event, the compositions never got a hearing.

Eventually, Elizabeth's larceny from cathedral endowments and the sixteenth-century inflation meant the disbanding of many of the surviving choirs. Musicians left the cathedrals for employment in noble households, and composers in these more secular circumstances turned to purely instrumental music for the first time. In the straitened conditions, church organs, which had mostly been installed in the early years of the sixteenth century, were often sold. Many ended up in taverns, and it shocked foreign visitors to hear these sacred instruments used for playing "dithyrambics and bestial bacchanalias."[47]

We should not overemphasize the opposition of the regime or of Protestants to choral worship, however. Thomas Becon's writings have served too often as a quarry for quotes disparaging musical services as vainglorious. True, we read that in 1568 a sort of musical iconoclasm broke out as Puritans disrupted choral services by "dancing and sporting themselves, until the sermons and lectures did begin, scorning and deriding both the service and those which were employed therein."[48] But this is only half of the story. As the exiles from Mary's reign returned from Geneva they brought with them a practice of congregational psalm singing which had reached a great vogue in France, even among Catholics and in courtly circles. Sternhold and Hopkins' versified English Psalter began its long career in 1548, and sixty-five editions were required by the end of the century.[49] Modern scholars cannot take this seriously as musical expression, especially when comparing it with the artistic loss of the same period. But religiously it may have been a more potent expression than choral masses. John Jewel, later a bishop, described how psalm singing helped to popularize Protestantism in London in the first year of Elizabeth's reign.

> For as soon as they had once begun singing in public, in only one little church in London, immediately not only the churches in the neighbourhood, but even in the towns far distant began to vie with each other in the same practice. You may sometimes see at St. Paul's Cross, after the service, six thousand persons, old and young, of both sexes, all singing together and praising God. This sadly annoys the Mass priests and devil. For they perceive by these means the sacred discourses sink more deeply into the minds of men, and that their kingdom is weakened and shaken up at almost every note.[50]

Some cathedral staffs tried to stop such displays, alleging a lack of respect for clergy and cathedral. It would not be the first time that a church objected to an outbreak of unauthorized religion. Sophisticated contemporaries like Queen Elizabeth made fun of the "Genevan jigs."[51] But psalm singing did not prove a momentary enthusiasm.

Psalms for masses may seem a poor exchange, aesthetically. But they did involve the laity in worship—in preference to a professionalized service—arguing for a sacralization in this area. Music became one of the ways in which religion reasserted itself in social and domestic life. Hymns in the Lutheran tradition were slow to become part of English culture, due to the Puritan prejudice against using words of merely human composition in worship. But even the greatest English composers—Tallis, Byrd, Morley—fell in with the new fashion and contributed psalm tunes. When books of domestic music were first published, most included musical settings of religious verses, along with secular songs.[52] Thus, as private music making reached new heights in Elizabeth's reign, a "devotional" music flourished even while liturgical settings declined.

At the professional level, however, the secularization of music was completed when the venue of musical performance changed from churches to halls devoted to instrumental productions during the Restoration. Music became an important part of London theatrical life, as plays were enlivened by musical interludes.[53] And a new, more dramatic and instrumental music found concert rooms of its own, outside of both church and theater. Taverns set aside rooms for music as early as the 1650s, and an advertisement of a public concert series appeared in the *London Gazette* of 30 December 1672. After that date London was never without at least one such series. A secular concert life developed earlier and more actively in London than in any other European city.[54]

Music for the theater even had an effect on the church music of the seventeenth century. Where music was still part of divine services, the choral polyphony of Elizabethan anthems gave way to the vocal solos and declamatory recitative derived from Italian opera.[55] More instruments were introduced, turning the anthem into something like the secular cantata. Charles II himself promoted such change; bored with the solemnity of Tallis and Byrd, he allowed a change in court worship which jarred the pious Anglican John Evelyn:

> One of His Majesty's Chaplains preached [in the Chapel Royal] after which, instead of the ancient grave and solemn wind musique accompanying the organ, was introduced a consort of violins between every pause, after the French fantastical light way, better suiting a tavern or playhouse than a church.[56]

In other words, it seemed like the music existed for its own sake and not as an aid to devotion. A modern critic concurs: "There is an element of ostentatious magnificence [in Restoration church compositions] that is wholly absent from the church music of the Elizabethans."[57]

By 1705 England was ready for regular performances of opera, the first secular musical form to attain "parity in esteem" with religious music.[58] As Dryden had remarked, the characters of this art "are generally supernatural, as Gods and Goddesses, and Heroes, which at least are descended from them, and are in due time to be adopted into their Number."[59] Of course nobody took such representations seriously as a religious expression. But the presence of demideities was a final tribute to the long association of grand music with religion.

The equivocal status of religious music was demonstrated in 1701 when the idea of a "Spiritual Concert" was brought to England. Anthems by John Blow and William Turner were performed for their value as entertainment, outside of their context of worship.[60] Such concerts were the background of the oratorio performances to which George Frederick Handel contributed. To be sure, his oratorios involved characters and events from religious history, but even *Messiah* was first advertised in Dublin papers as "an elegant entertainment."[61] Despite John Evelyn's sneer at French frivolity, French bishops had banned the plays by Racine on which Handel's *Esther* and *Athalia* were based, recognizing the loss of seriousness involved when turning religion into entertainment. Bishop Edmund Gibson successfully forbade the staging of *Esther* in London in 1732, but he could not prevent its being given in concert form.[62]

No doubt a religious interest at the center of entertainment culture reveals something about the tone of English society. And it is agreed that the themes that Handel found in Scripture proved more successful with the London public than the classical themes of his operas had done. Perhaps some in his audiences were having a religious experience. But in 1786 the Reverend John Newton, best known as the author of "Amazing Grace," published a book of fifty sermons decrying the frivolous or merely aesthetic atmosphere surrounding performances of *Messiah*.[63]

The secularization of literature presents similar ambiguities to those encountered with music. Taking "religious literature" in its widest sense, as books about religion, it is not clear that there was a decline in the production of religious works before 1640. Table 7.1, based on the research of Edith Klotz, shows the percentages which three subject groups represent of the total number of titles published in England.[64]

There is no general decline in the proportion of works on religion, but there is a consistent negative relation between religious works and what Klotz categorizes as "literary" ones. That is, in only two intervals (1540–50 and 1580–90) did religious and literary works increase or decrease together, whereas literary and social-historical titles moved together in eleven of the sixteen intervals. The

TABLE 7.1.   Titles published in England by subject category, by
percentage

Year	Religious	Literary	Social-Historical-Political
1480	71.4	0.0	28.6
1490	60.0	0.0	20.0
1500	32.6	30.4	32.6
1510	43.3	16.4	37.3
1520	26.8	17.5	51.5
1530	34.7	11.6	41.5
1540	41.3	9.8	33.7
1550	62.4	10.4	20.3
1560	36.2	24.2	26.2
1570	34.6	31.3	28.5
1580	48.7	19.3	21.9
1590	41.7	17.3	28.2
1600	36.3	32.4	23.6
1610	53.6	14.6	22.3
1620	47.1	21.2	27.1
1630	45.9	25.2	21.6
1640	43.5	27.0	23.9
average	44.2	21.6	26.2

demand for imaginative literature was apparently inversely related to religious concerns.

Drama offers the most obvious evidence of the secularization of literary effort. For centuries the Church had been the primary patron of dramatic performance, in the mystery, miracle, and morality plays which were a feature of its festivals. The first English secular play, *Fulgens and Lucres,* was written in 1497, and in 1519 there was a performance of Plautus at court. But the first impetus behind a secular drama came when extreme Protestants began to write plays satirizing the Church and promoting their own views of church history.[65] Henry promoted a certain amount of this satire until he found it getting out of hand, causing riot. In 1544 his government began to censor dramatic productions, complaining of plays performed "in divers and many suspicious, dark, and inconvenient places."[66] In Edward VI's reign the abolition of the feast of Corpus Christi (1548) ended the major occasion for the older religious drama.[67] And Queen Elizabeth's regime refused to license any play which made political or ecclesiastical statements.[68] Her court set the country an unsavory example in this regard, however. Upon her accession she countenanced parodies of the Catholic hierarchy, ritual, and saints. The first court masque dressed "crows" as cardinals, "asses" as bishops, and "wolves" as abbots; and the Venetian ambassador claimed that it even ridiculed God. So when several towns suspended their religious pageants because there was "no solemnitie," as the Norwich grocers complained, the crowds were only following the queen's lead.[69]

There had been no gradual decline of the old religious drama. Harold Gardiner asserts that "The plays did not die out through distaste but remained extremely popular until their last days, which came, not from any internal decay, but from an external force, the hostility of the Reformation."[70] City fathers in York repeatedly appealed to bishops to have the plays amended so they could be performed. The dean of York returned this order in 1568:

> As I find so manie things that I muche like because of th' antiquities, so I see manie things that I cannot allow because they be diagreeinge from the sinceritie of the gospell, the which things, yf they should either be altogether cancelled or altered into other matters, the whole drift of the play should be altered, and therefore I dare not put my pen unto it, thoghe in good will I assure you yf I were worthie to geve your lordshipp . . . counsel, suerlie mine advise shuld be that it shuld not be plaied, ffor thoghe it was plawsible to yeares agoe, and wold now also of the ignorant sort be well liked, yet now in the happie time of the gospell, I knowe the learned will mislike it, and how the state will beare it, I know not.[71]

Suppression always went back to the central government. However much we might agree with the dean's view of the debased religion of these dramas, they had been a source of religious views to many generations.

Some towns tried to keep up their productions, but in 1576 an order from Elizabeth's High Commission prohibited the plays on the grounds of their "superstition and idolatrie," especially their "prophanation" of the sacraments by having them performed on stage, and their portrayal of figures of the Trinity. The mysteries ended in Norwich and Worcester in the 1560s, in York, Wakefield, Chester, and Chelsford in the 1570s, and in Coventry in the 1590s. A few towns tried Protestant plays but they never continued long, having to compete with a more secular drama.[72]

As Patrick Collinson points out, so long as Protestantism had to make its way against government resistance, it had used the culture's own forms of protest, including drama, ballads, charivari. But once in power, and by 1580 at least, these popular arts were viewed as a threat.[73] So drama fell into more secular hands.

The drama of Elizabeth's reign did not grow out of an old tradition of religious or liturgical drama, but on top of its tomb. Elizabethan playwrights did not feel free to treat religious subjects in a serious manner, under the circumstances of their queen's ecclesiastical rule.[74] Nor were they constrained by the necessity of performing in churches. There were new theaters in which to perform the secular plays—something that England had lacked so long as church performance was the custom. In 1576, the year of the final order prohibiting further productions of the mysteries, John Burbage's original "Theatre" was opened in London—on the site of a priory. The next to open was likewise in a priory—the refectory of Blackfriar's. Within a decade the tragedies of Christopher Marlowe and Thomas Kyd were the rage of London. The change from morality plays to revenge tragedies, from saints' lives to political histories, must have been startling. All medieval English dramas were meant to explain the doctrinal significance of the festivals of which they formed a part. Much of Elizabethan drama, on the other hand, exhibited an aristocratic ethos rather than a specifically religious one, one based on a ethic of honor rather than of charity.[75]

The court masques so favored by Stuart monarchs represent a different challenge to religion. They can be seen as the replacement of the mystery plays (portraying the miracles of Christ) by a glorification of monarchs who appear to set the world in order. Kings became increasingly godlike through the time of Charles' personal rule: "From a hero, the center of a court and a culture," the king changed "to the god of power, the center of a universe." The heavens were a very prominent element in the set design. Blasphemy was only averted by disguising the king as Neptune or Jove.[76] But few converts were won to this worship of monarchy. Charles himself faithfully rehearsed his part every day through the tense days of 1640, but that masque turned out to be the last one performed in the English court.[77]

There is, of course, much literature in later centuries that mentions or "deals with" religion. But references to religion do not go to the heart of the change as literary historians have described it. Among these scholars there is broad agreement that the shift away from a Christian and humanist cultural base is a feature of the seventeenth century, and that by 1700 a watershed had been crossed. As Basil Willey put it, "The early eighteenth century did not, like the early seventeenth, witness a great intellectual revolution; it merely inherited the results and consolidated the certainties of the previous century."[78] A change in the ratio of awareness of natural and supernatural is, of course, part of what T. S. Eliot meant by the seventeenth-century "dissociation of sensibility." To him, the "metaphysical" poets were the last to have a unified sensibility which allowed them to live in both the scholastic and humanistic worlds, to deal seriously with both sacred and profane love, aristocratic and Christian ethics, science and mythology, and to engage in contemplation as well as in affairs of state. These balances were lost thereafter.[79] Religion would then appear in the form of the beliefs of the characters described, rather than with a broader sense of its ontological standing.

S. L. Bethell describes the change in terms of a narrower and simpler concept of "reason." Reason had once found room for analogy, intuition, feeling, aesthetic judgment as well as religious faith, but was increasingly defined as empirical investigation. The need for grace in right reasoning was assumed among Elizabethan writers; by 1700 even bishops such as John Tillotson and Thomas Sprat made their characteristic appeal to common sense, utility, and self-interest.

As Bethell wryly puts it, "There was more mysticism about the reason of the Elizabethans than the Augustans' faith."[80] Religious faith became one element within the characters' awareness, rather than the background of both nature and discourse.

Surveys of seventeenth-century literature commonly recognize some shift away from religious assumptions, sometimes overstating the case for emphasis. James Sutherland thought that it is roughly true that the supernatural had disappeared from poetry by 1700.[81] Douglas Bush declared that "The active belief in human life enveloped by divine power" was disappearing. Whereas "around 1600 the traditional patterns of thought and belief encountered little or no opposition; by 1700 the traditionalist could take nothing for granted." As for nature, Bush observes that it was no longer "a 'mystick Book,' the art of God, an object of contemplation, but a complex of forces to be measured and exploited."[82]

After showing how a number of seventeenth-century poets used biblical poetic genres to inform their own works, Barbara Kiefer Lewalski concludes that after 1730,

> Protestant poetics was radically undermined by an attenuation of faith in dogmatic Christianity and in its sacred Book. . . . Some lesser poets whose concerns and achievements were rather devotional than artistic continued to write in these terms, and biblical imagery and typological reference remain generally important in later literature. But major poets seeking to give lyric expression to religious impulses looked elsewhere for the grounds of a religious aesthetics—in universal religious principles, in romantic pantheism, in personal moral imperatives, in private mythologies, in ecclesiastic ritual, in existential *angst*.[83]

In other words, a nascent Protestant literary culture soon gave way to a more individualized faith.

There would, naturally, continue to be poetry and novels on religious themes, by authors whose personal faith, rather than their literary culture, was prompting them. But the rise of the novel in the early eighteenth century is particularly striking evidence of the emergence of a secular art. Ian Watt emphasizes that the "realism" of the novel did not allow divine intervention, except as it can be glimpsed through the subjective experience of the characters. We can see their faith, but we cannot see God.[84] Leopold Damrosch treats the novel as the response to a crisis in religious culture. *Paradise Lost* strikes him as the last great English work which could treat the Christian worldview in its traditional symbols: "For Milton the biblical story was the one true story of which all others were reflections." Even it was conscious of having to justify God's ways. This last great epic gave way to novels which sought to *discern* God's ways, in a culture that could not take them for granted.[85]

Damrosch thinks that as the older religious "myth" lost its ontological standing it was not rejected so much as psychologized and internalized. That is, it was secularized by transformation. To be sure, the novel long preserved a sense of a shape and closure in life that would be lost in an entirely secularized culture. But the works of Defoe, Richardson, Fielding, and others show the progressive disintegration of a religious autobiographical and narrative tradition.[86]

A sense of providential pattern was still pervasive in eighteenth-century literature. It cannot be said that Providence revealed any large-scale plans of its own, while preserving the virtue of serving girls. In fact, these providential resolutions had such an air of improvisation that it caused comment at the time: in 1677 Thomas Rymer coined the phrase "poetic justice" as if to suggest its artificiality. Theologians were forced to make the true marks of Providence more explicit— the disproportion between cause and effect, timeliness, association with great public figures or issues, vindication of the good, fulfillment of the hopes of the righteous. It all suggests a determination to believe, but not great faith. And if some claimed that these plays and novels were more effective than preaching in counteracting vice, this might itself be taken as evidence of secularization.[87]

For Protestants, the Word stood virtually alone as a medium of spiritual power. The early growth of English literacy would change the relation of art and print, shrivelling a religious sense which had been nourished by a variety of aesthetic idioms. This did not necessarily mean a purification of religion, as the Reformers had hoped; there were secular temptations to worship "idols of the mind" rather than wonder-working statues. Meanwhile, the state attempted to use the arts to glorify itself. But the masques, coronation anthems, and palaces produced did not begin to compete with arts which had achieved a truly autonomous, secular, existence.

8

The Politics of Reaction
(1603–1659)

When Elizabeth succeeded her sister Mary in 1558 Roman Catholic ambassadors in England reported their disgust at the blasphemously antipapal pageants of her coronation. They rightly sensed that this reign would be hard on religion as they knew it.[1] What they could not foresee was that extreme Protestants would also be offended. The secularity of Elizabeth's reign was so pronounced as to be sobering, and generated attempts at resacralizing the state and society. The irony of these attempts, by Arminian and Puritan alike, is that they would hasten the secularizing trends we have already noticed.

Elizabeth herself had some old-fashioned foibles; the presence of clerical wives so spoiled the atmosphere of cathedral precincts for her that she forbade clergy to have their families on college or cathedral grounds. Although she had to relent in order to have any resident clergy at all, married clergy always found advancement more difficult than their celibate rivals under this Virgin Queen.[2] Also, she covered the secular nakedness of her regime with the cult of the Christian prince, as we have seen in the symbolism of her court.[3] But hallowing the monarchy naturally meant insulting the Church, and when all of the bishops she inherited voted against her supremacy it confirmed her in a determination to ignore the Church's opposition.[4]

Religion, in the form of the established Church, found the courage to reassert itself. Toward the end of Elizabeth's reign, in 1589, Archbishop Richard Bancroft alluded publicly to the *jure divino* authority of bishops, opposing the assumption that episcopacy was an *adiaphoron*. Along with the Presbyterians' claim of a scriptural authority for their polity it was a first step toward an assertion of the

Church's preeminence. Bancroft was not necessarily attacking the royal supremacy, since he did not assert an intrinsic temporal authority for bishops. And it had
already been accepted that the monarch did not have the spiritual powers of the
clergy.[5] But in retrospect the claim was an important one. As the cult of sacred
monarchy lost its plausibility under James I, a new clerical assertiveness would
disturb the country—and bring down all religious parties.

James tried to take a relaxed attitude toward his subjects' religious behavior,
but he sensed that religious debate was having an unsettling effect on religious
culture. Accordingly, in 1622 he issued directions to his clergy to avoid contro-
verted points or the mysteries of the faith and restricted the increasingly popular
Sunday afternoon "lectures" to instruction on the catechism.[6] Thus James
showed that he preferred the practice of religion to the discussion of religion. In
Henry's time a man had gotten into trouble for saying that "a sermon preached is
better than the sacrament of the altar, and that he had rather go to hear a sermon
than to hear a mass."[7] But that had become a commonplace by the seventeenth
century. When James himself appeared at divine service he expected the officiating clergyman to break off prayers at once and proceed to the sermon.[8] But he did
not want his subjects to think of themselves as critics rather than worshippers.

Events had outrun such sentiments. The new sense of the importance of
sermons and of the Sabbath made James's *Book of Sports* a critical episode in the
religious history of England. In 1616 some Lancashire justices ran ahead of his
state in issuing regulations against violating the Sabbath. James felt that he must
make an issue both of his supremacy and of his responsibility for the religious
moderation of his people by resisting this puritanical rigorism. Accordingly he
issued *The Kings Majesties Declaration to His Subjects, Concerning lawfull
Sports to be used* (1618). After divine service, it proclaimed, his subjects could
follow a number of innocent sports for the sake of their health and spirits.[9]

The outcry shows a growing gulf between two views of religion, the king's,
which emphasized the solidarity of a nation assumed to be Christian, and another
that emphasized the holiness of a law that might someday make the nation
Christian. We have the moving words of one Cambridgeshire footballer who
remembered this episode as the central event in his life:

> When I was a young man I was greatly addicted to football playing; and as the
> custom was in our parish and many others, the young men, as soon as church
> was over, took a football and went to play. Our minister often remonstrated
> against our breaking the sabbath which however had little effect, only my con-
> science checked me at times, and I would sometimes steal away and hide myself
> from my companions. But being dexterous at the game, they would find me out,
> and get me again among them. This would bring on me more guilt and horror of
> conscience. Thus I went on sinning and repenting a long time, but had no
> resolution to break off from the practice; til one sabbath morning our good
> minister acquainted his hearers, that he was very sorry to tell them, that by

order of the King and Council, he must read them the following paper, or turn out of his living. This was the *Book of Sports* forbidding the minister or church-wardens or any other to molest or discourage the youth in their manly sports and recreations on the Lord's Day, etc. When our minister was reading it, I was seized with a chill and horror not to be described. Now, thought I, iniquity is established by a law, and sinners are hardened in their sinful ways! What sore judgments are to be expected upon so wicked and guilty a nation! What must I do? Whither shall I fly? How shall I escape the wrath to come? And God set in so with it, that I thought it was high time to be in earnest about salvation: And from that time I never had the least inclination to take a football in hand, or to join my vain companions any more. So that I date my conversion from that time.[10]

One never knows what God might use for the converting of a soul!

Stopping the momentum of secularization proved an uphill battle. For example, re-asserting the *jus divinum* of tithes made them a controversial issue. Grumbling over tithes was nothing new, but traditionally it had been over the administration of this revenue and not the Church's right to it. Indeed, the *Husbandman's Plea* (1647), subscribed by 5,000 Hertfordshire men, claimed that "husbandmen in those ignorant [pre-Reformation] times supposed that they had some spiritual benefit by paying of tithes."[11] But in 1606 George Carleton published his *Tithes Examined and Proved to Bee Due to the Clergie by a Divine Right*, acknowledging their controversial nature by that date. Treatises by Samuel Gardiner (1611), William Sclater (1612), and Foulke Robartes (1613) similarly argued a divine right to tithe, as against the notion that they were merely an expedient arrangement for the support of the clergy or a curiosity from the Jewish past.

So much argumentation on one side of this issue suggests growing scepticism, and in 1618 John Selden expressed this scepticism with considerable erudition in *The Historie of Tythes*. Legally, he showed tithes to be based in common law, not divine law. The implication was that they might therefore be regulated by utilitarian considerations. Selden could not stop short of sounding a tone of defiance to canon law, citing the Church's persecution of Friar Bacon "while Ignorance yet held her declining Empire."[12]

King James was alarmed at the destructive character of Selden's work. He required his presence at the palace of Theobalds to hear the royal displeasure over any attack on the Church's divine right to tithes. Selden was ordered to sign a declaration that he was in error in publishing it (though not in his facts) and was ordered neither to reply to his critics nor to allow any of his friends to do so.[13] Selden complained that he had only intended an historical treatment, as if that avoided the issue of the divine authority of the practice. Such disingenuousness was too obvious; he had relativized tithes by historicizing them, and contemporaries understood the implications. In rapid succession more works appeared, by James Sempill (1619), Richard Tillesley (1619), and Richard Montagu (1621), maintaining the Church's sacred right to tithe. Since they all were dedicated to the king it was clear that it was not safe to take any other view.

Learned argument is no way to bury something among the sacred foundations, but this debate did not die down. A Church campaign to assert the divine right to tithes was set for 1638 when it had to be postponed for fear of compromising the Ship Money issue.[14] But apologists in the 1640s were still trying to answer the utilitarian argument—that one only needed to make tithe rates answer the needs of the clergy. Sir Henry Spelman aggressively argued the claim of tithe to the subject's time and land as well as produce, using arguments from natural law and from the mystical qualities of the number ten. Actually, Spelman's most old-fashioned argument, from evidences of divine retribution, was the only appropriate (i.e., religious) response to the essentially secular, historical turn which this debate had taken.[15]

As we shall see, tithes were not abolished under Puritan rule, when so many other parts of the Church's operation were dismantled. But this was not from a residual respect for their holiness; it had more to do with the fact that almost 40 percent of all tithes were by then owned and collected by the laity. Since so much tithe income had already been secularized in this way, the debate over the right to them now turned on the effect that abolition would have on other forms of property right.[16] Tithe owners objected to proposals to maintain the clergy by some other means, since it would affect their own income. But they were perfectly happy to see tithe rights based on human law rather than God's.

Charles I's reign, beginning in 1625, saw the most deliberate efforts to restore God's prerogatives in England. Charles' ecclesiastical agent, William Laud, thought that the Reformation had gone too far: "the crime of those reformers" who wanted further purification was nothing less than "sacrilege too often pretending to reform superstition."[17] As archbishop of Canterbury (from 1633) Laud had the king's backing for a campaign to recover some of England's loss.

In the matter of monastic lands, Laud thought that once given to the Church they were sacrosanct and for the laity to hold them was sacrilege. He advised friends to restore such lands, perhaps gradually over several generations.[18] He seized the advowsons (rights of appointments in parish churches) belonging to lay owners when he could find loopholes in property law which would allow this. He also carefully developed the tactics and precedents for a full-scale resumption of the tithes which had been sold along with the Church's lands, winning the acquiescence of the common law courts.[19]

Ruling elites also worried when Laud reasserted the right of the clergy to the highest offices of government. He himself became chancellor of Oxford University in 1629 after a long succession of laymen. His sights were set even higher:

> A bishop may preach the Gospel more publicly, and to far greater edification, in a court of judicature, or at a council table, where great men are met together to draw things to an issue, than many preachers in their several charges can.[20]

What gospel? Not the Protestant gospel of free grace, surely. More likely the gospel of clerical dominance. At another time he said that the Court of Star Chamber was his pulpit—an ominous thought to an aristocracy which could still be cowed by that tribunal. Hugh Trevor-Roper protests that "To accuse Laud and his bishops of interfering in social and political affairs is ridiculous: for social and political affairs were their business."[21] This was certainly their own view, as it had been that of Cardinal Wolsey's generation. But it had ceased to be the view of the ruling classes of a secularized England.

They could only watch sullenly as Laud and his minions muscled their way into government. Queen Elizabeth had appointed only one bishop to her privy council, and even her High Commission for ecclesiastical affairs had a lay majority. Under Charles, High Commission had a clerical majority. Whereas Star Chamber had never included more than one bishop under Elizabeth, it contained three in 1633.[22] Clergymen were appointed justices of the peace throughout the country. In 1635 Archbishop John Spottiswood became lord chancellor of Scotland, and seven other bishops were named to the Scottish Privy Council with orders, apparently, to recover Scottish monastic lands.[23] In the next year William Juxon, bishop of London, was made lord treasurer, the first such appointment since 1469. He became lord admiral in 1638—surely an odd office for a cleric, and especially when the navy was becoming a focus of national attention.

Laud's goal in all this was to recreate the sense of England as a religious community. Among Juxon's duties, for example, was service on the Commission for the Great Level—a fen-drainage project—where he made sure that the newly recovered land was integrated into the tithe structure. As treasurer, he was also expected to squeeze London trade until the City accepted its tithe liability.[24] The Laudians opposed enclosure of common lands because it broke down traditional, corporate views of land ownership.[25] Also, even more than James, Laud recognized that religious discussion was socially divisive. A main concern of his campaign was to keep people from attending churches outside their own parish, to discourage the celebrity preaching which was such an unsettling aspect of Protestantism.[26] On the other hand, Laud was willing to restrain his "Arminian" colleagues as well, asking them not to publish controversial treatises.[27] And to set a proper example, Laud talked Charles into attending the whole of divine service, including prayers, unlike his father.[28]

Unfortunately, there was a new national consensus, and it was that Laud's views amounted to superstition and idolatry. Once, when Sir Nicholas Crispe casually set a silver flagon on an altar during a consecration service, Laud surprised him by saying the vessel had just been consecrated and that it would now be sacrilegious to take it home.[29] His anxiety whenever he saw anyone writing, sitting, or leaning on an altar led many to doubt that he understood a religion of faith. Laud tried to explain:

> The altar is the greatest place of God's residence upon earth, greater than the pulpit, for there 'tis *Hoc est Corpus Meum,* This is My Body; but in the other it is at most but *Hoc est Verbum Meum,* This is My Word; and a greater reverence is due to the Body, than the Word, of the Lord.[30]

Ordinary Protestants did not find this self-evident. Like St. John, they had come to think of Christ as the Logos, the Word of God; they had all but forgotten his corpus. For many of them the pulpit and not the altar was the place of Christ's presence.[31]

Laud did not give the new faith credit for sincerity. He complained of the Protestantism of his day that "'tis superstition nowadays for any man to come with more reverence into a church than a tinker and his bitch to come into an alehouse."[32] His friend William Chillingworth agreed:

> God has suffered the ancient, superstitious, histrionical adorning of his temples to be converted into the late slovenly profaneness, (commonly called *worshipping in spirit,* but intended to be worship without cost).[33]

In their view, the trouble had begun in King Edward's reign when the government rejected the notion of a sacrificial worship. As early as 1616, while dean of Gloucester Cathedral, Laud moved its communion table back to the east wall and railed it off from communicants. Not only was the congregation kept from overfamiliarity with the elements of worship, but the officiating priest would face away so as not to seem to address them. There could be no milling about the table during or after Communion, and worshippers would again think in terms of sacrifices and sacred spaces.[34]

Laud revealed more of his assumptions in discussing the Edwardian order that the "table" was to be set in "the most convenient part of the church." That order had not specified who was to decide what part was "most convenient," but it was obvious to Laud that it cannot have meant the churchwardens and parishioners. Obviously, it should be someone in the government. Having charge of these matters, Laud saw to it that altars were firmly against the east wall and that Communion was received kneeling. What objection could there be? It was clear that the east end is the most sacred area of the church and that the eucharist is the most sacred rite.

A pamphlet debate in 1635–37 showed that this was not self-evident. Laud was loath to be drawn into this debate, but in the draft canons of 1640 he suggested that

> this situation of the Holy Table doth not imply that it is, or ought to be esteemed a true and proper Altar, whereon Christ is again really sacrificed; but it is and may be called an Altar by us, in that sense in which the Primitive Church called it an Altar, and in no other.[35]

Laud was apparently admitting that he did not understand why the traditional usages were efficacious, but he retained that sense of the inherent necessity of the rite that showed that this was at the heart of his religion and not negotiable. Laud doubtless hoped that correct practice would in time be self-validating for later, happier generations. To that end, a benign compulsion was meant to create a consensus.[36]

The doctrine of *adiaphora* might have played into Laud's hands in this connection, since it always had the effect of increasing the area in which government could choose for its subjects without endangering their souls. Laud claimed, for instance, that the placement of the "altar" was being regulated on exactly these grounds. But others in his party showed their reactionary nature by acting as if such matters as private confession and kneeling at Communion were essential for salvation.[37]

Many of Charles's subjects feared the direction of these changes. There were riots over moving the table altar-wise and presentments for refusing to bow at the specified times.[38] When choral services were reintroduced in the cathedrals in line with Laud's views on God's dignity, disturbances broke out at Canterbury, Chester, and Worcester at least.[39] Even under a Laudian bishop like William Piers of Bath and Wells, only 30 percent of the parishes converted their tables into altars when ordered to do so.[40]

Given more time Laud would have gone farther. Where he had a freer hand, at the universities, there were complaints of the introduction in college chapels of all manner of "superstitious vanities, ceremonial folleries, apish toys and popish trinkets." Translated, this meant crucifixes, candles, copes, statues of Mary and the Christ child, paintings and tapestries, swinging censers, laundered surplices, organ music, Latin services, bowing, crossing, and a general rigidity of demeanor. Fellows of St. John's College, Cambridge, resigned rather than bow to the new altar. Another was given five lashes for ridiculing the practice of bowing at the name of Jesus. The hothouse churchmanship of the universities also brought back auricular confession, penance, and a doctrine of justification by works.[41]

Obviously, Laud's party showed a real feeling for the substance of religion. They installed stained glass in churches and chapels, reversing the trend of a century. They provided "Gothic" chalices and talked up the desirability of stone altars. Laud himself wished to be buried under the altar in St. John's College Chapel. His predecessor at Canterbury, the more Protestant George Abbot, had expressed the hope of dying in the pulpit, offering a neat contrast.[42]

The most outward and visible sign of Laud's restoration was the effort to refurbish a crumbling St. Paul's Cathedral in London. The medieval edifice was so busy and misused that one can almost believe the man who defended himself from a charge of urinating inside it, on the grounds that he did not know it was a church![43] Inigo Jones's new facade was to remind all those who saw it that it was, indeed, a house of worship and not an employment hall, a place of assignation, or a shortcut through the neighborhood. In addition, slums around the building were removed, to set the church apart, and posters were displayed which explained proper behavior inside.[44] Even this unobjectionable program caused grumbling. It was known, for example, that the fines from church courts were going to this pious and expensive purpose which meant that the penalty for adultery might be commuted to payments for St. Paul's. Like the sale of indulgences, this hurt the Church's image as much as the rebuilding helped.[45]

In all of this, Laud may actually have preferred force to argument as a means of restoring a religious culture. Culture, unlike faith, is the sort of thing one can impose by laws and force. But his associates insisted on arguing their positions as if they were creating a new faith. Richard Montagu expended his erudition in developing the doctrine of the permissible use of images and the sign of the cross, and in arguing terms like "consecration," "priest," and "absolution." He only succeeded in raising suspicions that he meant to restore the whole apparatus of Catholic religion, and in fact he did gingerly suggest the possibility of accommodation with Rome.[46] Peter Heylyn spent years of a busy life compiling a lengthy *Historie of That most famous Saint and Souldier of Christ Iesus; St. George of Cappadocia* (1633) to insure that England was not without a patron saint. He even tried to take George's relics seriously, establishing the saint's historicity in the approved, modern fashion.[47] The work breathes the spirit of a dusty pedantry rather than of naive devotion. In short, the Laudian movement became nearly as artificial as the Tractarianism that tried to pick up at this point in the nineteenth century.

Precisely contrary to his intentions, Laud made religion a matter of controversy. For instance, when he discovered that Lord Chief Justice Thomas Richardson had forbidden church ales while on circuit in Somerset in 1633, he determined to make as public an example as possible. So church ales were added to the list of sports permitted in a revived *Book of Sports*.[48] Charles reissued it, not because it would bring pleasure to the participants but because it would give pain to the Puritans.[49] In the same spirit, Peter Heylyn added further insult when he published *The History of the Sabbath* (1635), belittling the Puritans' Sabbatarianism. As a historicizing treatment of the subject, it had the same relativizing effect as Selden's history of tithes, and he taunted his opponents as superstitious, for "judaizing" the Sabbath.[50] This appetite for confrontation was unwise if the goal was promoting a religious consensus.

When a parliament finally convened in 1640 the country got a chance to show its feelings about Laud's piety. Altar rails were torn away and communion tables were moved about—most ostentatiously in St. Margaret's, Westminster, where the House of Commons took its corporate communions.[51] Church choirs were silenced and organs removed, accompanied by another round of iconoclasm.[52] John Aubrey, who went up to Oxford in 1642, remembered that:

> When I came to Oxford crucifixes were common in the glass in the studies' window; and in the chamber windows were canonised saints. . . . But after 1647 they were all broken. Down went Dagon. Now no religion is to be found.[53]

Royalist propagandists reported the destructiveness of Parliamentary armies, hoping to enlist a traditional attachment to the nation's churches. They spread the rumor of Parliament's intention to level all cathedrals so as to remove the memory of government by bishops. For their part, Puritans showed that Royalist troops were not above using church buildings for prisons, stables, and powder storage.[54] It was as though nothing were sacred any more.

Parliament enjoyed impeaching the *jure divino* bishops, primarily to keep them from voting on measures before the House of Lords. The bishops might then be released until the next major issue arose but eventually were excluded from Parliament altogether.[55] Laud's archiepiscopal palace at Lambeth was turned into a prison, while his newly scrubbed St. Paul's became a cavalry post.[56] Cathedrals seemed to invite special abuse in the Civil Wars: Durham became a prison, St. Asaph's a wine shop and ox-byre, while the episcopal palace of Exeter was made a sugar warehouse, and that of Salisbury a tavern.[57]

The glee with which superstitions were destroyed and the despondency of some who watched is caught in Bishop Joseph Hall's account of events in his cathedral at Norwich:

> Lord, what work was here, what clattering of glasses, what beating down of walls, what tearing up of monuments, what pulling down of seats, what wresting out of irons and brass from the windows and graves! What defacing of arms, what demolishing of curious stonework, that had not any representation in the world, but only of the cost of the founder and skill of the mason. What tooting and piping upon the destroyed organ-pipes, and what a hideous triumph on the market-day before all the country, when, in a kind of sacrilegious and profane procession, all the organ- pipes, vestments, both copes and surplices, together with the leaden cross which had been newly sawn down from over the Green yard pulpit, and the service books and singing books that could be had, were carried to the fire in the public market-place; a lewd wretch walking before the train in his cope trailing the dirt, with a service book in his hand, imitating in an impious scorn the tune, and usurping the words of the litany used formerly in the church. Near the public cross all these monuments of idolatry must be sacrificed to the fire; not without much ostentation of a zealous joy, in discharging ordinance, to the cost of some who professed how much they had longed to see that day.[58]

Perhaps the joy in this assault and the disgust at the loss of so much art were both authentically religious responses.

The list of things to be destroyed can be found in the "Root and Branch" Petition from London and other counties to Parliament (December 1640). Much of it could have been drawn up in Edward's reign, suggesting the extent of unfinished business. There were to be no more crucifixes, popish pictures, or vestments, no more gestures that aped those of Rome, no more standing at the Gloria and Gospel, bowing to the altar and at the name of Jesus, crossing in baptism, kneeling at the altar and adorning it with candles and images. There was objection to the consecration of churches, fonts, tables, pulpits, chalices, or church-yards and to "reconsecration upon pretended pollution, as though everything were unclean without their consecrating."[59] The Commons followed up with a resolution of September 1641, which required that "tables" be moved away from the altar-wise position, that rails, crucifixes, candles, and basins be eliminated as well as any pictures of God or the Virgin. Chancels were to be levelled with the nave if that were possible. On the other hand, the Lord's Day was to be observed, with sports and dancing forbidden and afternoon sermons permitted.[60]

The nation then had a chance to express its contempt for the remnants of a religious culture. Muskets were fired off in church to knock down hard-to-reach ornamental images. At one place, soldiers used a statue of Christ for musketry practice. They claimed to have removed "about a hundred other cherubims and angels" out of Peterhouse Chapel, Cambridge, and eighty superstitious pictures in Pembroke College Chapel. Parliamentary visitors confirmed such numbers in churches all over the country, sometimes meeting resistance to their campaign of destruction. On 2 May 1642 Cheapside Cross in London was the last major idol to fall.[61] Before his judges, Laud's defense was that, like altar placement, these images were "indifferent" and harmless, since they no longer inspired real worship.[62] Apparently, even in his view they had been reduced from holy objects to religious art.

The criterion for prohibiting these things was precisely that they were traditional and "popish." Thus, they were a human addition to worship and something that might inspire pride. Where human creativity was necessary, as in the design of chapels or the delivery of sermons, extreme Protestants would adopt a plain style, to the point that their humility was often taken for hypocrisy.

But Puritans also had hopes of making England more obviously, outwardly religious. Their positive recommendations for the nation's worship, however, tended toward generalities as befitted a faith. The *Nineteen Propositions* of 1642 spoke of

> such a reformation to be made of the Church government and liturgy as both houses of parliament shall advise; wherein they intend to have consultation with divines . . . taking away of innovations and superstitions.[63]

The *Solemn League and Covenant* of 1643 was no more specific, promising only to reform religion in England "in doctrine, worship, discipline, and government, according to the word of God and the example of the best reformed churches."

This would involve eliminating government by an episcopal hierarchy, along with all

> superstition, heresy, schism, profaneness, and whatsoever shall be found to be contrary to sound doctrine and the power of godliness, lest we partake in other men's sins, and thereby be in danger to receive of their plagues; and that the Lord may be one, and His name one in the three kingdoms.[64]

Parliament and the Assembly of Divines did not move to establish an enforceable religious culture. But there was renewed debate on the *jure divino* status of Presbyterian church government. The ever-watchful John Selden worried Parliament with the prospect of international, ecumenical Presbyterian assemblies which would surely assert their *jus divinum* and bring England under a foreign authority. Thus alerted, Parliament maintained England's freedom from theocratic pretensions.[65]

Interregnum religious policy amounted instead to preaching repentance to the nation. Parliamentary fasts gave the nation a chance to affirm its faith and its repentance. England's announced failings were not the ritual offenses that Laudians had worried over, but a careless ignorance, ungratefulness, profanation of God's name and Sabbath, luxury and waste, quarrelling, oppression and fraud.[66]

In the *Heads of the Proposals* of 1647—the design for a more constitutional monarchy—religion was only dealt with negatively, by repealing all acts imposing the *Book of Common Prayer*, church attendance, or restrictions on other religious assemblies.[67] With the announcement of the Commonwealth the royal arms were removed from churches.[68] Thus the supremacy of faith and conscience was acknowledged over all outward forms of religion. Anything which the state could enforce—any matter of ritual or culture—was by that very fact recognized as an *adiaphoron*, unnecessary to salvation. Individual faith, on the other hand, was treated as of such transcendent importance that the state dare not touch it. Liberty of worship seemed to General Oliver Cromwell and his associates to be of greater importance even than the religious unity which was the goal of the *Solemn League and Covenant*. In short, the individual, rather than the nation, had become the sacred unit.

Seen from another religious perspective, the army was declaring, in effect, that England did not need a social contract so artificial as the *Solemn League and Covenant*. The country's effort to destroy a false government and church had shown the nation's new righteousness. In God's new order there would be no need for a state church since society itself had demonstrated its religious character.[69] Viewed in this light, the granting of religious liberty was a recognition of the reintegration of sacred and secular. Holy war had resacralized the nation.

In hindsight, the religious toleration that finally was granted seems a mark of secularization, and we will treat it as such in our consideration of the secularization of power. For it was a recognition that social order could rest on another basis than religious agreement. But as it was first announced it was anything but an admission of religious failure. Rather it was the announcement of an almost apocalyptic success.

Meanwhile, the primacy of faith had become self-evident. The Levellers' unofficial *Agreement of the People* (1647) made it a main duty of government to respect the freedom of faith:

> Matters of religion and the ways of God's worship are not at all entrusted by us to any human power, because therein we cannot remit or exceed a tittle of what our consciences dictate to be the mind of God.[70]

Conscience was the guarantor of truth, therefore, rather than creedal formulas. The *Instrument of Government* (1653), England's only written constitution, adopted the terminology of the *Agreement* in its guarantee of liberty for all "such as profess faith in God by Jesus Christ." It hedged on support of an authorized clergy; England would continue "the present maintenance" of a clergy (i.e., by tithes) until such support could be put on another basis.[71]

The final irony of "Puritan" rule is the part that secularized tithe rights had in bringing down this last attempt to resacralize England. No substitute was found for the maintenance of the established clergy because the state feared the opposition of so many lay tithe owners. Quakers and others kept up a pamphlet attack, and in 1659 an embarrassed government was probably planning the abolition of this remnant of popery.[72] When General George Monck decided to move against that regime, initiating the Restoration, he announced that one of his tasks was to protect tithes.[73] He was not, of course, protecting a bit of religious culture, since tithes had already been secularized in an even more profane manner.

Looking back, Laud's efforts to salvage England's religious culture were clearly foredoomed. We notice, for example, that he paradoxically relied on the secular power to establish the independence of the Church.[74] Worse yet, the laity seems to have found the revived usages not familiar or comforting but superstitious, quaint, and ridiculous—frightening only as they enlisted the power of the state. It was not enough for Laud to assert the antiquity of his favored practices and accuse his opponents of promoting "innovations." His assertions did not seem to meet with contemporaries' inner conviction of their truth, as was true in Mary's reign.

In 1628 Charles I reminded the clergy of the need for a "settled continuance of the doctrine and discipline of the Church of England now established; from which we will not endure any varying or departing in the least degree."[75] He was expressing the sense that a religious culture depends on its settled character and that rites are hallowed by long habit. Unfortunately, the rites in question were matters of contention rather than habit. In their turn, the Commons treated these very practices as novelties, in the Three Resolutions of 1629 against "Whosoever shall bring in innovation in religion."[76] Both sides were right in accusing the other of innovations; neither party of England's Protestants was truly traditional.

In 1682 Bishop William Beveridge attempted to defend chancel screens in a day when they were hardly more than a memory. They went back, he protested, at least to Constantine's time:

> Besides our Obligations to conform as much as may be to the Practice of the Universal Church, and to avoid Novelty and Singularity in all things relating to the Worship of God, it cannot be easily imagined, that the Catholick Church in all Ages and Places, for 13 or 1400 Years together, should observe such a Custom as this, except there were great Reasons for it. What they were, it is not necessary for us to inquire now.[77]

There was a time when Christians had felt the need of a chancel screen; Beveridge was making the sad but unconscious admission that they no longer answered to any religious purpose. If revived, they would only be resented as an expression of the Church's power by people who thought that religion was above all a matter of conscience.

Given more time, Mary Tudor might have been able to manage a religious restoration among a generation which had grown up in the old habits. The reaction that overwhelmed Laud's much milder campaign accelerated the secularizing forces in English society and encouraged the forces of religious faith and freedom.

9

The Secularization
of Power

It should not be surprising to find that a secularizing of power was at the heart of our subject, since religion is best defined in terms of power. Certainly the activities of the state have been prominent in our considerations thus far, indicating that the secularization of English culture was largely due to a contest between two kinds of power. In 1486 the English government was glad to have the support of a papal bull which announced the Holy Father's "great curse" on those who did not acknowledge Henry VII; the king reprinted it in a proclamation. Supernatural power stood over political power and the Church had monopolized it. Two centuries later the English government refused to allow its emasculated church even to define blasphemy for legal purposes. This chapter traces the steps in the process by which religion lost its preeminent position and became one political issue among many.

The Reformation Convocation and Parliament

When Lacey Baldwin Smith studied the early Tudor episcopate it struck him that all those bishops who had been trained in civil or canon law ended up on the conservative side. On the other hand, all twenty-two of the bishops who were enthusiastic for Henry VIII's reformation were theologians by training. To the lawyers, religion was embedded in the rules of society; to the reformers, religion had a "prophetic" mission in calling society and its rules into question.[1] The conservatives' devotion to England's religious and political culture made Henry's job easier. They found themselves compromising with his changes in order to maintain the peace which was the necessary context of a ritual piety.[2] Earthly power can enforce a religious culture. But for the reformers, greater religious freedom seemed a precondition of true faith. The secularization of power, therefore, could seem either a challenge or a blessing to religious leaders, depending on their understanding of religion.

The issue of the state's opposition to the power of religion had a long history before 1500, of course. In the eleventh century, Pope Gregory VII asserted the independence of the Church against William the Conqueror, who had expected to appoint bishops, make ecclesiastical laws, override the decisions of church courts, and even decide when to acknowledge a particular pope's authority within England.[3] Gregory argued the absurdity of mixing temporal and spiritual powers, implying the secular character of the state. Later monarchs contested the boundary line between religious and secular jurisdictions, and Henry VIII never forgave the Church for Becket's victory over Henry II. His own secularization would amount to a wholesale transfer of power from the religious sphere to the state. Ironically, the Church had made this transfer easy by transforming itself into a rational-legal institution—the West's first "law-state."[4]

The situation as Henry VIII found it was confused. In the north of England, for instance, the bishops of Durham and Carlisle had to carry on government with very little guidance from a distant state—appointing justices, keeping jails, raising troops, enforcing outlawry. In the absence of effective temporal sanctions they sometimes used excommunication against border ruffians in order to turn a cowed or even admiring populace against those criminals. Secular punishments alone would not have been successful in 1500. At the same time, cases involving the Church's lands were typically tried in the secular, common-law courts rather than by the conciliar courts on which clerics often sat.[5]

England's lay and ecclesiastical courts often overlapped in jurisdiction, and business in church courts was actually increasing in the late fifteenth century in several contested areas, including sex offenses, tithes, wills, and debts. This was due in part to the fact that defendants in church courts had certain procedural advantages, stemming from the fact that the intent of the system was not punishment but reconciliation. The Church's reliance on spiritual sanctions and its generous understanding of equity represented a different model of government than the state had adopted.[6] Essentially it was the difference between spiritual and military power.

This very leniency may have been the initial cause of Henry's revolution. He was not the only one who was galled by the low conviction rate in the Church's courts. The early years of the sixteenth century saw an increase in praemunire conflicts, by which plaintiffs or judges tried to divert business to the royal courts. The Church's "rural" trial system based on oaths of compurgation and the ostracism of the excommunicated did not work as well in London, for example. Urban folk, especially, wanted something sterner.[7] So when in 1504 Richard Nix, bishop of Norwich, threatened to excommunicate all maintainers of praemunire as heretics, the stage was set for another contest of the spiritual and temporal power—the notorious Hunne episode and the debate between Henry Standish and Abbot Richard Kidderminster.[8]

Richard Hunne had been prosecuted for refusing a payment to the Church and on suspicion of Lollard heresy. When he was found dead in church custody, few people believed the verdict of suicide. In response, the parliament of 1515 determined to define the immunity of the Church's jurisdiction and personnel more strictly. This threatened a notable invasion of the Church's sphere by the state, and Abbot Kidderminster denounced Parliament's intention in a public sermon, declaring that any such statute would violate the law of God. When Henry VIII appointed Dr. Standish to debate Kidderminster on the subject, the former denied that even a papal decree asserting clerical immunity had any force in England. With the sides thus drawn, the Church's deliberative body, Convocation, summoned Standish to appear before it. Expecting to be accused of heresy, he appealed to the king for protection. The clergy tried to forestall royal action by claiming that clerics could not even be asked to answer, much less be tried, by a secular court. Predictably, royal judges suggested that the Church was guilty of a breach of praemunire. They went further, to say that this should be settled by a parliament without the attendance of the lords spiritual (bishops and mitred abbots). At this point Henry decided that England's peace was threatened and had Parliament drop the offending bill. The Church had maintained its independence, but at the price of making it an issue.[9]

When Henry later decided to force the issue, he had a resource that Henry II had not enjoyed: he could enlist the "consent of the realm" in parliaments that he manipulated. In the course of one such parliament (of 1529–36) the Church lost its power, not only over the laity but even over itself. Critical to this transfer of power was the fact that churchmen were part of Parliament. The very presence of the spiritual lords in this body provided hostages in Henry's campaign. At some times in the past the bishops and abbots had outnumbered secular lords. So Henry took the precaution of creating five new temporal peers for the "Reformation Parliament," making a lay majority of fifty-seven to fifty among the peers. Still, when the clerics lost crucial votes, they found it impossible to argue that they were not bound by the decision. Even when every one of the spiritual peers present voted against a bill regarding the powers of the Church, most observers did not doubt the validity of the resulting law.[10]

The existence of a parallel body, the Convocation of Canterbury, did not provide an effective counterweight, for it had been challenged and reduced even earlier. The weakness of Convocation was that its acts did not require the assent of the king. It was not considered the equal of Parliament precisely because it lacked this lay element. Parliament was England's true representative of the

"Commonwealth"—the term used for Henry's subjects both as English and as Christians. Even bishops thought their presence in Parliament was their more important function.[11] They only now began to learn the price that the Church would pay for its long association with the state and with a legalistic understanding of religion.

To be fair, we must remember the ambiguity of their situation. There was uncertainty over the exact meaning of "praemunire" and the "liberties of the Church." On a critical early agreement (1531) over a subsidy demanded from the Church there was ambiguity over what Henry meant by calling himself "supreme head" of the Church and what Convocation meant by its saving clause, "as far as the Word of God allows." As a measure of the confusion, it was necessary for Henry explicitly to relinquish his claim to the cure of souls—a priestly function.[12] Thus measures were passed without a clear sense of their significance, which would be defined later in Henry's courts.

The turning point came in 1532 and was registered both in Convocation and Parliament. Henry demanded of Convocation that he be allowed to approve all canons, giving him the same relation to that body that he had to Parliament. Convocation argued that spiritual jurisdiction proceeds from God and that the secular power could only confirm things that did not concern faith or ethics. Henry countered that only the king could call a meeting of Convocation, again like Parliament. The "Submission of the Clergy" which embodied Convocation's capitulation was passed by a majority of its upper house. At least twenty-six negative votes were registered in the lower house out of no more that sixty then attending. The official record vaguely states that it had been approved by these and "other bishops, abbots, and priors of the upper house of Convocation." So the Church's surrender was carried in a "Rump Convocation" and only after an intimidating visit by five leading councillors.[13]

Parliament then passed the Act of Annates which cut off payments to Rome. All the bishops present voted against it. In the seventeenth century theorists would raise the question of whether such a vote was valid, but it was not raised at the time.[14] Henry recognized the significance of the vote on this bill and came in person to watch the proceedings. He demanded a division of the house—the first in the recorded history of Parliament—and no doubt meant the experience to be intimidating. Some in attendance were actually imprisoned for their opposition.[15] Henry's bullying seems to have worked better with the clerical than the lay members, if one can judge from attendance figures. The only session of this parliament for which we have documentation (1534) shows a much higher lay than clerical attendance among the lords, which was uncharacteristic of earlier parliaments.[16]

Intimidation had formerly worked in the other direction, with a clerical lord chancellor presiding over a clerical majority among the lords. But the Reformation Parliament had opened quite differently, under a lay chancellor (Thomas

More) who did not make dark allusions to "hereticks and schismatikes" whenever criticisms of the Church were voiced. The chronicler Edward Hall, a member of the parliament, thought that the flood of criticism of the Church was only possible because of these factors and the king's obvious hostility toward the Church.[17] In addition, the clerical composition of that parliament changed, as the absentee Italian bishops of Worcester and Salisbury were replaced and other conservative prelates died. The theologically trained men whom Henry chose as replacements did not see religion so much in terms of ecclesiastical laws as of an evangelical faith. The summer of 1532 saw the death of the recalcitrant archbishop of Canterbury, William Warham, and his replacement with the pliant Cranmer, and the replacement of More with a less conservative lay chancellor, Thomas Audley.[18] Henry's transfer of power could now ignore the threat of obstruction.

In the next year an Act in Restraint of Appeals to Rome became England's declaration of independence from papal power. Through it, Henry announced himself supreme head over clergy and laity. The final court of appeal in ecclesiastical cases was now Convocation, not Rome. By a second Act of Annates (in 1534) cathedral chapters lost the right to refuse the king's choice of bishops. This meant that members of the upper house of Convocation would all be chosen by the king and unlikely to resist his power. And to demonstrate the change in church-state relations, Parliament in 1534 embodied the earlier Submission of the Clergy in a statute, to make clear that it was no longer in Convocation's power to withhold its erstwhile rights.[19]

According to the historian of the Reformation Parliament, "By 1534, Convocation had ceased to play a significant role in determining national ecclesiastical policy," having bargained away its independence. It was not asked its opinion on any of the religious issues of the 1534 session, and found itself begging the Council for a proclamation forbidding public discussion of theological issues.[20] Thus the Church found its Convocation useless and Parliament increasingly secular. The session of 1536, which began the seizure of monasteries, had only three abbots in attendance to defend them. There was more debate in this parliament on the Statute of Uses—a property issue—than on ecclesiastical matters. Changes came easily. Almost unnoticed was the fact that the act absorbing Wales (1536) extended the royal supremacy there and brought its monasteries into the king's possession. Parliament even ruled that the Church had fallen into doctrinal error in dispensing the levitical law governing the king's marriage: the Act of Succession declared that the pope's dispensation was "by authority of this present Parliament definitely, clearly and absolutely declared, deemed and adjudged to be against the laws of Almighty God."[21]

Thus a single parliament had given England legislative, financial, judicial, and doctrinal independence from the rest of Christendom. Henry took immediate advantage of his new powers. In 1535 he chose a layman, Thomas Cromwell, to be his deputy or "vicegerent" over spiritual affairs, when he might have named a cleric to the post. There was a gap of several months in 1535 when bishops were told not to exercise their functions without royal license, even in such areas as ordination, confirmation, and the blessing of altars, which the king himself could not perform.[22] In 1536 he presented the Ten Articles to Convocation to be their initial guide in doctrine—a formulation which rested simply on his royal supremacy. Later, in 1539 he decided to bring Parliament into this area, suggesting that a committee of Cromwell and eight bishops (four conservatives and four reformers) bring in a bill on doctrine. The wrangling was such that Henry introduced his own Six Articles for Parliament's approval. Thus the clergy failed in this last opportunity to give doctrinal leadership to English society.[23] And the power of religion, insofar as it had been embodied in the Church, was transformed into power over religion.

Administration and Jurisdiction

The declining presence of clerics in government offers an obvious measure of secularization, but requires some interpretation. In the medieval period bishops were always at the center of affairs, which indicates an integral regime— combining the activities of church and state. But they had often been promoted to the episcopate because they had already distinguished themselves in the royal service, which would indicate the Church's subservience to the state. On the other hand, when secular officials enforce the Church's rules at the Church's bidding, or when Parliament makes laws governing religion at the Church's request, it would indicate a sacralized regime. Matters are not always clear in this respect, but there can be little doubt about the situation under Henry. When his secular officials enforced church rules to keep the Church from doing so, and when Parliament transferred its jurisdiction to state courts, it could only be counted as a secularization of power.

Henry VII had a dozen or more spiritual councillors, and Henry VIII's first twenty years were dominated by one such figure. Even after Cardinal Wolsey's public humiliation Henry continued to appoint councillors who were trained in the Church. His presidents of the Council of the North and the Council of Wales were often bishops. Clerics were used as diplomats because they moved easily in international society.[24] And he did not follow the older practice of appointing men to church office entirely because of long state service and without religious vocation.

Edward's reign showed more clearly the difference that the Reformation made. Conservative bishops who had the training for administration had finally stiffened enough to resist the clearly Protestant policies of Edward's council. The first English liturgy was passed over the recorded protests of eight bishops and the probable opposition of five more. This time, they were not allowed to stay on for the sake of preserving order; seven of them were deprived for their opposition.[25]

The Protestant bishops, moreover, did not determine the ecclesiastical legislation in this more secular atmosphere. Nor did Queen Mary encourage ecclesiastical statesmanship. Only five of her fifty councillors were bishops, and only three of her nineteen episcopal appointments had degrees in law. Even Catholics now saw that the age called for religious leaders rather than ecclesiastical statesmen.[26]

Elizabeth wanted neither. She decided her ecclesiastical settlement without consulting Convocation, rather than trouble Mary's appointees about the matter.[27] She appointed only one bishop to her council—John Whitgift—and he was put there precisely to curb the forces of religious enthusiasm.[28] We have already noticed Elizabeth's practice of arranging disadvantageous exchanges of land with her bishops, and historians have justified this as the reasonable consequence of their declining importance in government. Since they were no longer important temporal lords they had less need of such extensive incomes.[29] Within the religious sphere, Elizabeth's bishops found their actions subject to her supremacy. An archbishop (Edmund Grindal) who refused her direct order to suppress some religious exercises was suspended from office and never allowed to resume his duties.

Extreme Protestants were alarmed at such actions. Some began to assert the *jus divinum* of Presbyterian church polity as a protest against the "Erastian," political basis of England's church. Only after this challenge did others begin to assert, on the contrary, a *jure divino* basis for episcopacy. This became especially urgent in the 1590s, given the prospect that a Scottish king, raised as a Presbyterian, might inherit the Anglican church. But while Episcopalians and Presbyterians squared off, most clerics seemed indifferent to these claims, and by the end of Elizabeth's reign there were moderates in both parties who declared the form of church government to be an *adiaphoron*.[30] For these writers, church government was to be arranged by the secular rules of practicality, which meant letting the queen have her way.

Below this highest level of administration the story is the same. By 1535 Henry's advisors were proposing to abolish church courts altogether. Henry chose to keep them, but this may have been because they were now more completely under his control than the common-law courts.[31] Cranmer offered to revise canon law to restore its spiritual intent, but a reform of the canons did not interest Henry if it meant recognizing an independent authority.[32] On the contrary, the study of the canon law enforced in church courts was abolished in 1535.[33] Laymen were permitted to exercise the remaining ecclesiastical jurisdiction by a statute of 1545.[34]

Elizabeth's reign saw a general shift of business from religious to secular courts, reversing the trend mentioned earlier. Some of this transfer was authorized by acts, which by their nature as statutes brought offenders into royal courts. For example, by a statute of 1549 (2 & 3 Edw. VI, c. 13) the clergy had to recover their tithes through the secular power.[35] Statutes even allowed the state to take over the punishment of heresy, simony, nonconformity, and sex offenses, relying on the secular penalties of fines and imprisonment rather than the penances of the past.[36] There was such a liberal use of writs of prohibition (which diverted cases to state courts) that clerics repeatedly asked that the practice be curbed, but to no avail.[37]

Social and economic changes encouraged the transfer which the state had initiated. With confused and overlapping jurisdictions, the ecclesiastical and common-law courts debated whether laborers' wages and merchants' profits were the "free gifts of God" and therefore tithable. Did the fishing industry deal in wild animals and were mining products nonrenewable, and therefore nontithable? How could tithes be assessed without the sanction of the confessional? When should they be extended to the colonies? Such matters were argued until the Restoration, when the issue fell entirely to the common law.[38]

By Elizabeth's time, the English people were feeling free to ignore the Church's jurisdiction. Often they simply failed to appear to face charges. Christopher Haigh has shown that in Lancashire in 1588 only three of sixty-two cited before one consistory court appeared. Between 1555 and 1592 the number of those who answered orders to appear at that bishop's visitations dropped from 84 percent to 27 percent. In Chester 781 sentences of excommunication in 1580–86 resulted in only eighty-five submissions. Excommunication depends upon society's willingness to ostracize offenders, and communities no longer seemed willing to honor the Church's judgments. Belatedly, Elizabeth showed some concern over this disrespect, but the special ecclesiastical commissions which she sent out (including lay officials) reported disappointing results. Six of 139 recusants summoned actually appeared before one such court in Lancashire in 1578. Commissioners might fine those who failed to attend, but those in Chester collected only £40 13s. of the £757 in fines which they imposed in 1580–83.[39]

Elizabeth's Court of High Commission was the one "church court" that thrived, although technically it was not a court Christian, resting as it did on the queen's spiritual prerogative and the Act of Supremacy. Unlike a true religious court, it did not aim at the reform but rather the punishment of offenders.[40] Indeed, this was the reason for its popularity with plaintiffs; it could fine and imprison and might therefore be effective. To its Puritan victims this secularized form of religious jurisdiction, with its power to force confessions, seemed to combine the worst of both systems.[41] While it used the intrusive procedures of the church courts, it lacked their transcendent purpose.

The ultimate humiliation of the Church was its loss of control at the lowest, local level, where it forfeited the respect of the humblest of its flock. The change is seen most simply in the transfer of advowsons from clerical to lay hands. In Essex, for example, on the eve of the Reformation this right of clerical appointment in 58 percent of the parishes was in the hands of bishops or abbots, 37.4 percent belonged to the laity, perhaps descendants of those who had first endowed the church, and 4.6 percent belonged to the king. At the death of Queen Mary only 16.7 percent were still in the hands of church officials, while 66.2 percent belonged to the laity and 17.1 percent to the king.[42] Translated into parish politics, it meant a more thorough subordination of parson to squire than ever.

On quite a different front, the state undertook a secularization of warfare. Henry VIII christened his twelve new cannon after the twelve Apostles, as befitted an alliance which he chose to call the Holy League.[43] His biggest ships were the *Henry Grace à Dieu*, the *Jesus*, *Peter*, and *Matthew*, with others called *Christ*, *John Baptist*, *Trinity*, and eleven which bore the name "Mary" in various combinations. Elizabeth's additions to the fleet did not invoke religious associations, but were called *Lion*, *Hart*, *Triumph*, *Swallow*, *Greyhound*, and the like. And this despite the fact that she faced an Armada, almost all of which bore saints' names.[44] Unlike the Spanish, the English viewed power with new eyes. Of course they saw God's Providence in their victory, but they no longer thought that they could insure that Providence. Military technology was no longer part of their religious culture.

Sacred Monarchy

In 1536 the rebels involved in the Pilgrimage of Grace stole a march on their impious government by appearing under a banner showing the wounds of Christ. This was at a time when the French were led by a sacred banner, the oriflamme, and the Scots fought under the Holy Rood. The rebels' act was a reminder that Henry's government had no such totem. In an earlier age Edward I would not have let his enemies get such an advantage; he kidnapped a famous piece of the True Cross from the Welsh in order to destroy their morale. But while the flag of the Five Wounds of Christ appeared again in the Prayer Book Rising (1549) and the Rising of the Northern Earls (1569) the sixteenth century would see the end of these wonder-working banners.[45]

In the medieval competition between the ever-changing royal arms and the various saints' banners (especially of Edmund, Edward the Confessor, and George), the latter were the more popular expressions. Kings came and went, while the cross of St. George, especially, retained its following. When James I created the first national standard he accepted the popular choice. Combining the various crosses as he did, however, gave the symbolism an abstract quality. And by setting St. George's cross on top of St. Andrew's he offended the nationalistic Scots. Cromwell would compound the problem by placing Ireland's harp over the center, breaking the crosses. Religious identification was lost in national symbolism.[46]

Power first tried to resanctify itself in the monarchy. Some of this effort involved the person of the monarch, rather than the office, and its discussion may be deferred to the next chapter. But Henry VII was trying to augment the sanctity of English monarchy when he presented the royal martyr Henry VI for canonization, citing the miracles wrought at his tomb.[47] Henry VIII struck out in a less traditional direction. He dropped the case for Henry VI in 1528 and in the Act in Restraint of Appeals fused the *corpus mysticum* and *corpus politicum* into one "body politic" with himself as head. The Tudors came to be noted for their use of terms such as "commonweal" and "body politic," which were consciously meant to symbolize a partnership with their people against any transcending religious authority.[48] The nation became a counter to the *corpus mysticum* of Christendom, whose head was Christ and whose servants tried to limit monarchs. A "liturgical kingship" which made medieval kings part of a religious order gave way to a greater association of the king with the law of this commonwealth.[49] The fact that Christianity had increasingly been presented in terms of law eased this transfer from a divine to a secular order in politics.[50]

Attempts were still made to clothe power in religious trappings. While Thomas Starkey was, for the first time, using the term "the state" in an impersonal and secular sense, other political writers sometimes referred to king, lords, and commons as a trinity.[51] The concept of divine-right monarchy was for almost a century the best way of expressing the new notion of sovereignty.[52] Even Thomas Hobbes would use religious symbols in this area, calling the unlimited state "a mortal god"—Leviathan. All this showed a true instinct; the new, sovereign state was going to make unprecedented demands and would need to awe its subjects with the language of divinity. Treason would have to invoke some of the horror of heresy: the quartering or boiling of traitors has been thought of as the equivalent of sacrifice to the gods.[53]

Queen Elizabeth had a lighter touch. We have seen how she used classical pagan and Christian religious motifs to generate loyalty to a reign whose legitimacy was in question. Accession Day jousts were offered as substitutes for saints' days, enlisting "chivalry and its religious traditions to focus fervent religious loyalty on the national monarch."[54] While young Edward had doubts about the military saint George and was designing new, scriptural insignia for the Order of the Garter, that was the one post-biblical saint whom Elizabeth's government maintained, as a national mascot.[55]

Protestant spokesmen had their versions of these royalist and religious themes. John Foxe, for example, likened Elizabeth to the Emperor Constantine, who was also born in England and was patron of the church of his day. Her Catholic subjects recalled a very different imperial symbolism: To them the emperor cult suggested the Antichrist, as it had done in the first century. Just as then, they saw Elizabeth's reign as a presage of confusion, destruction, and war.[56] Protestants agreed that some of the government's symbolism verged on a royal idolatry, but they encouraged the association of monarchy with Scripture. Whereas medieval court art had shown rulers receiving the Bible from the Church's representatives, Tudor artists portrayed the monarchs issuing the Bible to their grateful subjects. Title pages in the Coverdale Bible (1535), Great Bible (1539), and Bishops' Bible (1568) show the monarchs in this role.[57]

James might have liked to inspire a cult of sacred monarchy. But, uncomfortable around displays of weapons and gallantry, he let the Accession Day tilts lapse after 1619. Celebrations of divine monarchy moved indoors, in the form of masques.[58] And soon thereafter the increasingly secular situation of monarchy was demonstrated to the widest possible public, in the trial and execution of his son, carried on with every indication of due process. Many in 1649 felt the sacrilege of that episode. But their children did not lift a finger to save his son, James II.

Religion as a Political Issue

When Archbishop Laud tried to reassert the position of the Church he discovered how thoroughly power had been secularized. He took the easiest route and enlisted the royal supremacy. His famous order to move all "altars" back to the east end of churches had to come from the Privy Council.[59] Laud never found a way of making the relationship of church and state symmetrical again. Later, as power became diffused in the government of Restoration England, religion would become simply a contested area, between those who shared that power. That is, religion became a political issue, rather than an independent source of power.

Clericalism was one form which this issue took. Having Laud's example before them, the restored Parliament insisted on the Act for Removal of Ecclesiastics from Secular Office (16 Car. I, c. 27), objecting that

> bishops and other persons in holy orders ought not to be entangled with secular jurisdiction, the office of the ministry being of such great importance that it will take up the whole man; and for that it is found by long experience that their intermeddling with secular jurisdiction hath occasioned great mischiefs and scandal.

The contemporaneous example of the Puritans of Massachusetts Bay shows how generally these assumptions were accepted. Puritans are generally viewed as clericalists and had a tabula rasa spread before them in the New World. But when the churches of that colony consulted in 1632 on whether a person might be both a civil magistrate and an elder of the Church the decision was unanimous in the negative. At first, efforts were made to resolve civil conflicts by the counsel or discipline of the Church, but this quickly gave way to ordinary English legal usages. Education, poor relief, and even marriage law were accepted as the concern of the civil officials, as against the practice still prevailing in England. So even in that wilderness "theocracy" it proved impossible for the clergy to discipline the civil authorities.[60] The logical conclusion of this tendency was reached when Roger Williams of Rhode Island adopted the notion of a completely secular state, with no religious establishment whatsoever. England's Parliament approved his scheme in 1644 (confirmed by the Restoration government in 1663), marking the first time in the history of Western civilization that any government had instituted full religious freedom as opposed to simple toleration. As one scholar has put it, "To save religion, he [Williams] secularized politics."[61]

The Stuart Restoration of 1660 was a triumph of popular sovereignty over the previous attempts at theocracy. A restored Parliament kept power over religion in its own hands, refusing to recreate the High Commission or to revise the canons. In a notorious deal, Archbishop Sheldon gave up Convocation's traditional right of self-taxation, apparently in exchange for the state's agreement to use an archaic assessment. In effect, this was the end of Convocation, since it had lost its legislative, judicial, and financial powers even over the Church.[62] Naturally, Parliament's ventures into religious policy were clumsy. An egregious example was the Corporation Act of 1661 which used Holy Communion as a test for civic office, profaning the central rite of official religion as a symbol of exclusion and a bribe. And when the bishops had to offer England leadership one last time, it had to be outside normal or even legal channels.

Ironically, this last ecclesiastical initiative was in resisting James II's runaway religious policy—his Declaration of Indulgence for nonconformists (1688). After the Glorious Revolution, which followed the bishops' stand, they were not even asked to bless the coronation regalia, as in the past. The Coronation Oath was changed to have monarchs swear to uphold "the protestant reformed religion established by law" (1 Will. & Mary, c. 6). No longer did this mean the "laws and customs of St. Edward the Confessor" (which, in any event, had been lost in a numinous obscurity). Rather, it meant the ordinary statutes of partisan parliaments.[63] Those bishops who could not accept a change in what they considered a divinely sanctioned dynasty were deprived—by Parliament.[64] From 1689 on, bishops never united to represent the interests of the Church but found themselves absorbed into the ordinary parties and factions of their day.[65]

Even the riotous Anglican reaction in 1710–14 was the work of patently secular politicians. A Tory Parliament's stricter controls over press and education, the restrictions on the Toleration, new religious tests, additional churches for the metropolis were all meant to encourage the Church. But they fell far short of a cultural refoundation. Bishops found themselves divided even on this limited, if mean-spirited campaign.

Anglican reconstruction was finally blocked by an established party of secularism. The Whigs may be defined as those who insisted on keeping the Church out of power.[66] Worse still, a bishop, Benjamin Hoadly, was their most prominent spokesman in this matter. Tory and Whig bishops argued in print over the revival of Convocation, displaying their pedantry before a public which was being asked to decide the matter.[67]

In short, religion was no longer a power in English government; rather it was a subject of politics. Power over religion was the issue. Politicians might or might not be personally pious but they did not represent religion, which is the definition of a secular situation with regard to power. As J. C. D. Clark has demonstrated, eighteenth-century politics was much concerned with the position of the Church, and he documents a lively concern over the dangers from popery, the Jacobites, Dissenters, and Deists. Obviously there was a determination to keep any lively form of religion out of power.[68] But this politics was "religious" only in the sense of being about religion, as laymen made practical decisions concerning religious officials or institutions. It was not religious in the sense that religious officials or institutions exercised power in their own right. By 1700 few would have thought that England's politics were under the sway of spiritual forces, as many politicians of the 1640s had. Religious doctrines were hardly even guiding social or economic legislation, as would have been expected in the 1620s. Rather, religion itself was the matter to be defined, limited, or encouraged—by powers of another character. And clerics were allowed into the arena only after demonstrating their political leanings.

As Clark describes it, the "political theology" of the eighteenth century was rather abstract, arguing over origins—of government, of authority, of obligation. The only way in which it took God's active engagement into account was in respect of a choice of dynasties, opposing a divine providential right to the rival notion of a divine hereditary right.[69] Neither of these faiths sank deep cultural supports. The Jacobite doctrine of hereditary right kept itself alive in toasts, as an opposition ideology, inadequate to sustained effort. The Hanoverian appreciation of providence would fade into a secular faith in Britain's destiny. The phrase "confessional state" best indicates the changed status of religion in the new conditions. Confession suggests a free and conscious faith, a chosen allegiance and not the assumed, birthright loyalty more characteristic of a religious culture.

As Clark observes, "it was Dissent which did more than anything to break down the old order," rather than "Jacobin-atheist democracy."[70] This is not evidence against secularization of the kind we have been tracing. Sectarian Protestantism can very well be a secularizing force. There could even be, as Clark claims, an "almost universal" Christian belief and moral code in a society that had chosen to be secular in its political structures.[71]

Historians treat the cry of "The Church in Danger" as a exaggeration designed to inflame Queen Anne's subjects. But the truth is that the Church not only was in danger but had ceased to exist in any form recognizable to, say, Sir Thomas More. The government was under no obligation to seek the Church's approval for its actions, which is the mark of a church-state.[72] Whig dominance through the eighteenth century shows a determination to keep religion from becoming a power in its own right.

Perhaps the one individual who did most to end any flickering hopes of the Church dictating to the state was Robert Harley, at the turn of the eighteenth century. Harley was not a Whig and in fact called that party the "synagogue of the libertines," thinking the Junto leaders to be mere Deists or even atheists. But having come from a Dissenting background he could not always support his Tory allies either and undermined their plans for a resurgence of church power.[73] With the Hanoverian succession secured in 1714, the real question was how soon the disabilities for nonconformists would be repealed and toleration be replaced by full religious liberty. When the Occasional Conformity and Schism Acts were removed in 1718 Bishop Francis Atterbury took that to be the end of the Anglican constitution of England.[74]

Finally, just as Harley's Dissenting background inspired his secular view of politics, so the Dissenters pioneered the primary secular form of power—in political party organization. Quakers led the way by organizing to protest their extreme persecution. Naturally, the thrust of their political program was against ecclesiastical power. Minorities must organize in order to survive, and the Quakers soon learned how to coordinate local units, collect and disseminate evidence, use the media and petitions, lobby politicians, draft laws, and testify before committees. By 1732 their success was such that the other Dissenting denominational trustees (the various Fund Boards) organized their own lobby, called the Dissenting Deputies.[75] Doubtless they prayed as well, but the secular parties that copied them put their trust in these techniques.

Religious Toleration

The Dissenters' campaign for religious toleration brought the secularization of power to a conclusion. The issue here is not the growth of feelings of tolerance, but rather the steps toward a legal toleration. In fact the state was ahead of society in allowing this diversity and not responding to public sentiment, once again indicating that it was a primary force in secularization. Legal toleration showed the state's judgment that religious belief might be important to the individual but not to the social order.

When Sir Thomas More wrote *Utopia* in 1516 he had not yet met any heretics. It was easy to show a relaxed attitude toward imagined rationalists. By the time he was attacking real Protestants in 1533, however, he was calling heresy the worst crime of all, even beyond treason.[76] Taking that attitude as a baseline, we can hardly expect to see toleration as a blossoming generosity. Legal toleration was won by religious sectarians or separatists who feared the Church's power and their neighbors' hostility. Their goal was limited to freedom for their own group to practice its religion. They sought help from the state, from a sense that power was shifting in its direction.

Since the time of Wyclif the English state had recognized the need to aid the Church in combatting heresy, agreeing in 1401 to burn those whom the Church condemned. Henry VIII is known to have executed at least fifty-one heretics under this arrangement, more than all previous kings put together.[77] Edward VI's Protestant regime took the jurisdiction over heresy out of the Church's hands altogether, giving royal courts that responsibility. And only two heretics are known to have been executed in that reign. Mary's reaction resulted in at least 284 executions before her own death cut short that campaign. Elizabeth executed only five specifically for heresy, feeling secure enough to deal with most challenges as matters of nonconformity, punishable by fines, while the separatist congregations arising in London and Kent were simply banished.[78] The idea that an organic society's health and welfare depended on universal orthodoxy and ritual purity was already giving way to the notion that the formal, legal order of the state could preserve the commonwealth. Some of Elizabeth's Puritan subjects were not convinced of this and urged her to more extreme policies.[79]

James I reacted pompously against the secular trend, declaring himself "a defender of the Catholic faith" and "willing to maintain and defend the holy church." But burning two provocative heretics in 1612 turned out to be a disagreeable experience. James then lectured Parliament that persecution had never exterminated a religion, nor had force ever established one. After 1616 there are records of prosecution for heresy at common law, but the convicted were allowed to sit out their lives in prison.[80]

In 1645 Parliament considered this issue, being faced with an alarming rise of Socinian or unitarian preaching. The difficulty was in deciding the boundaries of heresy. There had been a time, centuries before, when theologians might have had some success defining blasphemy, but with the laity now debating the issue there was no agreement. The Blasphemy Bill (1648) as amended in 1650 imposed the extreme penalty, but only on those who actively declared themselves to be God, or to be beyond guilt, or denied the holiness of God or the existence of an afterlife. Christians might well have found such a minimal definition disappointing. Worse still, in 1650 the Elizabethan Act of Uniformity was repealed, and everyone was simply directed to attend some religious service.[81]

Perhaps some leaders shared a hope that religious liberty in an enlightened nation would lead to greater convergence of opinion.[82] In any case, the *Instrument of Government* offered not simply toleration but religious liberty—for all who "profess faith in God by Jesus Christ" and did not try to undermine the government by maintaining Catholicism or Episcopalianism, or preaching "licentiousness" (antinomianism).[83] That is, the government would not inquire into a faith that did not threaten the political or social order. In practice, "Religious discipline under the Protectorate, even as stepped up in the last years, was looser than in any other period in the seventeenth century."[84]

Restoration governments adopted a less tolerant policy. Less secure than Cromwell, they felt that greater restrictions on religion would be needed as an aid against sedition.[85] Accordingly, the restored Parliament imposed a number of civil disabilities on nonconformity without making it illegal in itself. The Corporation Act, Act of Uniformity, Conventicle Acts, Five Mile Act, and Test Acts did not proscribe any particular beliefs. They did not aim at spiritual rehabilitation or doctrinal correction. They simply punished the political offenses of the past and the refusal to accept Parliament's power over religion. It is a misnomer to term this "religious legislation"; nobody would have related these matters to salvation.

So England moved from the extermination of heresy to the harassment of nonconformity. But there was confusion and bad conscience about political persecution in a religious guise. Few expected to see entire religious uniformity again. Many nonconformists were highly respected, and their position seemed intolerable. It was unclear what laws they lived under, whether certain Elizabethan statutes still pertained, and whether ecclesiastical censures still governed those who admitted no allegiance to the Church of England. Sympathetic justices happily used prohibitions against the ecclesiastical courts to quash proceedings.[86] The 1401 statute for the burning of heretics was repealed in 1677. On the other hand, some justices arbitrarily denied basic civil rights in farcical trials. And Parliament rejected a whole series of "Comprehension" bills which would have allowed most Dissenters to establish some connection with the Church of England. The prospect of a legal toleration for true sectarians was even less popular, especially since it was promoted by kings who were suspected of having Catholics principally in mind. The attempted indulgences of 1672 and 1687–88 were their most unpopular initiatives.

The issue came to a head in 1689. Again, a comprehension of respectable Dissenters was proposed along with a grudging toleration for Protestant sectarians, all by way of acknowledging the overriding Catholic threat. By a Tory miscalculation, however, a deal was struck in which the more objectionable toleration was voted through while the comprehension scheme was shelved until Convocation could be revived. Cynics may have foreseen that Convocation would never deal with the issue and only hoped to gut the bill. And so it happened. Presbyterians had to take their place with the despised sectarians in permanent separation under the ungenerous terms of the toleration.[87]

Law had run ahead of public opinion. The Toleration Act of 1689 turned out to be a more significant change than Parliament intended. It only suspended some of the civil disabilities which Parliament had earlier imposed, but many thought even that was too generous and wanted to view it as a temporary measure for the generation then living. Bills against "occasional conformity" to the Church of England were introduced, to make sure that Dissenters did not qualify for public office by pretending to conform. Nothing shows more clearly the political character of this struggle. The clergy should have been happy to see Dissenters coming to Anglican worship if there had been any religious intention behind that requirement. Archbishop Thomas Tenison pointed this out at the time.[88] But Tories assumed that their rivals had only political motives in their "occasional" participation in Anglican rites. What could have put that into their minds? Perhaps their own motives in profaning the Sacrament as a political test.

By the 1690s the only issue left in regard to religious toleration was the definition of blasphemy. Naturally, the Interregnum ordinance was no longer operative. Judges had sometimes taken the position that Christianity was a part of the law of England. The great seventeenth-century jurists Edward Coke and Matthew Hale had lent their weight to this identification of English culture with religion. Technically it meant that a statute made against "Christianity" was void, and in the absence of a common-law precedent judges sometimes quoted Scripture in their decisions. The practice seems to have died out in the 1680s.[89] Until then it had created a common-law jurisdiction over blasphemy in the absence of effective control by church courts. There was a need, therefore, for statutory provision. Accordingly, in 1698 the Blasphemy Act (9 Will. III, c. 35) prohibited those raised as Christians but who held to Unitarianism or denied the Scriptures or "the Christian Religion" from holding any public office. A second conviction disabled one from initiating civil suits, acting as a guardian or making wills, and carried a three-year prison sentence. No religious penance was mentioned.

In 1721, worried by the widening bounds of tolerable belief, Archbishop William Wake wanted to strengthen these penalties against blasphemy, atheism, and profaneness. It seemed impolitic or unseemly for him to introduce the bill himself, and so he got a layman to sponsor it. Eight of thirteen bishops present voted against the measure, which failed.[90]

The idea that an archbishop might be accused of conflict of interest for trying to restrict atheism and that most of his episcopal colleagues would vote against such an effort shows how far the Church had been displaced from public life. Wake was far from claiming a right inherent in his spiritual office. Rather, he was begging the secular arm to define and sanction the nation's religion, or its majority religion. Parliament would not do so, nor allow the Church to do so. By now the Church's powers were confined to disciplining its own officials.

England's change from a religious culture to religious faith made toleration possible. The first stage of this development had a religious purpose, as Separatists begged for freedom for their group. Of course each sect expected to exercise compulsion over its own members. A second stage would be reached in the eighteenth century when the issue really became tolerance—a feeling that belief or lack of belief was no one else's business. Sceptics might thereby win freedom from religion. The first stage showed a religious fear of church-state power; the second suggested a secular indifference to society's opinion.

By 1700 the state was poised to seize the final power over religion—the power not only to define what is true religion but what is religion per se. Families which agree that the husband will decide the big issues and the wife the little ones may find that they cannot agree on what constitutes a big issue. Similarly, when the state promises to protect the exercise of religion it is crucial to know who decides what is authentically religious and what is arrant nonsense. Medieval statutes had relied on the Church to render judgment by "God's Law" before calling on the state to carry out sentence.[91] The acts against profanity in 1624 and 1695 did not give judges or juries any guidelines in recognizing a profanation of religion.[92] They were expected to recognize it when they heard it. The Blasphemy Act prohibited the denial of the Scriptures or "the Christian religion," which proved too broad to be helpful in the more sophisticated and secular culture of 1700. No wonder judges and juries failed to convict anyone under the act.[93] That may even have been the intention of the legislators. It did not bother them that they could not define religion authoritatively—so long as no one else could do so.

10

The Secularization
of Personhood and
Association

After the Reformation English society had no place for saints, pilgrims, beggars, kinfolk in purgatory, or monks or friars or nuns or hermits—or even priests, in anything like the old sense. English society was greatly simplified when these roles disappeared. On the other hand, the individual soul became more complex. Religious salvation itself changed from a collective to a more individual matter: conservative clerics in Henry VIII's time had thought of society as existing within the circle of God's grace, being preserved from error and perdition; Reformers may be defined as those who thought that society had fallen into error and needed to be brought into line with God's law, especially through the spiritual transformation of its members.[1] The triumph of the latter view involved the secularization of all the bonds that united English men and women.

In a proclamation of 16 November 1538, Henry's council announced the demotion of England's most famous saint, Thomas Becket, for treason. Sources disagree on whether the saint's bones were actually burnt or only scattered among other bones in order to frustrate his worshippers.[2] It was the first shot in one of Henry's less heralded wars, for many other saints watched over England. Not only was there a national patron in St. George, whose thigh bone had found its way to England, but there were royal saints like St. Edward the Confessor, and rebels like Simon de Montfort who were canonized in public opinion. Henry also had to worry about other obscure saints (some of whom survived from a pagan past) who held the hopes of the dispossessed.[3] Perhaps he felt that his rule would be more secure without these saints, and certainly his treasury was fatter as he melted down their shrines. But a good deal of England's traditional religion vanished with the saints' cults.

England was not as rich in native saints as most countries, perhaps because the progress of Christian missions had been comparatively peaceful, creating few martyrs. Nevertheless, saints were the focus of a distinctive religious activity throughout the Middle Ages. In short order they disappeared, along with their holy days and shrines, leaving the calendar and the English landscape without its familiar religious features. The public reading of saints' legends, which had been a regular parochial activity, disappeared along with their commemoration days.[4]

Worshippers turned elsewhere for supernatural assistance, which was precisely the Protestants' desire. Pilgrimage to those shrines had once been a release from social ties and a liminal passage into a new religious community. Protestants could only allegorize pilgrimage, as an individual and interior passage, a sectarian exile from "the world." Pilgrimage became a metaphor for the life of faith, meaning the abandonment of one's culture and society.

In an earlier age, Mary Tudor's martyrs would have become cult figures. But Protestants did not recognize spiritual forces of this nature. The Marian martyrs were heroes, of course, but heroes exist at an historical distance, not hovering near their relics or watchful of their devotees. Marian Catholics did not necessarily give up such forms of devotion; the skulls of monks executed by Henry were preserved as relics.[5] But public devotion ended as the Protestant state disbanded the company of sacred intermediaries.

As we have noticed before, the state looked for ways to substitute itself as a focus for petition and entreaty. In this case, the trappings of a sacred monarchy were embroidered by the Tudors. Henry VIII took a perverse pleasure in sending "cramp rings" to his ambassadors in Rome to pass out to epileptics on the pope's doorstep. Epilepsy, like scrofula ("the King's Evil"), was one of these puzzling diseases whose remissions might be proof of a concerned king's power and legitimacy. In the fifteenth century Lancastrian and Yorkist partisans had argued over whose touch was proving more efficacious in healing these afflictions. The answer might decide the dynastic issue between them. An increase in the alms distributed at these healing services may even have been a bribe for the sick to patronize their claimant.[6]

Already by Elizabeth's reign there are signs of change. Unlike Mary, she did not consecrate and distribute cramp rings, although she continued to touch for scrofula. Perhaps this was her idea of a compromise; having heard criticism from Puritans who thought royal miracles were part of medieval superstition and from Catholics who considered her a heretic, she responded by reducing but not eliminating such practices.[7] James I, for all his talk of the divine right of kings, was almost too squeamish to touch the sick. As a Protestant he protested that the age of miracles was past. Eventually, his evident desire to be a religious as well as political figure got the better of him, and he managed the healings by covering the sores with a cloth.

It is hard to say how the public received royal healing. When Charles I was executed by his unbelieving subjects there were jokes about the matter; Henry Marten suggested that the Commonwealth might touch the scrofulous with the Great Seal.[8] Others, however, thought it was fitting that when Cromwell's son-in-law, Robert Rich, died of the King's Evil the Lord Protector could not lift a finger to help him.[9]

Royal healing was even an important part of the Restoration. Indeed, the unlikely Charles II may have touched more sufferers (perhaps 100,000) than any other English monarch. This was not yet entirely incompatible with scientific interests, but William III was too Protestant to continue the practice. No one pressed him to do so. If Anne, who rejected the doctrine of divine-right monarchy, still took up healing, it may have been to counter the claims of her half-brother and his Catholic supporters, who were also attempting cures. The Hanoverians flatly refused to stoop to such cheap advertising.[10]

In short, none of these monarchs enjoyed a sacred aura which would unite England behind them. Henry VIII dropped a claim to priestly functions (*potestas ordinis*), which was perhaps thought to be inherent in his anointing. Elizabeth's royal supremacy was recognized as essentially parliamentary and not the caesaro-papism of Henry's aspirations.[11] Catholic writers ridiculed female headship over the Church as a more patent absurdity than that of a layman in that role.[12] Charles I's royal martyrdom did something to revive religious claims for his office. Handkerchiefs soaked in his blood were said to have effected cures, and Parliament gave him a day in the calendar. It was kept with solemnity by part of the nation—to spite the other part. Thus a sacred respect for monarchy became a sectarian matter rather than a religio-cultural bond.[13]

Only recently have historians become aware that a king's charismatic author-ity could rub off on his intimates—the Gentlemen of the Privy Chamber—by their physical contact. It is hardly surprising that this relation went unrecognized for so long, given its puzzling connection with royal defecation. Evidently, initia-tion by contact with the monarch's excrement related to the quasi-sacramental character of his anointing. Study of the full importance of the Privy Chamber in the politics and diplomacy of Henry VIII's reign may yet hold some surprises. But by 1700 awe or even respect for body service to the monarch had virtually disappeared. It was in the 1660s that the title of Groom of the Stool was deliber-ately misrepresented as "Stole" by embarrassed contemporaries.[14] Clearly, sacred monarchy could not fill the void left when the saints were demoted.

At the other end of the social scale, Reformation society took steps to elimi-nate beggars. As we have seen in connection with gild charities, the medieval religious economy had a recognized place for the poor, not seeing them primarily as a "problem." Queen Mary's funeral required a hundred paupers bearing torches, for instance, to follow her hearse.[15] Almshouses were typically meant to house twelve (or thirteen) inmates, for the number of the Apostles (plus Jesus).[16] Even Henry's first injunctions (1536) remembered the religious status of the poor, in quoting the adage that "the goods of the Church are called the goods of the poor."[17] As it worked out, the goods taken from the Church were not such a boon to the poor as to some other groups. Soon, other arrangements were being made for beggars. The Poor Law of that year stipulated that the poor be housed at public expense, removing them from public view. In 1538 mendicant (or begging) friars, who had once given English men and women a chance to exercise their charity, were eliminated when their houses were seized.[18]

The prayers or blessings of beggars and friars had been viewed as a return for one's charity.[19] As they lost that religious function the poor seemed merely useless. Such problems call for solutions, or elimination. Medieval charity did not have the elimination of beggars in mind, but philanthropists and reformers gave increasing thought to this possibility.

Historians have been more interested in England's loss of its monks and nuns. Modern scholarship questions the view that there was a long decline in monastic vocations. The number of the "religious" was actually recovering from the effects of the Black Death, so Henry's dissolution was not simply a recognition of decline. In 1530 there were about 7,500 monks, 3,000 friars and 1,800 nuns, accounting for almost one percent of the adult population. Their job, too, had been to pray for the nation.[20]

After the dissolution, former monks and friars could be used in the parochial priesthood, so that they would not necessarily fade into lay society. England had a chance to fill the vacant churches held by pluralists. In fact, however, the numbers of parochial clergy actually began to fall. This was partly due to the deprivations that accompanied each reversal of religious policy, partly to the discouragement of new vocations as monks and friars momentarily flooded the job market, and partly to falling clerical incomes because of the great inflation. Pluralism (trying to serve several churches) became even more necessary, especially for married priests with family responsibilities. As a measure of this trend, the number ordained as priests in the diocese of Lincoln dropped steadily from over one hundred in 1523 to a mere five in 1546, with similar figures for Durham and Exeter. By Edward VI's reign it might have been necessary to dissolve the chantries simply to provide enough priests for the ordinary parish ministry.[21] Numbers were falling so fast that in 1560 Archbishop Matthew Parker instituted the office of lector or lay reader to fill in for deprived or nonresident clergy.[22] Minor orders of clergy were abolished in 1550, which mainly had the effect of laicizing the university population.[23]

By 1600 the whole clerical estate has been estimated at between 11,000 and 13,000.[24] The number of those who were identified with sacred duties had therefore fallen to about 0.6 percent of England's adult population.[25] The clergy of

Leon and Castille (Spain) in 1626 and of Angers (France) in 1769 appear to have been close to 4.5 percent of their adult populations.[26]

One is tempted to count cunning folk and witches with England's clergy, given our inclusive definition of religion. Recent studies have made us aware of how busy they were in the sixteenth century, mediating occult powers to their society. Historians suspect that as the Church withdrew from the practice of magic there must have been an increased demand for the services of these practitioners. There is, of course, no hope of estimating their numbers. The curve of witchcraft prosecutions, even if we had much better court records, would only indicate the level of public fear and not the incidence of activity.[27]

While we cannot graph the trend of this commerce with occult or demonic powers there were developments in the status of witches which we may note. Witchcraft was first made a statutory offense in 1542, under Henry VIII. Protestants begrudged witches even this much official recognition and repealed the law during Edward VI's reign (1547). But they soon reconsidered and under an Elizabethan law (1563) ushered in the great age of witch hunting. Forty years of this was enough to raise questions, and in a famous case of 1602 medical experts were brought in to examine such a demoniac. The results were mixed—two doctors diagnosing spirit possession and two hysteria. Opinion was shifting; James I's view changed from that which he had expressed in a book on the subject in 1597. He began to take pride in being able to discover impostures, spotting one out of a group of nine others who had already been hanged. A string of acquittals followed.[28]

By 1620 the severity of the courts was declining. A resurgence of witch hunting during the hated Interregnum may even have helped to discredit belief in witches.[29] Pedantic debate on the phenomenon continued, but those who defended the belief seemed increasingly defensive. As another measure of feeling, the acquittal rate in the Restoration rose to a point higher than continental levels. The last execution for witchcraft in England was in 1685, the last condemnation in 1712, and the last law on the subject was repealed in 1736, replaced by penalties for the claim of magical or diabolical powers. Hassling witches continued very unofficially even into the nineteenth century, showing once again that the state was in advance of general opinion.[30]

There was a corresponding decline in the awe or charisma surrounding the Christian clergy. It is true that the medieval Church was criticized for its proud bishops, greedy priests, and sodden monks. But that church's job had not been to provide a moral example so much as to mediate grace, through the clergy's sacramental ministry. Theory taught that those sacraments were efficacious despite the moral failings of officiating priests. The laity, no matter how moral, lacked the consecration that would allow them to traffic with that other world.

But Reformers redefined the sacraments as witnesses to God's grace rather than as operative causes, and therefore the clergy of England ceased to be a sacerdotal priesthood. The cleric's role had once been as impersonal as a medium's. Now it was bound up with his individual personality, and human personality is inevitably a distraction in worship. Also, with the redefinition of the role to emphasize the teacher rather than the priest, the critical feature was education rather than consecration.

In effect, the clergy was becoming a profession rather than an estate, differing from other men in degree rather than in kind. If their main distinction was in knowledge of the Scriptures, it was soon clear that lay men and women could challenge their expertise. If it was as counselors and moral examples, the piety of others might be a rebuke to them. If they made too much of the spiritual nature of their call, sectarians could often claim even more striking credentials. Quakers, for example, aggressively debated whether a pedantic knowledge of the Bible or a clear "Inner Light" was the mark of God's spokespersons. While clergy now came out of the universities, prophets still mainly came out of the wilderness.[31]

Symbolic of the change in the clergy's position in society was the change in ecclesiastical dress. The tonsure disappeared at the Reformation without any known directive. All eucharistic vestments were forbidden by the *Prayer Book* of 1552. Elizabeth reconsidered the matter and allowed the surplice for parish use, and cope, chasuble, alb, and stole for collegiate churches. She expected square caps and academic gowns for street wear, in one of her indications of a religious, or at least a conservative, sensibility.

On the other hand, "Puritan" initially referred to a party opposed to distinctive dress for the clergy, in the Vestments Controversy of 1563–67.[32] Moderates such as Phillip Stubbs hated to see Protestants split over a practice which was "mere indifferent." Some distinctiveness in dress might add dignity to the profession, he thought, and could therefore be a proper concern of the magistrate.[33] But real Puritans insisted on the secularization of clerical dress, and retained only the professional costume of academics. By 1660 the clergy had "adopted to a greater or lesser degree contemporary fashionable dress" with minimal indications of their function.[34] Naturally, Catholic priests still operating in England also had to assume a lay disguise.

Far more shocking was the fact of clerical marriage. Celibacy was indicative of the detachment which the clergy needed in order to preserve its special place in society. Clerical marriage argued the clergy's mundane character. This is not to say that it lowered the clergy's moral reputation, but that was not the issue. One of the puzzles for modern students is to find that contemporaries were more shocked by married priests than by fornicating ones.[35] At first, Church courts viewed things the same way. When Robert Barnes wrote the first justification of clerical marriage in English (1534) he asked his readers whether it made sense to treat priests who married more harshly than those who kept concubines. Why were the former executed, when incontinent priests were not even transferred?[36] Whether one saw things Barnes's way depended on whether one found holiness primarily in the sacraments or in a moral life. Contemporaries were apparently troubled at the confusion of human and divine loves in the lives of their priests. Some refused the sacraments from the hands of married clergy and called their children bastards.[37]

As a further example of the feeling on this issue, Henry VIII released the "religious" from their vows of poverty and obedience, but not from chastity. According to the Act of Six Articles, marriage against that oath was punishable by death upon a second conviction. The distinction between these vows seems to have been self-evident. By contrast, Barnes's argument that celibacy was "unnatural" was beside the point; to be natural was to be profane.

Edward VI's Protestant government allowed clerical marriage in 1549 (2 & 3 Edw. VI, c. 21), although the law began with a preamble which discouraged it. By the time of her accession Mary had to deprive about a quarter of the parish clergy for marriage. It was the only criterion she used for winnowing her clergy, while she ignored doctrinal offenses. The numbers of those removed varied by region, from a third in London to only a tenth in York and a twentieth in conservative Lancaster.[38]

Feeling still ran high on this issue. The body of one reformer's wife was disinterred from the cemetery of Christ Church, Oxford, for fear of contaminating the relics of St. Frideswide.[39] There was also something disgusting in the idea of clergymen worrying over inheritances and the advancement of their own children.[40] And sure enough, sons of clerical families soon came to be greatly overrepresented in the Church, as would have been the case in any ordinary profession. By 1700 more clergymen came from clerical families than from any other type of background, more than a quarter of all clergy in some counties.[41] The idea of a "vocation" for the ministry, in the literal sense of a divine summons, was hard to maintain in such circumstances.

Paradoxically, the government's reduction of the time-honored clerical immunities known as "benefit of clergy" may have actually brightened the clergy's reputation. Clergy had enjoyed immunity from temporal jurisdiction, giving them the right to be tried in church courts even for felonies. But benefit of clergy had long since ceased to be limited to the clergy itself. Since literacy was the traditional test of clerical status in this respect, by 1500 that group included many who had never intended to take orders. There was grumbling over the misuse of this privilege by the laity, and the clergy's unique status was compromised when these rights were extended to so many others.

Henry VII began the limitation of "clergy" in 1489, when the immunity was restricted to a first offense (4 Henry VII, c. 14). In 1513 another statute (4 Henry VIII, c. 2) removed benefit of clergy from a variety of felonies for the many persons in minor orders. It was this that triggered the parliamentary debate of 1515 described in chapter 9. The Reformation Parliament did not revise these clerical immunities, perhaps because they allowed a way around some unreasonably harsh penalties of the common law.[42] But a series of sixteenth-century statutes did erode the benefit by removing various classes of persons and offenses from its operation. Felonies created after 1530 specifically prohibited such benefit. The rule that a "clergyable" charge would subsume a nonclergyable one was reversed in 1566—establishing the superiority of the secular jurisdiction. An act of 1576 ruled that benefit of clergy no longer meant that claimants would be given into the custody of bishops. Meanwhile, since statute now regulated religious belief and practice, those in holy orders found themselves appearing before secular judges even in religious matters.[43] Thus the clergy lost the power to govern itself in line with the special requirements of its calling.

If the identity of the clergy was undergoing change, so was that of the heretic. We tend to restrict that term to those holding heterodox doctrine, but it had a wider meaning in 1500, including simple blasphemy or disrespect. In Henry VIII's reign heresy and treason were difficult to distinguish; disrespect was generalized. Henry executed Elizabeth Barton, "the Nun of Kent," for treason, arguing that the "blasphemy" of her political prophesies was subsumed in that secular charge. Later Protestants insisted on a distinction here. Initially, they had a hard time explaining how they could be loyal to the state while wanting to change the religious establishment. What they wanted was a secularization of treason, and Queen Elizabeth started in this direction by claiming that the Jesuit missioners of her time were being executed for treason and not for their faith. But as late as 1575 two Anabaptists were burnt for the "heresy" of denying that Elizabeth's privy councillors were Christian magistrates.[44]

Heresy was still a rather general charge. Elizabethan "atheism" might not touch the issue of God's existence, but only be a denial of the Trinity, Christ's divinity, Scripture's truth, Providence, the immortality of the soul, or lesser matters. Fine discriminations of doubt were not common in that nervous age. Any scoffing at religion might be branded atheism, since it was assumed that the particular point which was being ridiculed only masked a universal rejection.[45]

In that respect, the seventeenth-century changes are significant. After James burnt two Arians in 1612, either the public outcry was greater than in Queen Mary's reign or it fell on more sensitive ears. At any rate, James allowed the next such heretic to be imprisoned for life.[46] The difference is considerable. In a bygone age nothing had more clearly demonstrated the country's desire to be fumigated from the pollution of heresy than an auto-da-fé. To allow a heretic to continue to breathe the same air as good Christians was a remarkable admission of their common humanity. Many expected God to punish England for this carelessness.[47]

As in the previous chapter, we see that the issue of blasphemy was transformed into that of nonconformity.[48] Toleration became a matter of degree and of political negotiation, rather than a violation of absolute, sacred judgment. In brief, diversity was expected in a more secular society, without seeming to threaten its foundations.

Just as the character of the heretic was changing, so did Antichrist change in this period, with consequences for English nationalism. At the outset of the Reformation nationalism could define itself in reference to Antichrist, identifying it with the papacy or an apostate Roman church. Christopher Hill has shown that such a belief was not confined to cranks but was almost universal among Elizabethan intellectuals. Things changed in the 1630s. Archbishop Laud and his Arminian allies preferred not to antagonize the Catholic Church and questioned the identification of pope and Antichrist. It was a provocative act. Puritans now saw that a conspiracy of evil had reached into England itself, and at the highest level. Persecution of Puritan leaders was evidence that the hierarchy was actively serving Antichrist, whether wittingly or not.[49]

All this meant that Antichrist had ceased to mean a foreign threat and now divided the nation itself. Bishops could be stigmatized as Antichrist. Independents began to suspect Presbyterianism of being the "Mark of the Beast," and found that the numerical values of the letters in "Solemn League and Covenant" add up to 666—the number which Revelation 13:18 associates with the Beast. Their opponents did the same with Cromwell's name and official titles. Separatists made any religious establishment or imposition of belief the mark of the Beast. Civil War polemics made such constant references to these issues that poets had to abandon the term "beast" in favor of "animal."[50] With religion dividing the country, rather than uniting it, English nationalism needed a new basis.

Nationalism had started out on a more positive religious footing. In the early years of the Reformation much was made of the fact that God's favor to England began when the biblical Joseph of Arimathea reached its shores, or with St. Helena and Constantine's residence there, and that Britons had been the first nation to adopt Christianity. But John Foxe and his heirs touched gingerly on these legends, choosing rather to emphasize Wyclif and those monarchs who had suffered the opposition of papalists as the heroes of English independence.[51] David Loades suspects that an antipapal xenophobia came to be a greater impetus for the Reformation than Protestantism itself.[52] And Caroline Hibbard shows the importance of the "Popish Plotting" of the 1630s, real and imagined, in sustaining the later Rebellion.[53]

As for outsiders, the Spanish and French were despised largely because of their clericalism and superstition, which the English had now outgrown. What the English said they detested in those groups—their cruelty to native Americans, English seamen, the Dutch and Huguenots, the poverty engendered by their systems, their grovelling piety—was associated with their religion, not their race.[54] The Catholicism dominating those societies stood for the arrogance of power, hypocrisy and lies, avarice, manipulation through ignorance and fear, and unnatural chastity. And if religions were to be judged by their works, everyone knew what clericalism had contributed to history—Mary's executions, St. Bartholomew's Day, political assassinations, Gunpowder Plot, the Irish Massacres and London's Fire.[55] Travellers to France made a point of complaining about how many clergy there were and what odd clothes, diets, and customs they affected. They pitied continental Catholics for their worship of relics and despised them for forcing Protestant minorities to honor processions of their empty symbols and robed children.[56]

Anti-Catholicism was the national ideology of seventeenth-century England. Seamen, who lived on the cutting edge of this nationalism, shared a fierce antipopery which was "a negative substitute for religion."[57] In J. R. Jones's view,

> Anti-Popery was one of the forces making for national unity; it appealed at different levels to each section of society, it could be supported by crude prejudice, traditional anti-clerical sentiment, patristic scholarship and rational argument.[58]

In short, English nationalism focused on the religion of those whom the English most despised—French, Spanish, Irish, and highland Scots. Celebrations of English unity took a largely negative form, especially in the pope-burning processions of November 5 and 17.[59]

In 1667, when the scientific bishop Thomas Sprat made an effort to explain English national character in more positive and naturalistic terms, he mentioned climate, air, insular geography, the composition of the English blood, and "the reasonableness of their faith."[60] Presumably he meant their tepid devotion. English pride centered on their coolness toward clericalism and superstition—formerly known as religion.

Below the level of national identity, many social groups underwent a secular transformation. We have already seen the decline of occupational gilds, and their spiritual responsibilities to families and the larger community. Medieval religious confraternities had also provided a larger community than family and kin. They were designed primarily to be helpful when members died and families were thereby disrupted. To this end they provided funerals and masses, charity for widows and orphans, sometimes in the form of almshouses and schools.[61] In London alone there were somewhere between 100 and 160 such confraternities before the Reformation, but they existed in rural areas as well.[62]

Charles Phythian-Adams has described the central position of such confraternities in the life of Coventry. The various fraternities of that town, including the crafts, contained perhaps 80 percent of the householders. Prominent members presented themselves for election into the two purely religious gilds of Corpus Christi and Holy Trinity, whose officers regularly moved into Coventry's municipal offices. Before the Reformation, the mayor and his retinue were expected to attend church daily, and the most prominent civic activities were the confraternity charities, obits, and fellowship banquets.[63]

All this ended in 1547 when the Chantries Act seized their funds, for none of those activities were judged to have any religious value. Some scholars have thought that the vitality of Corpus Christi celebrations sponsored by the gilds and fraternities had already begun to decline before the Reformation. They had once been a means of holding social unity and differentiation in tension. Now, in London at least, the power of the magistrate was too great to "need to come to terms with the oppositionist elements, political and social."[64] Whatever the cause, religious-civic processions and plays ended in the sixteenth century, as "ceremony and religion together withdrew indoors from the vulgar gaze."[65]

Meanwhile, the alehouse or tavern assumed a new prominence as feasts, fraternity meetings, pageants, ales, and games were banished from the church. Alehouses had been rare in medieval England, but Peter Clark estimates that their number doubled between 1580 and 1630. If his latter figure of 30,000 is close, they outnumbered churches by a factor of three. And they offered very direct competition. Christenings and funerals were sometimes adjourned from church to alehouse, and clandestine marriages were often performed there. Ritual aspects of drinking developed, like toasting and healths. Citizens complained to magistrates that communities were being divided, especially on Sunday morning.[66] For now that religion was a matter of contention, the tavern could serve as headquarters for those who disliked their parson, whether for his Puritanism or his High Anglicanism.

Even the social solidarity of local religious congregations was dissolving. John Bossy has shown how many features of medieval religion—often puzzling to us—contributed to the cohesion of communities. Communion, charity, confession, and restitution were activities that had primarily a social reference. After the Reformation they became individual acts or performances, showing a shift from solidarity to civility. Church pews and family burial plots damaged community in the very heart of its religious setting. Most striking of all is the Protestant willingness to treat marriage as an entirely civil matter, at just the time when the Tridentine Catholic Church had finally established the ecclesiastical character of the institution.[67]

The Protestant Church of England never regarded marriage as a sacrament and the most puritanical spirits, like the Brownists of Elizabeth's time, objected to any clerical intrusion into the rite. In New England, by 1647 the magistrates of Boston had ordered ministers not to perform marriages but only to be on hand to add an exhortation to the newlyweds. So it was no great surprise when Cromwell's parliament of 1653 made marriage and divorce secular acts, under civil regulation.[68] The Restoration returned to the traditional, muddled law of marriage which confused the authority of family, state, and church. Nevertheless, Dissenters showed the way toward the eventual secularization of this essential social bond. It was their grievance at having to be married by Anglican rites that kept the issue alive after the Restoration. Finally, they would take satisfaction in Lord Hardwick's Marriage Act of 1753, which was bitterly attacked by Tories as the secularization of the family.[69]

A consideration of oaths is a topic of even more importance to the secularization of person and society than to the secularization of language. Oaths had been used to establish one's character and also one's social bonds and were among the most familiar of religious acts. They were meant to be a fearful matter because they invoked God's presence in one's affairs, although by Falstaff's time they were too commonly profaned. By the end of our period, however, they were feared because they they were extorted by the state and could incur the legal penalties for perjury.

It is hard for us to credit the constant resort to oaths in Shakespeare's time, but their popularity is attested by the great variety of those recorded. Men and women swore by the Mass, cross, book, rood, angels, saints, Mary, and more facetiously, by various parts of God's anatomy. Personal styles developed, and it was remembered that various monarchs had had their favorites: "God's Resurrection" (William I), "St. Luke's Face" (William II), "Our Lord's Death" (Henry I), "God's Eyes" (Henry II), "the Feet of God" (John), "Soul of God" (Richard II), and "Mother of God" (Henry VIII himself).[70]

Vows and oaths were popular because of their use in an aristocratic society: they advertised one's personal honor. By swearing to accomplish something one dared others to doubt one's determination. Some playfulness in the use of oaths is not necessarily evidence of irreligion. There was still room for shock at "profanity"—the unthinking use of the most solemn oaths, like "God's wounds" ('zounds) and "God's blood" ('sbloud).[71] Nor does the fact that oaths were frequently broken argue against their religious seriousness. It only shows that religion inspired higher aspirations than humans usually reached. On the other hand, there is evidence that oaths made a difference: when Cardinal Wolsey first made taxpayers swear to their tax (subsidy) assessments in 1523 it was quite unpopular, as if consciences were being stirred. When Elizabeth's government stopped the practice the returns became much more dishonest.[72]

Once again, the secularization of oaths involved both government and Protestantism. For a start, the state had a natural interest in a jurisdiction over perjury, which had once been the province of ecclesiastical courts. Three statutes were passed in 1495 to regulate the offense, creating a civil jurisdiction over what was essentially a religious act.[73] Then Reformation legislation began restricting the use of oaths, ending their use in tithe suits (1548), perjury cases in secular courts (1563), and in subsidy assessments (1563).[74]

But Henry VIII's reign had a much more destructive effect on oaths than these modifications. Shakespeare registered the change when he had Richard III insinuate that:

> An oath is of no moment, being not took
> Before a true and lawful magistrate
> That hath authority over him that swears.
> 3 *Henry VI*, I, ii, 22–24

By Shakespeare's time, then, government had encouraged the notion that the sanction behind oaths was the legal penalty for perjury and not the punishments of hell. It had done this by forcing an increased use of oaths for its own purposes, devaluing them like an inflating currency.

Henry VIII made a habit of imposing oaths by statute. The first instance was the Act of Succession of 1534, which ordered all adult males to swear their acceptance of the new religious policy. Clarifying legislation declared any prior conflicting oaths to be "vain and annihilate" (26 Henry VIII, c. 2). Being imposed by statute, any offenses would naturally be tried in the state's courts. It was the first use of this spiritual instrument for a political purpose.[75] But could a secular authority release one from an oath made before God? Not many wanted to test the point.

Sir Thomas More's efforts to refuse the entanglements of this oath dramatized the issue of a secular power which could override conscience and divine law. From his perspective, the irony of the episode was the profaning of a spiritual instrument for an unholy act. Ironies multiplied two years later when Anne Boleyn's fall required the nation to forswear that oath with another, imposed by a new succession act (28 Henry VIII, c. 7). Again, it made previous oaths "vain and annihilate." In 1543 there was still another reversal, by which time it was obvious that religious oaths were not more binding than secular statutes but less so.[76]

Edward VI's Protestant advisors made one last attempt to restore a religious character to oaths and imprecations by including a ritual curse or "comminiacion of sinners" in the 1552 *Book of Common Prayer*. It was a substitute for the excommunication anathema of the old religion, and was presented as an interim arrangement until some new form of penance could be adopted. None was forthcoming. In 1563 a new homily did pronounce God's curse specifically on those who misused oaths—false swearers and blasphemers. As it observed, oaths hold society together, end conflicts, support the justice system. But the problem was not the private disregard of oaths so much as the systematic undermining of the practice by its political use.

Under Elizabeth a comprehensive statute brought perjury within the purview of the state's courts (5 Eliz., c. 9). At the same time, Parliament found the courage to object to one secular extension of oaths. This concerned the queen's new Court of High Commission and its use of the ex officio oath, which might force self-incrimination. The aim of proceedings in that court was not reclamation from error, as in true ecclesiastical proceedings, but punishment for crime. That made this secularization of procedure an anomoly.[77] Against Catholics, however, Parliament was willing to create oaths to trap them into self-incrimination. King James I asserted that the Oath of Allegiance (1606) was a wholly political matter, so that the idea that a pope could invalidate it was preposterous. Hard-pressed Catholics fell to quarrelling among themselves over the casuistry of equivocation in the taking of oaths. By this time it would have been a very simple believer who could still view an oath as a straightforward religious act.[78]

Having undermined the religious character of oaths, the government sought to eliminate profanity from books and plays. James I's act of 1606 did have an effect: Shakespeare's subsequent plays saw such references fall, from an average of around one hundred to only thirty-odd instances in *Lear* and a dozen in *Macbeth*. Playwrights were driven to the use of "By Jupiter" and other stilted phrases, and by then there was a puritanical section of English society that openly complained of the persistence of this unseemly and mindless habit.[79] When one of Oliver Cromwell's chaplains, John Howe, was asked by an aristocratic but tiresomely profane admirer to name any favor which he could do him, Howe replied "There is one favour which I should be happy your lordship would grant me— leave to swear the next oath."[80]

In the end the state failed in its attempt to sacralize the law by combining sacred oaths and secular sanctions. Ten conflicting oaths of loyalty were tendered between 1640 and 1660.[81] They were meant to unite the country and failed. Alternatively, Restoration politicians used such oaths to divide the country in their favor. Specifically, the Corporation Act required all local officers to take three oaths and to make a public declaration that the Solemn League and Covenant was "in itself an unlawful oath" (13 Car. II, s. 2, c. 1).

Who kept the consciences of those who took and renounced all these oaths? The Corporation Act required magistrates to keep a record of the oaths taken before them. Presumably, God could not keep track of them all. Meanwhile the Test Acts of 1673 and 1678 created oaths to religious disbelief—denial of transubstantiation, the invocation of Mary or the saints, and the sacrificial character of the Mass. Secularization could not go further than that.

Oaths might have declined even without the state's clumsy actions. Christopher Hill reminds us that the seventeenth century saw the rise of bourgeois values of self-interest and free contract to rival the aristocratic virtues of self-respect and honor. By contract, businessmen and women put the keeping of their consciences in each others' power.[82] And they might get quicker redress from the state for broken contracts than from God for broken oaths.

Finally, the Revolution of 1688 demonstrated how quixotic oaths had become in a secular world. Several bishops and clergymen refused to break their oaths to James II in order to take fresh ones to William and Mary, even though it cost them their positions. But most of their colleagues thought like John Tillotson. In 1681 he had declared that society could not subsist without oaths, but when the time came he found no difficulty in taking the oath that Archbishop William

Sancroft could not take—and took his job as well. The archbishop of York, John Sharp, shrugged off scruples by observing that "The laws of the land are the only rule of our conscience in this matter."[83] Even bishops only thought of oaths as hostages to the state.

By this time, only Quakers and perhaps some Baptists still feared oaths as a matter of religion. In 1696 the Affirmation Act was enacted to meet such scruples. Clergymen were opposed, primarily because it would make the enforcement of tithe difficult, since tithes were still assessed upon oath.[84] The preamble of the act offered no justification for the use of solemn affirmation; Parliament was simply acknowledging that there were now secular ways of creating the obligations which oaths had once made.

At the beginning of our period, Bishop Stephen Gardiner had expressed an older view of the sacred character of community when he asked rhetorically, "Shall we, after 1,500 years, begin to inquire whether the state of our religion be established in mere idolatry as they do nowadays term it in blasphemy?" The idea that the Christian society of England could have passed so many centuries in error was preposterous to this conservative. His colleague, Edward Bonner, echoed the same thought: "In matters of state, individuals were not to be so much regarded as the whole body of the citizens."[85] The state betrayed them. In Henry VIII's new world, ideas could challenge a long-standing social consensus.

Protestants turned the authority of Scripture against their society. Bishop John Hooper countered the conservatives' faith by asking them to "Consider, that many times the true church is but a small congregation." His colleagues, Bishops Ridley, Latimer, and William Turner even spoke of standing alone against "the world," as if society were founded in evil.[86] Even their relation to an all-too-human church became increasingly problematic, as their faith became more individual.

As social relations were secularized the sanctity of society was replaced by the sacredness of the individual. It was souls that were saved now, and not whole churches. Legal toleration, however grudging and constricted, was the state's recognition of the sacred rights of conscience. It seems only logical that an Englishman, Thomas Hobbes, should be the first social theorist to take the individual rather than society as the unit of his analysis, and that John Locke could assume that society was bound together by agreement on things like property, rather than on God.[87]

11

The Secularization of Scholarship and Science

One might expect to find the secularization of thought treated prominently among the causes of a more general secularization. Studies which treat any decline of religion as the result of new trends of thought concentrate on the areas which we are only now considering. But this chapter and the next are largely concerned with the results of the larger process. The secularization of historical scholarship, social thought, political theory, natural philosophy, and theory of religion came so late in our period as to suggest that they were responses to the earlier developments that we have considered. Some of the new ideas of the period are of interest only to the intellectual historian, as showing when they were possible. Our emphasis will be on the ideas that were prevalent or under general discussion. Many works of an intrinsic interest and of importance to the long-term development of our philosophical tradition were not yet widely known or accepted. So we will look for the reaction to Hobbes, for example, as much as at Hobbes himself.

The delay of secular trends in thought is more surprising in that the patronage of scholarship was transferred to secular figures very early in the Reformation. Given the attack on the Church's wealth, one would naturally expect a change toward lay patronage in scholarship. Christine Nasie Wilkins has measured the shift of intellectual patronage away from religious leaders and toward lay figures.[1] Using Franklin Williams' *Index of Dedications*, she compared the number of printed titles dedicated to the two archbishops as against those dedicated to monarchs and their heirs from 1500 to 1640. The pattern is clear. Until 1529 there were as many dedications to archbishops as to monarchs (eight to nine), but during the 1530s twenty-four books were dedicated Henry VIII, while only one named an archbishop as patron. This was, of course, exactly the period of Henry's attack on the Church's power, and the pattern continued into the following reigns. In the 1540s and 1550s, 112 dedications went to Henry, Edward (and his guardians Somerset and Northumberland) and Mary, while only twelve went to the archbishops.

Interestingly, the first two decades of Elizabeth's reign (1560–79) saw a resurgence of ecclesiastical patronage. The queen received fifty-eight dedications as opposed to thirty-seven directed to her archbishops and another thirty-five to men who would later be advanced to that position. Many of the latter works were proposals for further reform of the Church by members of a growing Puritan movement. Elizabeth did not welcome this tendency, and in the balance of her reign (1580–99) we see the effects of her more determined leadership in church affairs. The number of royal dedications rose to 118, while dedications to the archbishops only edged up to forty-six (with another thirteen to future appointees). This was at a time when the total output of the press was increasing from about 150 titles per year (1560) to about 265 (1590).[2] James I's reign continued this dramatic rise in royal dedications relative to book production. In the period 1600–24 there were 546 dedications to the king and his heirs, while the output of the press increased to about 410 titles per year. Dedications to the archbishops came to 137 in the same period, with another 21 to prospective appointees.

Wilkins observes that this shift in book dedications reveals a change in the authors' perception of their audience. For literary patronage was not simply a way of insuring financial support. A book dedication was an advertisement which implied, rightly or wrongly, that the patron had approved its content. Authors looked for patrons with long purses, of course, but also for names that would carry authority with the reading public. Increasingly, that meant secular rulers, implying that authors expected the state to have greater credibility than the Church in the minds of readers.

We must note that this decline in ecclesiastical patronage had nothing to do with a decline of interest in religious questions. The sale of religious works was not declining during this period. Table 7.1 indicates that as late as 1610 almost 54 percent of all titles published were on religion (including some few on philosophy), and by 1640 this figure had fallen only to 44 percent. So the decline in church patronage is to be understood in terms of its political power rather than reader interest. Still, as attention was diverted toward the state, the Church and eventually religion itself would be less in the people's thoughts.

Historical Scholarship

Changes in historical scholarship show how slowly the secularization of thought proceeded in comparison with areas in which the state's power was brought to bear more directly. The significant change, of course, is toward a sense of history as development, and independent of Providence. Secularization was not simply a purging of the old chronicles' references to miracles and relics. To be sure, this was done—to Robert Fabyan's *New Chronicles of England and France* (1516) in a new edition of 1542, for example. But more significant steps toward the new historiography were taken by theologians. May McKisack shows how the Reformation itself inspired a radical approach, in the effort to recover England's past. Early humanists had looked to history for moral lessons,[3] but the first histories which offered a connected sense of national development were John Bale's *The Image of Both Churches* (1545?) and John Foxe's *Acts and Monuments of these latter and perillous Dayes* (1563).

These transitional works found their principle of organization in Deuteronomic or in millenarian concepts. When the key to understanding the past was in the biblical books of Deuteronomy or Revelation, such histories amounted to a continuation of Scripture itself.[4] But in Scripture's history of a covenanted people, Protestants recognized a religious meaning even in an unrepeatable, directioned history. History was not exactly trackless; there were "types" or models which recurred and gave the nation clues to its duty. Whereas the humanist Polydore Vergil had mentioned the fact that the first Christian emperor had an English mother and was proclaimed as emperor while in England, for him this was a fact without consequences; for Foxe, Constantine was a prototype of Elizabeth, and England was being given another chance to fulfill her covenanted destiny.[5] Despite such patterns in God's Providence, there was the possibility of tragic failure. Queen Mary's reign was a case in point, when the faith of Protestants was tested and proved sufficient. In short, there was still an understanding of sacred time within Protestant scholarship, but it was not of a kind which would simply suggest a ritual repetition.

By the end of the Tudor century the most obvious change was simply in the greatly increased interest in history, as shown by the printing of new chronicles, pocket chronicles, history plays, historical romances, epics, and ballads. These all encouraged a nationalism—born of England's Protestant isolation—that caused English readers to lose their sense of a common religious identification with the rest of Europe.

F. J. Levy observes that the sixteenth-century literature also suggested the view that God's plan was according to a reasonable order, so that scholars might concentrate on second causes without denying Providence as a first mover. But Levy concludes his survey of sixteenth-century historiography with the disappointed observation that:

> Men were as strongly convinced in 1625 as in 1480 that they lived in a basically orderly universe. Even the kind of order remained the same, for the Copernican theory was only beginning to be assimilated. Everyone knew that God ruled the world in accordance with a plan known in its entirety only to Him.[6]

As a case in point, Sir Walter Ralegh continued to use the typology of the four monarchies of the book of Daniel as an organizing principle in his *History of the World*. In essence, he was writing to justify the ways of God, and in his work God disposed what humans proposed.[7]

The seventeenth century saw greater change. A newly formed Society of Antiquaries included only two clerics among its forty known members, and in 1614 its bylaws forbade the discussion of religion (and politics). That was so that members could get on with the business of secular scholarship rather than Deuteronomic memorial or prophetic speculation. John Stow's *Survey of London* (1598) suggests the change; although he was suspected of popery because of his obvious depression over the damage to London's priories and churches, Stow was really only interested in what Londoners had done for those churches, not in what religion had done for them.[8]

Writers continued to assign much to Providence, whether by convention (culture) or conviction (faith).[9] But contemporary arguments over the law and constitution of England initiated a more radically secular understanding. The search for origins led to the discovery of unsuspected institutions such as a "feudal" system underlying England's political development. In other words, scholars were learning to understand themselves and their society through a study of the past, rather than simply looking there for confirmation of their beliefs. If taken seriously, this historicism would suggest a true human autonomy—humanity creating itself in time. Thus it was in some mid-century histories—of common law, feudal contract, parliaments—that we find the beginnings of a secular historical consciousness. To scholars like Sir Henry Spelman, William Dugdale, and Robert Brady, England's development followed a unique course, without a predetermined pattern.[10]

The fruits of this new historical method did not reach the market until late in our period. Spelman's epochal discovery of the feudal origins of parliaments was first published in 1664 and began showing up in the work of others in the mid-1670s. After all, the Restoration itself had been a triumph of the unhistorical notion of an ancient, immemorial constitition, and in those tense circumstances there were political constraints on the study of history. Ideas of an autonomous, secular development of societies were first to be followed up, not by English scholars but by Vico, Montesquieu, and Voltaire.[11]

Social Thought

Social philosophers showed the same hesitation in breaking away from traditional views. Sir Thomas More's *Utopia* of 1516 was a promising new beginning. Utopian literature, after all, shows a capacity to relativize social institutions. In particular, "utopias" usually offer critical reflection on the position of religion in the life of society. More himself did this, to a surprising degree for someone who would be a champion of the traditional position of his church. Such literature did not catch on immediately, however. *Utopia* was not translated into English until 1551, and there were only five more ventures in the genre in England before the end of the century, all after 1574.

The seventeenth century saw more such activity, however. There were at least forty-six utopias published in that period, and England overtook Italy's lead in the genre.[12] Of course none became the blueprint for actual change, but together they show an increasing use of imagination in social thought. When religion was mentioned, it was with some sense of its functional role in society. In Francis Bacon's *New Atlantis* (1626) scientism created the ideological bond which religion had always provided. This awareness of the instrumental value of religion would undermine the traditional understanding of the Church's intrinsically spiritual character.

When English writers approached social questions more practically, the emancipation of their thinking went somewhat haltingly. Arthur Ferguson has shown how Reformation changes prompted the first serious debate on social questions. At first the discussions were in the moralizing mode of medieval satirists, and analysis did not go deeper than a discovery of sin and greed. But Henry VIII's far-reaching actions forced commentators to consider institutions as well as personalities.[13] The disposing of the monastic endowments, for instance, stimulated thought about human creativity in transforming society. Also, for some reason, there was a greater desire to deploy statistics in support of one's position, even in such humble tracts as Simon Fish's *Supplicacyon for the Beggars* (1529?).[14]

Henry's debasements of the currency and the mid-century depression of trade stimulated greater efforts at economic analysis. In time, such analyses would divorce policy from moral prescription, but this was slow in developing. Ferguson believes that in the sixteenth century only the *Discourse of the Common Weal of this Realm of England* (1549?, probably by Sir Thomas Smith) broke through to an analysis of anything as extensive as the market "mechanism." Smith was capable of seeing self-interest as something besides a spiritual failure. He took the view that while government might *guide* this very natural impulse, it was useless to resist it. Accordingly, he suggested the possibility of using the government dynamically to guide social change, whereas earlier the state seemed useful protectively, in maintaining stability. Finally, Ferguson notes a pervasive change in the meaning of the term "wealth." A word which had once meant "weal" or "welfare"—a quality of life—was coming to mean "money." Such a redefinition would greatly facilitate the future literature of analysis.[15]

The seventeenth century saw greater analytic advance. Joyce Appleby credits Thomas Mun with the first real theory of market relations (in the 1620s), cutting economic thought free from religious prescription. She sees the 1650s as the period in which moral and religious considerations—always so prominent in discussions of usury, enclosure, or the price of bread—gave way to a widely shared realism.[16] In fact, a new term, "interest," came into use to replace the loaded "usury." Debate now focused on the level of interest that was acceptable, rather than on the principle of the thing. Greed was treated as a cornerstone of the new science of economics, given its reliability as a motive. And economic regulation was judged by its effect rather than by the righteousness of its motive.[17] In short, economics now tried to find laws, not impose them, and it found them in society rather than in Scripture.

R. H. Tawney should have titled his famous study of these changes *Secularization and the Rise of Capitalism* since its real theme is the separation of economic activity from religious direction. Of course, he was tracing the importance of "Puritan" doctrine in turning self-interest, thrift, and enterprise from sins—or at least distractions from virtue—into virtues of a sort. The term "secularization" did not seem appropriate to a change which grew out of the heart of doctrine, and Tawney viewed this development as ironic. But we have seen that Protestantism has, by its nature, a secularizing tendency. What is important here is Tawney's confirmation of our chronology, finding the Restoration to mark the triumph of the secular values of capitalism.[18]

Scholars disagree, however, over the emergence of a full-blown concept of "the economy." William Letwin finds the Restoration to be critical for the appearance of comprehensive systems of economic thought. In the English analysis of Dutch success, in the fascination with commercial and demographic data, in the debate between proponents of free trade and mercantilism, he sees major advances in systematic thinking. Josiah Child, Nicholas Barbon, and Sir William Petty came increasingly close to comprehensive theories before Sir Dudley North achieved them in the 1680s. But Keith Tribe emphasizes the failure of most writers of the period to bring subjects like exchange, productivity, property, price, or value together in a comprehensive analysis. The ground for such concepts was still typically political, centering on the "commonwealth."[19] Still, scholars were beginning to imagine a society held together not by divine sanction or a common piety or even political force, but by something as natural as prudent self-interest.

Political Theory

Studies of political thought sometimes take a concern for liberty over order as the edge of secularization. There is an ambiguity here; order can be something "given" in God's creation or something which humans create. For Henry Parker (1640s) and his disciples, society and the political order were human creations— an exercise of power—over a natural disorder.[20] Liberty is also open to interpretation and not necessarily inimical to religion. Indeed, *On Christian Liberty* might stand as the best statement of Luther's faith. But to emphasize religious liberty over religious order indicates a new understanding of religion, certainly. In the terms of our analysis, order has to do with religious culture, while liberty is closer to the concept of religious faith.

According to Christopher Morris, sixteenth-century English political philosophers had theories of society (the "Christian Commonwealth") but not of the state. Early treatments of this socio-political order viewed religion as integrated with all aspects of government, and discussed church, conscience, God, along with king, laws, and people. Throughout that century Catholics argued from divine law and from a reason that partook of the divine, while Protestants argued from Scripture and divine will.[21] Similar though they may seem, there was a significant difference. By concentrating on will, Protestant thought tended to supplant order with power, and power would be secularized when it appeared that God's power could not withstand man's. Order itself was secularized when it was shown to be based in power, and human power at that.

Another way of registering the early modern shift in political thinking is to trace its changing epistemology, from rational order to empiricism. Francis Bacon tried to *find* laws of human behavior from experience, rather than to accept them from philosophy. James Harrington tried to discover the causes of the Civil War in a way quite unlike Shakespeare's overlay of moral lessons on the Wars of the Roses. William Petty tried to abstract the relations within society in order to suggest utilitarian policies.[22] In each of these approaches we see an intellectual commitment to mundane reality over received laws.

Perhaps the secularization of political theory is best seen when sharpened to a focus on sovereignty—an earthly authority not shared with a divine master. Here again there is irony, since the concept of sovereignty begins with the doctrine of divine-right monarchy. We are so used to approaching the history of political theory with other questions in mind that we need to be clear what is relevant to a search for secularization. We need not be concerned with the struggle between royal, parliamentary, and popular sovereignty or between any of these and "fundamental law," natural law, or common law. By the time there were contests between these possibilities, secularization was well advanced. The critical change was when rulers or ruling groups ceased to worry about sharing their authority with the Church or bowing to any formulation of God's will. Strangely enough, that development began with the doctrine of the divine right of kings.

Divine-right monarchy is, after all, a transfer of political authority from ecclesiastical figures to more temporal ones. This is why it was not a favored theory of the medieval church. Only after the break with Rome could the divine right of the English monarchy be safely propounded, suggesting an independence from outside religious authority. As J. N. Figgis recognized, it was an expression of anticlericalism, useful against Presbyterians as well as papists.[23] In effect, it was the first way the English found to express the notion of national sovereignty.

Had divine-right theory really sacralized the English monarchy we might hesitate to treat it as secularization. But Henry VIII's extensive use of Parliament in religious legislation, his choice of a layman as his minister (vicegerent) for ecclesiastical affairs, his failure to insist on exercising priestly functions show that a true sacralization of his role was hardly contemplated. The papal title "Defender of the Faith," which Henry had worked so hard to get (in 1521) had turned out to be the wrong way to increase his authority, and he all but disowned the book that helped earn it.[24] In effect, Henry borrowed the religious connotations of divine right to fend off a more truly religious power.

Henry had other rivals, however, and divine right was useful in countering the limiting concepts of fundamental law and natural law. The sovereignty implied in divine right meant that his state had the power to create law, whatever history or philosophy might say. Once the superiority of power over law was established, the contest between royal, parliamentary, and popular sovereignty could begin.[25] Of course, even popular sovereignty might be described in terms of the divine right of the people, and refer to vox populi as *vox Dei*. But this terminology appeared too late to be convincing.[26] When Locke and his contemporaries asserted that the sovereign power resided not in the state but in the people, they did not make that authority a religious one.[27]

The fading rhetoric of sacred rule has proven an absorbing subject for historians. It was long thought that Locke spent his energy in attacking Robert Filmer's works in order to destroy the grip of religious authority, since Filmer had argued that kings inherited the biblical Adam's authority. But more recent scholars have noted that Filmer quoted somewhat less Scripture than did Locke and used Scripture for the sort of "anthropological" evidence that comes from any history. In fact, it is now believed that he was trying to abandon scriptural arguments (as opposed to scriptural examples) in order to put the theory of royal supremacy on a naturalistic basis.[28] Filmer insisted, for instance, that obedience to the king's law superceded obedience to other formulations of divine law.[29]

On the other hand, Locke's secularity has often been exaggerated. It has been shown that his view of economic relations explicitly involves God, as first maker and possessor.[30] And he did not think that society could be bound together without considering obligations to the creator, as well as to one's fellows. Scholars were embarrassed by Locke's statements on the political untrustworthiness of atheists, until they recognized that this was consistent with the rest of his views; John Dunn points out that his proposals on toleration would have excluded David Hume, for example.[31]

The English still liked to imagine that they were properly devout and demonstrated this by their loud rejection of two notoriously "secular" figures, Machiavelli and Hobbes. Machiavelli's works entered the English consciousness in the sixteenth century, when medieval ideas of moral order and natural law were still dominant. Readers were not quite prepared to acknowledge his ruthlessly utilitarian language, or to treat religion so frankly in terms of the ruler's convenience.

Accordingly, *The Prince* was not published in English until 1640. Yet there were almost four hundred allusions to Machiavelli in the dramas of that period; clearly, he stood for something that the public recognized well enough. Nothing was more common than for writers and politicians to accuse each other of Machiavellian deceit in their use of religious justifications.[32]

But according to Felix Raab, Machiavelli began to drop out of discussion almost before he was formally acknowledged, because the religious assumptions underlying political analysis were disappearing so rapidly. In their place, he says, an analysis in terms of group "interests" was being adopted:

> The undeniably pragmatic character of English politics, 1640–60, had a mighty effect here in demonstrating that in so far as religion was not wholly a political device, it belonged to an ethical sphere totally unrelated to the political world.[33]

Thomas Hobbes's materialist philosophy was also troubling to a society which found itself both repelled by, and drawn to, a secularized politics. Samuel Mintz's study of Hobbes's reception concludes that "It was atheism then which was at the heart of the controversy about Hobbes."[34] When Hobbes defined God as matter, contemporaries understood him to mean that God did not exist, just as defining human beings in wholly material terms robbed them of their essential character.[35] Actually, when Hobbes said that the religious sense came from a fear of the unknown and led to a first cause—"that which men mean by the name of God"—*he* did not claim that this was illogical or that those fears were groundless. Yet it was universally assumed that he was being crudely ironical and meant to reduce religion to unreality. It is possible that the bad faith was on the part of his detractors; they attacked in Hobbes doubts that they could not acknowledge in themselves. Over a hundred refutations appeared by the end of his century, when only one should have sufficed for people of a more robust faith. Their tone often suggests a feeling that they were a beleaguered minority in a sea of unbelief. And, once more, playwrights were careful not to present "Hobbist" characters sympathetically.[36]

Recent scholarship seems agreed that Hobbes was a sincere, if heretical, believer. He was, after all, an open Socinian at a time when that was not only socially unacceptable but actually dangerous. Hobbes took his usual care in making his religious ideas internally consistent, and he based them on truly biblical and dynamic concepts rather than the Greek metaphysics favored by orthodox theologians.[37] But in a sense his contemporaries were right. Nature could substitute for God in Hobbes's thinking, and history for Providence. A theology which boxes its God into a perfectly unitary reality does not allow for a religious response. So while we may speak of Hobbes's theology, we cannot speak of his religion. At most, religion for him would mean following the state's direction when bestowing one's deepest respect.

Hobbes's unpopularity, then, was due to his practical atheism as much as to his absolutist political philosophy. But the terms of his political philosophy, somewhat modified, would become standard currency, and his metaphysics would put him in the mainstream of the new science. The difficulty was in his forthrightness; the new Royal Society of London for Improving Natural Knowledge refused to admit him despite his great interest in their activities. He became the main target of a whole school of idealist philosophers—the Cambridge Platonists—and inspired belated attempts to prove the existence of a spirit world by the evidence of apparitions and of witches.[38]

Apparently Hobbes's contemporaries thought that one could not even whisper one's doubts in that day of failing faith for fear of inspiring a wholesale repudiation of religion. After all, had not the most famous atheist of the Restoration—the poet John Wilmot, earl of Rochester—admitted in his deathbed repentance (1680) that the philosophy of "Mr. Hobbs, and others, had undone him, and many more, of the best parts in the Nation."[39] The reaction of contemporaries was an admission that Hobbes had discerned the direction of English philosophy.

Natural Philosophy

To consider the secularization of English natural philosophy is to speak of the mechanization of the worldview, along the lines that Hobbes had envisioned. A mechanistic outlook was not universally acknowledged among the most prominent scientists or philosophers of the time. It was, however, the part of the Scientific Revolution that proved most momentous for the future of philosophy. A mechanistic view would be an essential denial of religion defined as we have, involving another world of supernatural agency. Since this was the definition of religion at the time, it explains the uneasiness and even the resistance of so many pious scientists.

The seventeenth century began with other possibilities. Aristotle might have been replaced by some animistic view of the world, or by Paracelsian or Hermetic approaches, with magical, alchemical, or occult techniques. In the words of one historian, these "sciences"

> were as much religious as worldly, as in alchemy with its techniques of self-purification and salvation, and their processes resemble rituals as much as they do laboratory experiments.[40]

Some of these methods operated symbolically, viewing reality in terms of signs which were more real than their "representations" in nature. The ultimate reference of such signs or metaphors was a mystery, but it seemed closer to gods or spirits than to the sort of reality envisioned by Galileo and Descartes.[41]

There was tension between these competing approaches during the seventeenth century, and historians puzzle over the exact relationship between them. Isaac Newton's alchemical studies are frequently cited to show the persistence of occult science even among the heroes of modernity. But the future would belong to a more open and demonstrable science, in which verification (or at least falsification) and alternative theories were possible. This open, scientific culture would supplant a closed, religious or magical one, in which claims to omniscience had always blocked study.[42]

As another way of describing the mechanization of outlook, Carolyn Merchant has presented the new view of nature as a change of emphasis from order to power, and a new understanding of both:

> In the organic world, order meant the function of each part within the larger whole, as determined by its nature, while power was diffused from the top downward through the social or cosmic hierarchies. In the mechanical world, order was redefined to mean the predictable behavior of each part within a rationally determined system of laws, while power derived from active and immediate intervention in a secularized world. Order and power together constituted control. Rational control over nature, society, and the self was achieved by redefining reality itself through the new machine metaphor. As the unifying model for science and society, the machine has permeated and reconstructed human consciousness so totally that today we scarcely question its validity.[43]

Order is not intrinsically religious, nor power secular. But as Merchant notes, power emphasized God's transcendence while order had suggested divine immanence. And transcendence tended to remove God from human contact, which is conducive to secularization.[44] In addition, humanity found that power could affect order, as it learned to input power to an ordered system. Thus, the scientist's approach to the world became more like the secular technology of the mechanic and less like the supplication of the magus.

In England, Francis Bacon was the foremost proponent of this view, announcing human power over creation. His terminology emphasized how nature could be forced, dissected, altered, interrogated, "tried"—as nature lost its position as humanity's teacher and became its slave.[45] Hobbes rushed forward with the mechanistic view in his De Corpore (1655). His analysis of animal life in terms of appetite and aversion, and of man as machine, did not appeal to contemporaries, and there was a predictable reaction. Bishop Thomas Sprat nevertheless hoped that there might soon be discoveries of the "Actions of the Soul . . . without destroying its Spiritual and Immortal Being."[46] The Cambridge Platonists' idea of a "vital vegetable plastic nature" was designed to avoid the atheistic implication of mechanistic views and to allow for God's intervention.[47] But it was obviously not designed to further scientific research of the kind that was becoming interesting.

How did thinkers decide among these worldviews? Keith Thomas has described the resilient and "self-confirming" character of magical and religious explanations. For society to be convinced of the truth of a "scientific" explanation, it would already have had to accept the presuppositions of that science. Changes of basic outlook and "paradigm" are not mediated by evidence or argument so much as by a shift of belief. Thomas Kuhn has even called it "conversion."[48]

Theologians played a part in effecting this conversion. In 1620, with the publication of *Novum Organum*, Bacon was still pleading for science in an age of religion. Specifically, he hoped to convince readers to divide religion from science, since the two seemed to be corrupting each other.[49] He need not have worried. Theologians soon began to argue for God's existence, not from the irregularities in nature—miracles, for example—but precisely from the regularities. Many clergy became members of the Royal Society even though it forbade any discussion of religion.[50]

One reason for clerical support is that the religio-magical tradition had discredited itself by association with religious "excesses." Sectarian radicals had been especially eager for a restoration of Hermetic knowledge, and this made Churchmen and Dissenters embrace a more staid, less immanentist philosophy.[51] Faced with the aberrations of these religious radicals, it was natural for establishment theologians, such as the Platonist John Smith, to declare that there should be nothing in religion that "alienates the mind." True religion enlightens, he thought, while false religion "ravishes" the mind.[52] This observation was understandable in light of England's mid-century upheavals, but it makes a striking contrast to previous stages in Western religion.

Michael MacDonald has shown that the clergy was in the forefront of naturalistic analysis when it came to subjects like mental illness. Here again, they were motivated by fear of being associated with the explanations and treatments common among the sects.[53] Keith Thomas's *Religion and the Decline of Magic* is likewise concerned with the encouragement that Protestant clergy offered science in destroying the magical, astrological, occult, and generally miraculous elements in English religion—even before science had been able make good on its promises. After all, scientists were still tripping over their first baby steps, embarrassing themselves with mistaken calculations of cometary returns, for instance.[54] But if modern approaches to science needed religion to get a hearing in the early seventeenth century, by the end of that century utility had become a sufficient argument.[55]

Advances in technology did not necessarily work to weaken faith. Marjorie Nicolson has shown how the telescope and the microscope created a new awe at God's handiwork. Scientists, poets, and men and women of fashion wondered at the poverty of their earlier religious ideas when they began to see things through God's eyes.[56] Such feelings could awaken faith. But they did not necessarily give confidence in traditional religious culture.

While clergy were sometimes promoting naturalistic philosophies, scientists often showed some wariness of the mechanistic secularization of thought. When William Harvey's model of the human body—described in *Exercitatio Anatomica de Motu Cordis et Sanguinis* (1628)—came out as a frightening maze of pipes, filters, pumps, and valves, he felt that he had to include some vital spirits as well.[57] It was typical of the scientists of the day to worry about deadening the world under their dissection. The notable biologist, John Ray, also pictured nature as "plastic"—infused with spirit. The randomness of atomism and the fact that it was the favored philosophy of libertine aristocrats worried the pious chemist, Robert Boyle. He developed a "corpuscular" theory which avoided the worst features of atomism. Other scientists tried something more in the Cartesian line which suggested the analogy of a tremendous clock—implying an intelligence behind creation.[58] Even at the end of our period, Isaac Newton needed God to maintain his world machine by a kind of continuous miracle. He and the most notable philosophers of the time, Samuel Clarke and George Berkeley, struggled to avoid identifying God with the notion of "Absolute Space" for fear of freezing Providence. Newton himself revised the *Principia* in 1713 to include his affirmation of God.[59]

All this did not work, at least for the general public. There was a momentum in these views that could not be resisted, at least by weaker minds. God's omnipresence was the same as God's absence. Despite Newton's protests of faith, he encouraged

> the conception of God as a retired engineer, and from this to His complete elimination was only a step. For scientists who nevertheless wanted to preserve their faith there was hardly any other possibility but to keep religion and science strictly apart.[60]

Science became a public faith just as the public ceased to understand it. As Newton united heaven and earth under universal laws, he could only express the relation in a mathematics which was beyond the public's capacity. Words would no longer do to describe reality at an ultimate level—whether ordinary language or theological terminology. But if mathematics was truly the language of God, then traditional theology was not the way of enlightenment.[61]

The public was perfectly willing to judge these matters, even if elites were wary. Their conversion to the new mechanistic faith was perhaps in direct proportion to its incomprehensibility. The "paradigm shift" toward a mechanical model was partly due to the change in the social composition of the jury which now decided such issues. Thomas Kuhn has pointed out that "as in political revolutions, so in paradigm choice—there is no standard higher than the assent of the relevant community."[62] The relevant community had changed. There was a real streak of anti-"intellectualism" in Restoration England as polite society took over from a discredited philosophical elite.[63]

So it would be a mistake to think that philosophers were dragging an unwilling public into a more modern world. For example, it is not so important to know that Isaac Newton was spending more time on millennial calculations than on physics than to know that he was keeping them secret. When Robert Boyle, the "father of chemistry," endowed lectures "for proving the Christian religion, against notorious Infidels, *viz.* Atheists, Theists, Pagans, Jews, and Mahometans," it was an acknowledgement that the public was apt to rush in where great scientists feared to tread. The first set of these lectures in 1692 skipped Mahometans and such and got right down to *A Confutation of Atheism.* Newton helped Richard Bentley with these lectures. At the same time he was arguing with John Locke over the "Hobbist" determinism in the latter's recently published views on the human mind.[64]

The public was also deciding issues of more practical concern, as when witchcraft and plague brought them into contact with scientific debates. Again, religious thinkers such as William Perkins and King James I helped by theorizing that the devil's actions in these catastrophies might be supernatural "in respect of our nature" but are "naturall unto himself." That is, the devil was bound by the laws of his nature. This mystification of the subject, with its terminology of "quasi-natural," "hyperphysical," or "preternatural," at least showed a new desire to naturalize the supernatural. This was part of the Reformation's thrust, in demoting sacred objects, acts and words, in order that God would stand alone.[65] Jeffrey Burton Russell concludes that Francis Hutchinson's *Historical Essay Concerning Witchcraft* (1718) was the final chapter on the debate over witchcraft in England. After that date the devil almost disappeared from literature, reappearing only as an aesthetic symbol with the Romantics—hardly an object of literal belief and sometimes a sympathetic figure.[66]

Paul Slack's discussion of plague also illustrates the popular transformation of English thought. The variety and unpredictability of plague had always suggested its supernatural character. Until 1530 community response had taken the form of religious processions with the Host or candles. Protestants stigmatized this as superstitious, and such practices were last recorded in London in 1543. For their part, Protestants recommended private prayers, making the religious response less a community than an individual matter. They also suggested that "natural medicines were a divinely ordained gift and should not be neglected." On the other hand, there were Calvinists who took a religiously fatalistic position which disdained quarantine or any attempt to flee an outbreak of plague.[67] These religious responses were not informed by science, which was then split between Paracelsian and Galenic approaches.

With no better direction than this, local government officials simply took matters into their own hands. They insisted on what Slack terms a "secular approach to epidemic disease" which emphasized controlling the population through quarantine and the prohibition of flight. It was secular, not in being scientific but in ignoring religion. Slack contrasts this with the approach of Ottoman authorities, where Islamic fatalism maintained its sway over government.[68]

In time, English science caught up with the thinking of magistrates. There was a lively public discussion of natural causes, stimulated by the publication of the mortality figures which towns were now recording. Newspapers printed these "bills of mortality," noting the plague's seasonal cycles and its concentration in suburbs. All this encouraged the idea that plague was

> a limited social problem rather than a universal and divinely ordained threat. By making plague familiar and measureable, the bills of mortality undermined those supernatural interpretations which are reserved in most societies for unusual afflictions and sudden calamities.

Scientists were still baffled by the variety which plague could present and officials still daubed "Lord Have Mercy" on quarantine homes. But the search for natural explanations continued, in spite of the lack of progress in treatment and the demonstrable failure of the government's policy of isolation. In line with our earlier explanation of Protestant opposition to radical religion, Slack notes that the clergy supported the government's policies of control, for fear of the disorderly effect of religious enthusiasts who might try to conjure away the threat.[69]

Education

In the fifteenth century education had already begun slipping from the hands of the Church, which saw no threat to orthodoxy in that area. There were secular statutes regulating schools as early as 1406. Common law was used to settle cases involving schools where this could be done without trespassing on the Church's rights. Educational expansion in this period was normally at the initiative of town authorities. These tendencies were dramatized when St. Paul's School in London was put into the hands of lay trustees and given a lay (and married) headmaster.[70]

Henry VIII saw the significance of education to his program of change, and considered how to encourage lay schools in order to erode the Church's monopoly. As head of the Church it became his duty to regulate the universities. And his new cathedrals (formerly monastic churches) were fitted out with "King's Schools."[71] By the time of his death, in the words of Joan Simon, "there had been a wholesale transference of rights over schools to the crown, bringing to a climax a long process of lay encroachment on ecclesiastical powers over education." Schools continued the usual prayers and catechizing along with an increasingly humanist curriculum. But they were more conscious of the need to meet lay needs, including preparation for state service.[72]

Not surprisingly, the kind of orthodoxy which was watched most closely was the political variety. Elizabeth required teachers to take oaths declaring their political allegiance (5 Eliz., c. 1, s. 4). But in 1580 the Privy Council also directed bishops to insure the religious orthodoxy and morals of all schoolmasters; an act of the next year (23 Eliz., c. 1, s. 5) established the duty of the Church to license all teachers—something not done even in the Middle Ages.[73] The most active intrusion of government—to remove schoolmasters who were heterodox, profane or immoral—was first attempted during the Protectorate.[74] Such an increase in oversight is what one would expect in a period dominated by religious ferment and conflict.

The Restoration marked a decline in religious oversight. The Act of Uniformity (14 Car. II, c. 4) reinstated the bishops' duty to license schoolmasters, but there was uncertainty over whether teachers in the growing number of nongrammar schools had to be licensed.[75] State courts interfered increasingly with canon-law jurisdiction, until Cox's Case of 1700 gave a clear precident for limiting ecclesiastical control to Latin grammar schools. The Tories' Schism Act of 1714 was meant to restore an earlier or imagined clerical authority over education, but with the triumph of the Whigs the law never went into effect.[76] Beyond this, the laity constituted an increasing proportion of the teaching force, especially in the nonclassical and charity schools. But grammar schools were also affected; by 1700 in Leicestershire, two-thirds of all schools were taught by laymen. Lawrence Stone considers this loss of a clerical monopoly the central feature of the "educational revolution" of this period.[77]

Laicization would not necessarily mean a secularization of educational content. But the curriculum also suggests a fading religious presence. Before the advent of humanism the curriculum could easily be related to a Christianized culture. Even English literacy began with religious texts—the paternoster, creed, commandments, and prayers—which were already familiar to the pupil, greatly facilitating the task. Prayers were said in school, and the pupils were catechized and taken to church in accordance with the founders' wishes.[78] But interest in the ancient rhetoricians began to change this in the sixteenth century. Erasmus popularized the view that those authors so combined beauty and virtue that a humanistic education would have a moral effect fully in keeping with religious faith. By the end of the sixteenth century, however, classicism was tacitly admitted to be secular, and divinity constituted a separate subject.[79] And by 1546 grammar schools were being founded with statutes that mentioned no religious function and had a "markedly humanistic curriculum."[80]

By the eighteenth century England's schools were considered to make quite a contrast with those on the continent in offering no effective religious instruction at all. In the schools' defense, one contemporary retorted that

> instruction in religious and moral principles ought to come from a parent. For
> this reason it is, perhaps, that in many schools there has been no provision for it,
> and that boys have been well acquainted with the classics, and at the same time
> ignorant of the most obvious doctrines of religion.[81]

Apparently many schoolmasters agreed. By 1700 there were several spelling
books which made a point of containing nothing but secular material, and the
eighteenth century saw the decline in the percentage of religious content in
"readers" as well.[82] Even in the universities, where there was supposed to be
academic instruction in divinity, less was done to prepare clergy for their duties
than in any other Protestant country, in Bishop Edmund Gibson's view.[83]

During the Renaissance there had been talk of founding alternative educational institutions—more secular "academies"—for the children of the ruling
classes. This would leave the fusty scholasticism of the grammar schools and
universities entirely to aspiring clerics. Nothing came of this talk. Instead, the
universities themselves became aristocratic in tone, encouraging the secularization of all higher education. In the sixteenth century the course of study for the
bachelor of arts became entirely autonomous, unrelated to the theological course.
Religious exercises were only recommended to students as a devotional and
voluntary exercise. The only religious requirement left was attendance at chapel
and at university sermons.[84]

Even the rhetorical theory and practice at the heart of a literary education
became more secular. The Reformation included a frontal attack on a culture that
depended on reference to an array of religious, but Catholic, commonplaces. Peter
Ramus, a French Protestant, was successful in his campaign to spread distrust of
those figures, tropes, and metaphors which had been the coin of rhetoric and of
thinking in the Middle Ages and into the Renaissance. Thus he generated a rival
fashion for plain matter and new methods of argument even in religious discourse. In an earlier age, the dominance of those rhetorical figures made it almost
impossible to articulate challenges to current religious culture. The new science,
on the other hand, could not have been expressed in those figures at all, since they
were not suited to concrete descriptions of reality.[85] Thus, Protestantism and the
new science left their mark at the heart of a changing education.

Meanwhile, for the first time, the universities were presided over by lay
chancellors. In 1535 Cardinal Fisher was replaced as chancellor of Cambridge by a
layman, Thomas Cromwell. Cambridge had only two clerical chancellors after
that, both in the reign of Queen Mary. The chancellorship of Oxford remained in
clerical hands until 1552 when Sir John Mason assumed the office. Cardinal
Reginald Pole replaced him under Mary, but Mason was pointedly restored to the
office under Elizabeth. There were only fourteen years after that when it was not
in lay hands.[86] The position may be largely symbolic, but it is symbolic of the
government's determination not to trust the clergy in an area critical to religion.

Theory of Religion

One effect of all of these changes on English thought was to contribute to a comparative study of religions and to naturalistic explanations of religion itself. These are indications that the secularization of thought was complete and that a speculative atheism was finally possible. Even if an awareness of theories about other religions did not cause English men and women to lose all faith in their own, still they would understand that their faith was a personal, individual matter.

Readers had long been aware of other religions, of course. Well into the seventeenth century writers referred to them in order to confirm Christianity, either because they agreed so closely or, alternatively, by their outlandishness! The ease with which other religions could be made to reflect credit on the English religious tradition—whatever the logic chopping involved—is evidence of a secure belief. Likewise, the recognition that Christians, and especially Protestants, were outnumbered in the world did not immediately promote cultural relativism or feelings of insignificance. It only suggested the need for missions.[87] At first, then, a greater acquaintance with alien religions only confirmed the English in their religious culture.

The first writer to take other religions seriously was Lord Herbert of Cherbury, whose *De Religione Gentilium* was published (in 1663) some years after his death in 1648. Herbert took the amount of agreement which he found among the world's religions to be a mark of their common truth.[88] While the notion of converting to Islam or Judaism was not a psychic option in seventeenth-century England, a Deism based on Herbert's irenical approach would certainly soften Christian commitment. Of course, there is some question whether Deism was ever a religion in the sense of an access to power. Herbert claimed to converse with his God, but other Deist writers envisioned a figure who was not free to intersect with their world. So contemporaries were probably right in claiming that Deists were hardly different from the "atheists" who swarmed in their imaginations.[89] Not every philosophy that mentions God is a religion.

Soon, what Paul Hazard has termed the essentially negative character of Deism became evident. Deists were in the forefront of attempts to explain religion naturalistically. Their notions of a "Law of Nature" paralyzed any divine will. To them, spirit was more like a moral instinct than the capacity for ecstatic transcendence. They dismissed any paradox within religion as a violation of the requirement that the truth be clear and distinct.[90] In works like the third earl of Shaftesbury's *Letter Concerning Enthusiasm* (1708) psychological balance became the touchstone of religious truth.[91] It is worth noting that Shaftesbury and the other prominent representatives of this position—Anthony Collins, Thomas Chubb, Thomas Gordon, John Trenchard, Thomas Morgan, Viscount Bolingbroke, John Toland—were from Dissenting backgrounds.[92] They can be seen as extending the early Protestant attacks on popish superstition to something of a logical conclusion.

Just as Catholics had once accused Protestantism of masking a blank unbelief, so pious Protestants now viewed these liberals as closet atheists. Apologists for religion in Restoration England sensed that they were in a new situation. Anti-atheistical authors had once discredited atheists by accusations of libertinism, intellectual laziness, luxury, or melancholia. But Restoration apologists were forced onto the defensive, facing difficulties in their own position. Miracles, the afterlife, spirits, scriptural inspiration all needed justifying.[93] They were coming to realize that it was not this or that doctrine that needed buttressing, but the notion of religion itself.

As many have observed, the contemporary reaction to atheism seems out of all proportion to the threat. Some of the seventeenth-century refutations cannot seem to name any actual atheists except Hobbes. Examples are usually gathered from Italy or from classical antiquity. English cases seem "folklorish," copied from book to book. Of course, there was a philosophical tradition of concealing dangerous truths from an uncomprehending public, so there may have been more genuine atheists in England than the two whom historians have discovered so far—Christopher Marlowe and Anthony Collins. But it seems likely, as some have suspected, that religious apologists were compensating for their own inner doubts.[94]

What is at issue in the denunciation of atheism is not the religious belief of the English masses, but the faith of religious apologists. Can we not take their concern and their proselytizing activity as partly an effort to convince themselves of the truths they promoted? The first indications of the penetration of naturalistic and reductionistic explanations of religion come from apologists for religion. They did not wait for freethinkers to declare themselves but put the words into their mouths. Contemporaries wryly noted that the champions of orthodoxy only succeeded in raising doubts in innocent minds.[95]

Something had shifted. At one time, the fact that pagan traditions resembled certain Christian doctrines had been proof of the prefiguration of the Gospel; it was now treated as proof of some natural cause. Whereas the main reductionistic explanations of religion—from feelings of fear, awe, gratitude, ignorance of second causes, the craft of priests and kings, the apotheosis of heroes, the allegorization of virtues—had long been known from ancient authors, these only became a subject of interest in the late seventeenth century.[96] Lucretius' long-ignored discussion of the fears which brought the gods to birth required ten editions in England from 1675 to the end of the century.

Quaker illuminations and Ranter ravings, which had once been explained in the spiritual terms of demonic possession, were now explained psychologically in John Trenchard's The Natural History of Superstition (1709).[97] Indeed, in the view of Frank Manuel, the study of psychology largely began in the effort to discredit the religion of those who were now feared as fanatics. Exceptional piety became a disease.[98]

Even religious apologists found themselves operating from within this naturalism. For a long time, they had favored naturalistic explanations of atheism in order to discredit it. Robert Burton explored this possibility in *The Anatomy of Melancholy* (1621); and Thomas Jackson (1625) and Thomas Fuller (1642) offered further suggestions, including prosperity and mental illness, as causes of unbelief.[99] In the last decades of the century authors suggested that peace (or alternatively sectarian strife), prosperity or the absence of hardship, or the commercial spirit, might be to blame.[100] Thus, long before modern science ventured its explanations, the naturalistic approach was widely considered appropriate to the study of religion and irreligion.

Marking the end of our period, along with Trenchard's seminal work, was England's response to the episode (starting in 1706) of the French Prophets or Camisards. These immigrants shocked opinion by outbursts of "charismatic" religious activity which England had not seen since the 1650s. The usual explanations were repeated, from demon possession, hypocritical deception, enthusiastic contagion, to plain insane delusion.[101] What is of interest is that the published attacks came principally from religious apologists rather than from freethinkers. Perhaps the case was all too obvious to the latter, so that the opposition to such expressions of religion as prophecy, healings, resurrections, convulsions, and glossolalia could be trusted to religious leaders, both Anglicans and Dissenters. Remnants of the movement would survive until similar outbreaks in the Methodist revivals. But any possibility that these religious expressions would find respectful recognition within English culture was clearly past.

While this book is not about the growth of atheism, we can now see how previous changes made an entirely naturalistic philosophy possible. The secularization of time made possible a more secular history. The secularization of the person and social relations allowed a secular social theory. Secularization of power prompted secular political theories. Secularized space was necessary to the new natural philosophy or science. And the secularization of language and of literature encouraged a secular education. All of these, in turn, would give support to theories of religion, which marks the final stage of a secularization of culture. Religion was now something to be explained, rather than the basis of all explanations. All that remained was the very uncertain process of diffusion of that relativistic view of religion through society. Of course, it is not necessary that religious *faith* disappear as a result, any more than it is necessary that irreligion take the form of a reasoned atheism.

If the secularization of thought was not a cause of the secularization of other aspects of English life, it is the fullest expression of that process. For it marks the full consciousness of secularization and of the issue of faith. And yet the process had begun at a much more basic level: At the beginning of our period the organization of scholarly reference works followed a thematic pattern, and the index of subjects typically gave God, angels, and other spiritual matters first place. By 1600 such works were simply alphabetized.[102] That kind of shift shows the end of absolute reference points in English culture and the failure of religion to order thought. It was as revolutionary as Newton's cosmology.

12

Religious Responses
to Secularization

By the 1660s English men and women were aware of a decline of religious piety, giving rise to such works as Richard Allestree's *The Causes of the Decay of Christian Piety* (1667). With at least fourteen editions before the end of the century, this was one of the best-selling books of the Restoration period.[1] Allestree's "causes" are all moral and meant to discredit the impious. We have seen them complained of before: ignorance, theological disputes, sensuality, self-interest, pride, misplaced zeal, excessive curiosity.[2] Nothing in modern life was presented as creating a new situation with regard to belief. In Allestree's view the Gospel only had to contend with the same moral flaws as always. And yet the latter seemed to be gaining ground.

So there was some ambivalence about the state of religion in Restoration England. Probably most approved of the changes which we have associated with secularization—the separation and purification of religion. But many also worried over whether a more enlightened and conscious faith was giving the needed intellectual and moral discipline to society. Out of these concerns grew England's first religious movements and sects, offering a new organization to the nation's religious life.

At the heart of the new faith was a recognition of the individual. In its revulsion from a corrupt society and wayward culture, Protestantism brought an intensified sense of the value of the individual soul. In time, even the state recognized this in its official toleration of the sacred rights of conscience. Whereas before the Reformation it had been usual to think of the salvation of the Church, now one was concerned with the salvation of the individual. Modern individualism has been a further secularization of this attitude, and historians credit Dissenting groups with being its foremost supporters and exemplars.[3] But even Catholics were touched by the new attitude: James II was England's first born-again king; he sounded the new note in his self-reproach, seeing the Revolution as God's act "to scourge him, and humble him . . . in order to save his soul."[4]

Science as well as Protestantism contributed to this heightened sense of the individual. A mechanistic science left human beings feeling that they were uniquely personal in an otherwise impersonal universe. And while humanity could relate to God, it could only manipulate the rest of creation. The politics and the psychology that we associate with John Locke also echoed the new religious individualism. His "civil society" was something different from Christian society—individuals being bound together by respect for property rather than by orthodoxy.[5] It was characteristic of the times, however, that Locke should shrink from his own conclusions, trying to locate a place for faith in his discussion of "human understanding."[6]

Art also encouraged individualism. Studies of the early novel show how the "Puritan" sense of the individual's spiritual autonomy gave rise to a new literary form. The more mundane world of these novels did not at first mark a decline of religion. In fact, they promoted "a faith that sees human life as a narrative invented by God but interpreted by human beings." Early novelists were showing that nothing in life, even humble lives, was pointless or random when seen from the standpoint of God's character-building project. Samuel Richardson could let Christian values develop more naturally than Milton had, precisely by abandoning the epic sweep for an individual perspective.[7]

Central to the new, individualized faith was Scripture itself. Of course the Bible was respected under the old regime too. It was carried in procession as an object of worship. It was used in sorcery, was one of the sources of scholastic theology, and inspired much of the folklore of popular piety. In her coronation procession, Elizabeth was presented with a Bible, kissed her hands before receiving it and then kissed the Bible and hugged it, thrilling her newly liberated Protestant subjects. Some of them could not resist a totemistic devotion to Bibles. Though Protestant ministers often objected, Bibles were used among their people for divination, as a medicinal charm, for warding off devils, swearing oaths, and detecting thefts. In New England, partisans in a dispute between ministers carried a Bible atop a pole as an ensign.[8] Even ministers could not resist outward signs of devotion; in Dissenting chapels the only color was apt to be a scarlet pillow for the Bible.[9]

But there was also a more spiritual appreciation of Scripture. Quite aside from the theological uses of the Bible, Protestants used it religiously; the presence of the Bible was as the presence of God. It furnished the archetypes by which people understood their lives, experiences, and identities. Indeed, many began to keep diaries and bind them, turning their lives back into books, and continuing Scripture's account of God's purposes.[10]

We have made a great deal of the fact that the Protestants' more literal use of Scripture had a corrosive effect on the religious culture of England. But this should not obscure the positive uses that Protestants found for Scripture. They strove to enter into its world. An imaginative projection into apostolic times became one of main ways to reach the holy. Expository sermons transported believers into the world of the patriarchs and prophets, and gave them the experience of the real presence of their Lord. The motif of Christ as bridegroom gave scope to their affective mysticism.

Insofar as a new religious subculture was developing, that "Protestant culture was sermon culture."[11] There had been sermons before, of course, but they became more important in the new era. For Protestants, sermons were not simply to encourage virtue or teach doctrine; they were nothing less than a means of grace. Indeed, they were often said to be the primary means of grace.[12] That followed naturally from the doctrine of justification by faith, for preaching from Scripture was the ordinary means of awakening a saving faith. Had not St. Paul written that the preaching of the Gospel is the power of God unto salvation to every one that believed (Romans 1:15–16)? Sermons and supernatural power were linked by the message of the cross, which was foolishness to those who would perish but the power of God to those who are saved (I Corinthians 1:18).

At the outset of the Reformation, Tyndale laid it down as a principle that "hereby mayest thou know the difference between Christ's signs or sacraments and antichrist's signs or ceremonies: that Christ's signs speak, and antichrist's be dumb."[13] When the old church used sermons, they might surprise hearers with symbolic parallels or miraculous accounts, or terrify them with cautionary stories. But the sermon was never the heart of the service. It was a prelude to the sacraments. For Protestants, on the other hand, sermons became more holy than Communion itself.[14] There was a resonance between Scripture and the indwelling Spirit that could shake the heart. Protestants had difficulty explaining how hearers could prepare their hearts for God's calling, in view of the arbitrary character of "election." But those who wrote on the subject always assumed the prominence of sermons in the process. Indeed, their books on the subject are collections of sermons![15]

Devotion to the sermon became all the greater when the most extreme Protestants found their movement blocked by the church. After Elizabeth crushed Puritanism as a political movement around 1590 it became an evangelical enterprise, appealing to the nation through preaching. Its message was a life of faith as pictured in the images by which the Puritans are still remembered, of warfare and pilgrimage. Their earnestness made them critical of the sermons of Laud's Arminian faction. Puritans disparaged the "witty" preaching of such court favorites as Lancelot Andrewes, whose "metaphysical" conceits sounded more like the wisdom of words than the Word of wisdom.[16] In response, Laud disparaged the primacy of sermons. He understood that England could have either a religious culture or an evangelical faith but not both. As it happened, the monthly fast sermons before Parliament in 1642 became a political force in toppling Laud, radicalizing the events of that fateful year. The apocalyptic preaching that the Commons heard in St. Margaret's Church offered a vision of inconceivable change and cathartic violence. For a time it was irresistible.[17]

But depending as it did upon faith it was subject to reverses and doubt. Restoration clergy attacked a pulpit rhetoric which aroused more emotion than obedience. Samuel Parker, bishop of Oxford, wondered if there should not be an act of Parliament against the use of metaphors. And the more respectable Dissenters likewise disavowed a rhetoric of "enthusiasm," asserting that God instructed "in a calm and sedate way."[18] Sermons became less cosmic in their scope and less fervent. So by the 1730s the revival of evangelical preaching by George White-field and John Wesley was sufficiently novel to cause a sensation. The susceptibility of this piety to fashion is a feature of the new, more secular situation.

In general, spirit-filled worship was distinguished by spontaneity—which meant that the faithful were not to depend on a book or memorized forms. Extempore prayers were thought to show greater devotion and were recommended by the *Directory of the Public Worship of God* which the Westminster Assembly issued in 1645. This *Directory* was unlike previous liturgies in giving only general directions for the services and not setting the words themselves. Less officially, spontaneity was also achieved by glossolalia and spiritual healing. All of these were more likely to be indulged by the radical sects than by Puritans or Anglicans.[19]

The institution of congregational singing was one novelty that created a cultural form. Musical worship had formerly been a matter of professional performance, but early in Elizabeth's reign the returning exiles introduced London congregations to Genevan psalm singing, as described in chapter 7. Contemporary hymns also entered English culture in the seventeenth century, both in Anglican and sectarian worship, despite initial resistance to elements of worship that were not directly from God's Word.[20]

Despite secularizing trends in literature, the seventeenth century saw the flowering of a consciously religious poetry and verse, from Catholic, Anglican, Puritan, and even Sectarian sources. The magnitude of this effort can be seen by the list of those who still command the respect of anthologists: John Donne, Mary Herbert, Thomas Campion, Giles Fletcher, Jr., George Herbert, William Drummond, William Austin, Robert Herrick, William Habington, Francis Quarles, Abraham Cowley, Thomas Washbourne, John Milton, Richard Crashaw, John Austin, Henry More, Andrew Marvell, Henry Vaughn, Joseph Beaumont, Nathaniel Wanley, Thomas Ken, John Norris, Edward Taylor, and of course,

Anonymous.[21] In the next century their verse would inspire the greatest age of hymn writing in the language.

Yet in reading this literature one is left with a sense of constriction. John Donne is exceptional in finding God wherever he looks in the midst of a wide-awake life. The other authors, powerful as their talents may be, seem to incorporate a narrower range of experience. This is, of course, what T. S. Eliot noticed in the literature of the whole century. In short, the religious poets were little short of being hymn writers themselves, in proportion as their verse deals more with "religion" and less with "life."

Protestant devotion to the word created a subculture, at least. Sabbath duties, private reading of Scripture, extempore private and family prayers, the keeping of spiritual diaries, and religious poetry could create a framework for life. But unlike the older religious culture, it was a matter of choice. In fact, it amounted to cultural nonconformity and thus met rejection, incomprehension, and hostility in the wider society.

And it might be more proper to speak of several Protestant subcultures, institutionalized by the various sects. These denominations constitute another religious initiative, another response to secularization. No one, perhaps not even Queen Elizabeth, thought that her compromise church was perfect. "Anglicans" were willing to let the state decide the shape of worship for the sake of peace and the hope of fostering a new religious culture in England. But others insisted on further purification of a religion which was still too idolatrous. In Elizabeth's own time a few of these were willing to risk their lives to form "gathered churches" to carry on worship in the more purified forms. Thus began the tradition of Separatism—of what sociologists call "sects."

Despite the very small numbers involved, the principle of Separatism was well known to the English public from John Foxe's description of the conventicles which met in defiance of Queen Mary. Separatist principles of restricted membership, believer's baptism, parity of elders, and congregational decision making were disturbing even to those who had never met such sectarians.[22] "Puritans" must always have felt a tug in that direction, though they stayed within the Church so long as there was a chance of purifying it.

When that chance came, in the 1640s, Puritans were unable to agree on the reorganization of the Church which could establish their religious culture. On the one hand, state authority over religion troubled them, having seen its compromises. But Separatism frightened them too because of its current excesses. They heard of practices which could not be reconciled with their notions of religious solemnity:

> In *Gangrena,* published in 1646, Thomas Edwards dwelt upon the horrors of religious and social anarchy caused by the absence of any national ecclesiastical

discipline. He claimed to have been sent a report from an eye witness the previous year of a love feast attended by eighty Anabaptists in a great house in Bishopsgate Street in London. At the feast five new members were baptized; afterwards the community fell to prayer, each one kneeling by himself apart. Edward Barber, their minister, went to every member in turn, men and women, and laid his hands upon their heads, praying that they might receive the Holy Ghost. (By this action, Edwards later explained, Barber gave authority to such persons as had gifts to preach publically.) These ceremonies finished, they had eaten a meal together and after that participated in the Lord's Supper. The evening ended with a disputation over whether Christ died for all men or only for the elect. Edwards knew of other General Baptist churches in London, one conducted by Lamb, a soapboiler, in Bell Alley off Coleman Street, another to which Kiffin acted as minister. Young men and wenches flocked in particular to Lamb's meetings where such confusion reigned that a spectator might have thought he was at a play.[23]

Puritans like Edwards felt some attraction to a spirituality which could not be institutionalized. But in 1662 these reformers were forced to choose between allegiance to the tatters of a religious culture and the acknowledgment of a socially marginal faith. Those who chose the latter maintained the hope that some accommodation ("Comprehension") might be worked out with the Church. They resisted the impulse to organize separate religious institutions or associations. Presbyterians and Independents even maintained some elements of a cultural heritage—in confessions, liturgical practice, and theological literature. They instituted their own burial grounds, academies, charity schools, and achieved social cohesion through endogamy. And they shrank from the final break which would result from ordaining their own clergy.[24]

Quakers and Baptists, having accepted their pariah status more forthrightly, were the first to organize national associations. These were for political as much as religious purposes, to protect hard-pressed believers. The General Baptists held their first national assembly in 1654, and the individualistic Quakers were paradoxically the most tightly organized of all.[25] Sectarian organization among the more numerous, prosperous, and educated Dissenters was delayed until 1689, in the aftermath of the Toleration.

Denominational organization was not, therefore, the happy reaction to toleration. It was a depairing response to the failure of comprehension, and the recognition of permanent isolation. Such organization began with regional clerical associations which met to consult on congregational problems, to ordain new ministers, establish funds to support promising students for the ministry, and maintain the clergy's widows and orphans.[26] Dissent had been forced to find a way to perpetuate itself across the generations, and change from a movement into sects.

These new "gathered" churches created a very different religious atmosphere from that of the traditional parish. There was an heightened sense that the bond between worshippers was not their common birth or locality but their common belief and commitment. Walking to meeting house or chapel would be a reminder of one's estrangement from society. To Dissenters, religion meant an act of faith in God alone and not trust in Christian society. On the other hand, there was an intensity in their fellowship that must have surpassed anything the older church provided.

In time, some "Anglican" clergy came to feel the need for something of this sort—for new forms of religious association and a more serious recognition of belief. In short, during the Restoration one can see the beginnings of Anglicanism as a religious movement—a group organized to promote some major change in the nation's institutions by noninstitutionalized means.[27] Active involvement or churchmanship was no longer satisfied with the ecclesiastical establishment but looked for a more spontaneous commitment.

During the Interregnum the Church of England's distinctive liturgy and doctrine had disappeared, along with its hierarchy. Religious establishment was in disarray, and the children of exiled bishops sometimes converted to continental Catholicism. But there were some in England who did not lose hope that their church would someday be restored.[28] Clandestine services gave the liturgy a glamour that had not been noticed before. Ejected clergy turned to a campaign of scholarship, propaganda, and devotional writing in order to keep the remnants of a religious culture alive. They created an awareness of the distinctiveness of the English Protestant tradition—of its liturgy, its apostolic ordination, its heroes. Anglicanism became self-conscious.[29]

These seventeenth-century works do not, perhaps, evoke that shimmer of a romantic beauty in the Church that we find among Victorian Tractarians. But nostalga gave some emotional depth to the new Anglican piety. There was real beauty too. In the early years of the seventeenth century Richard Hooker's philosophical apology for the Church, Lancelot Andrewes' prayers, and George Herbert's poetry had already created a legacy of beauty. In the 1650s the clerical biographies by Izaak Walton, the devotions of Jeremy Taylor and of Charles I (as edited in the *Eikon Basilike*) added to that heritage. The biblical, patristic, and theological studies of John Pearson, John Bramhall, Herbert Thorndike, and James Ussher gave Anglican clergy a literary culture to replace their lost institutional security.

Thus, the threat to the institutional existence of the Church of England made people conscious of its traditions. During the Interregnum, when the episcopal government of the Church was abolished and its liturgy was proscribed, some had assumed that it was gone forever. Others realized that these traditions could be put on a new footing. In the absence of legal establishment there were efforts in the 1650s to make Anglicanism popular. Works of practical instruction by Richard Allestree and commentaries such as Henry Hammond's *Paraphrases and Annotations upon all the Books of the New Testament* appealed to the free allegiance of the public and not just to its cowed submission. It was a far cry from

Archbishop Laud's attempt to reconstruct the political establishment. English men and women were learning to recognize a spiritual distinctiveness in Anglicanism that was more than simple chauvinism.

In the Restoration the published sermons by Robert Sanderson and Robert South added to this popular Anglicanism. Devotional books by Anglican clergy began to compete with those by Puritan authors in popularity, expressing pride in a distinctive English piety.[30] Perhaps Edward Lake was trying to be provocative in declaring that his *Officium Eucharisticum* (1673) was compiled from such "Devout Fathers" of England's church as Lancelot Andrewes, John Cosin, and "that Great and Good Man, Archbishop Laud."[31] Bishop William Beveridge was more typical when his best-selling *The Excellency and Usefulness of the Common-Prayer* (1682) expressed the satisfaction that the English could take in a liturgy that had weathered attacks by both papists and Puritans.[32] His dean, William Stanley, picked up this theme of the moderation of Anglicanism in *The Faith and Practice of a Church of England Man*. In Stanley's view the Church of England was like one crucified between two thieves—of superstition and fanaticism.[33] The timing of Stanley's work is suggestive. It appeared in June of 1688 when the institutional survival of Anglicanism again seemed threatened by a papist monarch. In this crisis, Stanley was heartened to think that "It hath been of old observed, that where and when the Church had less secular aid, there God did in a more special manner vindicate it himself."[34]

In short, Anglicans were learning to think like sectarians. Laud would not have welcomed an appeal to popular opinion, much less lay leadership in an Anglican revival. Restoration clerics sensed a more supportive spirit, however, and enlisted it for a church which again was threatened by the secular power. This new lay piety deserves a name, and "Anglican" is the only real candidate, always remembering that it is the historian's substitute for a variety of even more awkward contemporary usages such as "confessionalist," "communicant," "churchman," "Church-of-England man."[35]

The formation of Anglican religious societies gave this movement substance. This initiative, and semi-monastic communities, had been discussed at the Restoration, to preserve the sense of conspiratorial fellowship fostered under Puritan despotism. Nothing came of them until 1678, when the Popish Plot warned of danger to the restored Church. In that year Rev. Anthony Horneck founded the first religious societies, especially involving young men. Besides the obvious Catholic threat, it was claimed that these societies were also a reaction to the reports of clubs of atheists.[36] Just as Stanley pleaded with the gentry to countenance the Church by a more ostentatious adherence, so the societies were meant to be a public witness of devotion to the Church—something more than the dumb obedience of conventional believers.[37] "Communicant" was taking on a new meaning in a secular society, when the penalties for nonattendance had lapsed and monarchs smiled on recusancy.

Horneck's societies, mostly in London, were modest in their aims at first, promoting frequent Communion and urban charities. After the Revolution of 1688 they felt more secure and aggressive. There were new Societies for the Reformation of Manners, which were not religiously devotional but promoted the enforcement of public morality. They had the encouragement of the monarchs, who made their support unofficial—in line with the voluntaristic thrust of this movement. These societies demanded the enforcement of existing laws against public profanity, blasphemy, gambling, drunkeness, debauchery, and Sunday trading—laws which had been forgotten during the Restoration. It is relevant to our theme that they preferred to bring their cases before the temporal authorities rather than to use the moribund church courts. By 1701 about twenty such societies operated in London itself.[38]

There was a much greater number of societies with more specifically religious motives, whose meetings included the sharing of spiritual concerns of a personal nature. By 1714, 27 percent of London parishes scheduled services to accommodate such societies, and twenty-seven other towns had them by that date. Samuel Wesley, the father of the founders of the later Methodist Societies, began a society in his parish of Epworth.[39] In 1699 four laymen and a cleric capped this effort by organizing the Society for Promoting Christian Knowledge to evangelize the largely unchurched lower orders through schools and tracts. A Society for the Propagation of the Gospel in Foreign Parts (1701) took up the problem of ministering to English colonists, their slaves and their native American neighbors. These and other societies all encouraged other charities and missions.[40]

The church was split over the propriety of these new, lay initiatives. Many of the bishops gave the societies public encouragement, but others resented the implication that the Church was not adequate to guide England's spiritual life. After all, as late as the 1630s Bishop Matthew Wren required his Visitors to ferret out those who discussed religion in their homes—automatically suspecting them of some kind of heresy. The clergy sensed that the interlocking directorates of these organizations posed a threat to their leadership. Prominent Tory clerics such as Henry Sacheverell and Francis Atterbury criticized the societies openly.[41]

Fears of the movement's independence of mind were not groundless. Latitudinarian clergy suspected the SPCK's charity schools of spreading Jacobite, Nonjuring (pro-Stuart) sympathies. They could not be sure that this Anglican devotion to an idealized church implied the same respect for the state. For example, among the lay leaders who had refused the oaths to the revolution regime was Robert Nelson. Nelson was one of the central figures among the societies, and the principal author of *A Companion for the Festivals and Fasts of the Church of England* (1704), the most characteristic expression of a self-conscious Anglicanism before the Oxford Movement (tenth edition in 1717, twentieth in 1752, thirty-sixth in 1826).[42] Thus, the religious establishment felt it was threatened by a proselytizing "High Churchmanship."

The societies succeeded in making religion an issue in a secular society, if we can judge from sarcastic newspaper references. They could even be accused of courting notoriety. Some grumbled that it was hard to get a shave on a Sunday, so intimidated were barbers by the threat of legal action against Sunday trade. It was said that swearing was falling out of fashion, at least in uncertain company.[43] In 1712, the SPCK announced that it had established no fewer than five hundred charity schools, showing that the movement of lay Anglicanism had penetrated the country generally. In 1713 their schools in London organized a procession of 4,000 well-scrubbed scholars to the public thanksgiving for the Peace of Utrecht at St. Paul's. There was a similar performance the next year in celebration of the Hanoverian succession.[44]

Some well-wishers to religion concluded from these activities that Christianity could compete in a freer environment. Bishop Edmund Gibson was still trying to revive canon law and Convocation by the celebrated publication of his *Codex Juris Ecclesiae Anglicanae* in 1713. But the future would not lie in this direction. In retrospect, the Tory ascendancy of 1710–14 was the last effort to reassert anything like the old system of religious compulsion. Their campaign envisioned a renewed censorship over press and education, secured the appointment of a bishop to the Privy Council, tightened religious tests for public office, encouraged Church-and-Queen riots, and promoted the building of fifty new churches for a growing London. But all of this was undone when the Whigs came into power with George I in 1714.

Voluntary societies did not maintain their vitality for long. When the Wesleys tried to revive them in the late 1730s they seemed exhausted.[45] This is what one should expect of religious movements. They may create a sincere enthusiasm, but it will be temporary. The life expectancy of movements cannot be long unless they somehow institutionalize the charismatic impulse—if that is not a contradiction.

The best example of the momentary character of faith may be seen in one other religious response, the efflorescence of millenarianism. There was nothing new about it; Richard I made sure to meet Joachim of Fiore in 1191 to hear his prophecies regarding Saladin before his crusade.[46] Galfridian prophecies, in animal shape (with hints of heraldry), were popular in England on the eve of the Reformation. Henry VIII's government took seriously their potential for inspiring rebellion and went to the lengths of publishing counterinterpretations.[47] In 1541 Parliament made it a felony to pretend to supernatural predictions (33 Henry VIII, c. 14). Not everyone believed in these apocalyptic statements, or in all of them, of course. Satirical treatments had appeared as early as the fourteenth century. The first generation of Protestants, including Tyndale, did not favor literal interpretations of the Book of Revelation, thinking that it had lent itself to superstition and triviality.

It was the Turkish menace in the 1530s that caused continental Reformers to reconsider the relevance of prophecy. English exiles from Mary's reign became aware of this heightened faith and were receptive because the present held so little hope for them. When they returned to England they brought the continental interest with them, where the dramatic reversals in politics made believers of a whole nation. In foreign affairs, the Armada episode and the high stakes in the Religious Wars made a prophetic view of events inevitable.[48]

Through the reigns of Elizabeth and James, millenarianism was not a sign of alienation from English society, but rather of involvement in it. God's enemies and England's seemed to be the same. A new stage was reached when Laud's rule raised suspicions that Antichrist had found friends in England.[49] From this time on, millenarianism would divide England rather than unify it.

When government broke down in the 1640s, politics momentarily took a millenarian form. A secular polity was not yet ready to give guidance to the nation during unprecedented change. As censorship collapsed there was a striking increase of interest in millennial and other prophecies.[50] The sense that events were touching the fringes of God's power made this a major religious expression. Millenarianism was "the most striking and fundamental characteristic of the formal preaching before the Long Parliament."[51] Petitions to Parliament included "expressions of grateful wonder at the dispensations of providence which became virtually obligatory in the preambles."[52] The fall of Archbishop Laud confirmed several specific prophecies of the 1630s. Granted such excitement, it is little wonder that the Irish Rebellion was taken as the literal onset of the Great Tribulation which was to precede the End.[53] History was being swallowed into eternity.

Obviously, all this was not the scholarly eschatology of a later time but a political cry which could mobilize a whole nation. Its strength was in its ambiguity; the biblical language was too thrilling to translate into ordinary political terms. Some radicals did specify their expectation of the end of tithes, canon law, and the national church, but for the most part millenarianism left details open.[54] For a brief time, then, politics was truly a branch of religion.

The 1650s witnessed a rapid decline in millennial expectations. God had proven even more inscrutable than the Calvinists had imagined. The best theological minds in England, meeting in the Westminster Assembly, failed to chart England's millennial course and only discovered widening differences over these and other matters.[55]

Eschatological scholarship did not die out entirely in Dissent or even among Anglicans. But there was now a gulf between popular and scholarly millenarianism.[56] It is notorious that Isaac Newton came to spend more time on his millenarian scholarship than he did on science. This is now taken to show how little we understand the age of the Scientific Revolution, or how odd geniuses can be. Worldly-wise politicians maintained an interest too, as when Bishops William Lloyd and William Sancroft sat down together during the Revolution in 1688 to try to rethink prophecy in the light of current events. In 1712 Lloyd had an audience with Robert Harley and Queen Anne to explain how prophecy seemed to bear on the Catholic Church at that juncture.[57]

But familiarity had given prophecy such a bad name that scholars were more reticent.[58] So we see the modern pattern developing, in which popular prophecy is a mark of social and cultural marginality while scholarly interest is overspread with commentary glosses and embarrassment. It is true that millenarianism "persisted" up to the French Revolution and beyond. But even with that revolution's hubristic attack on Christianity, apocalyptic prophecy did not provide the symbols for England's struggle with France.[59] In part, millenarianism was secularized by transformation into the idea of Progress. When restless intellects such as David Hartley, Richard Price, and Joseph Priestley turned these doctrines over in their minds, they were bound to come out differently. Thus one of the most vital expressions of religious belief was secularized from a transcendant realm into an immanent utopia.[60]

Millenarianism had given scope to an unprecedented religious creativity; but Christopher Hill's *The World Turned Upside Down* shows the secularizing tendency of these initiatives. Nothing was more common among mid-century religious radicals than to "demythologize" traditional doctrines: Christ was within the individual and nowhere else, the Resurrection has already taken place within those who are in on the secret, the Second Coming will be a new consciousness, heaven is a happy life here and now. Sin is only in the consciences of those still in bondage, hell is a state of mind, and the devil is some principle of life—a part of the God who is also Nature.[61]

One can only maintain the delight in such realizations for so long. They evoke a religious sense in the midst of everyday life, but only for a generation raised in the traditional piety. Later generations will be left with the wonders of unadorned Nature. So as Hill remarks, "we see radical religion passing into rationalism" in these redefinitions. For seventeenth-century radicals, "their escape route from theology was theological."[62] It was necessary that it be so. Secular thought could not spring from nowhere; it had to grow out of religious concepts to get any hearing at all, even a hostile one.

The late seventeenth century saw active religious interests and initiatives. These often have the appearance of reactions against an alarming decline. Still, Protestantism succeeded in hallowing some aspects of life. There was a new sense of England's mission in history, a strict observance of the Sabbath, a taste for vernacular Scripture and sermons and hymns, and respect for individual conscience. English society generally shared in these, making them a matter of culture. But the new religious organizations, whether sects or societies, had the effect of dividing society, marking off subcultures. In such a situation, one was free to choose which elements of this nascent culture suited a personal faith.

Faith is that part of religion that cannot be legally established or enforced. Culture can be enforced, being a matter of practice or outward profession. Thus faith is harder either to foster or to destroy. The success of Restoration efforts to encourage a more personal religious faith is hard to measure by the historian's methods. But the responses to secularization at least showed that many in the seventeenth century understood that religion would have to be put on a different basis than culture and compulsion, both to survive and to be worthy to survive.

13

Antecedents, Causes,
and Conclusions

Perceptive historians have puzzled over how the seventeenth century could witness the simultaneous "intensification of both religiosity and secularism."[1] It has made them wonder about the assumption of a law "of the conservation of historical energy" whereby an increase in a secular direction is necessarily compensated by a decrease in some religious direction.[2] This is less of a mystery if one thinks of secularization as affecting institutions and culture until 1700, and actually encouraging religious faith by way of a reaction.

Secularization has often been taken to mean an erosion of religious belief, resulting from some combination of intellectual and technological advance. This study questions that assumption. While seeing secularization, initially, as the loss of religion's social functions, we can also see it as a refinement or spiritualization of faith. Certainly the various processes of secularization corresponded to a heightened emphasis on certain elements of Christianity. But as cultural changes sharpened the intellectual focus, serious questions arose concerning religion.

Lucien Febvre was doubtless right to point out that true scepticism required a new vocabulary if it were to sustain itself, and if Europe were to break free from the envelope of a religious culture. This study has attempted to show how England's cultural grammar was transformed. Notions of space and time, approaches to work and art, patterns of power and association changed to create a secular culture and an autonomous individual. Only then could scholars and philosophers express the new outlook and speak of religion with entire objectivity. Treating the change as a topic in social and cultural history did not mean that it had to be presented as unconscious, inchoate, or inevitable. To a large degree, the secularization of England was a conscious choice, carried out in a political campaign. We can make a good guess as to the motives involved.

Protestants saw only gain in a more spiritual and reflective religion. Secularization might have come even without their aid in justifying the state's actions, but they gave the process much of its impetus. Protestants believed that the essential features of their religion could not only survive the separation from other aspects of culture but would be purified by the process. As the victors in England's cultural revolution, we have accepted their rather intellectualized definition of religion, so that we are hardly surprised if an historian identifies religion as the bare proposition that "God exists."[3] Atheism, which at one time was too arduous an intellectual effort to contemplate, has come to seem like a simple negative. We are a long way from the culture of 1500, in which critics could only express their opposition by an inversion of religion, in blasphemy, heterodoxy, or demonism. The spiritualization that made stark unbelief possible was also the price of a free faith.

But there were political motives as well, and the political antecedents include the 1370s when John Wyclif was redefining religion's position in society. The parliaments of that time seemed receptive to suggestions on how to humble the Church. Dissatisfaction with clerical dominance had created an anticlerical party under John of Gaunt. Covetous eyes were cast on the Church's property, and taxation of the Church and statutory restrictions on papal power were enacted. Parliament resolved that the highest state offices should go to laymen. So Wyclif was encouraged to develop his theory of the separation of spiritual and temporal lordship, and he did not stop there.

In some respects the Lollard understanding of religion became more radical than that of the first generations of Protestants. Lollards were even more likely to view the Eucharist entirely as a memorial, promote an extreme iconoclasm, slight the liturgy in favor of preaching, and denounce tithe support.[4] But the shocks of papal schism (1378) and the Peasants' Revolt (1381) took the momentum out of this campaign. Church and council drew together out of a fear of disorder, and Wyclif lost his patronage.[5] Threats to the Church did not disappear entirely. The government conducted a survey of all gild wealth in 1388, perhaps envisioning confiscation.[6] Gaunt's son, as King Henry IV, inherited some of his father's distaste for the Church and executed an archbishop in 1405 over papal protests.[7] The high point of the anticlerical campaign was a carefully conceived scheme to disendow church property, introduced in 1410. The same year saw unsuccessful attempts to reduce clerical immunity and to end burning for heresy.[8]

Why, then, did England not carry through its secularizing project at that point? After all, Henry VIII's reformation was based on those fourteenth-century Statutes of Provisors and Praemunire, and Wyclif was an inspiration to Edward VI's reformers. And yet a century and a half went by, in which the Church not only survived but flourished. No doubt the embryonic character of the state made politicians wary of destroying any institutions of the political or social establishment. The state was not ready to sustain both a theological and constitutional revolution until Henry VIII's time, and even then there was real risk.[9]

The other retarding factor, no doubt, was that Wyclif had only his pen and his preachers, and not a press to spread the new ideas. Even John Foxe was aware of the part that printing was playing in the sixteenth-century Reformation.[10] Printing is the most obvious contribution that technological development made to the sixteenth-century Reformation and secularization. As often observed, it not only spread the new ideas but it made the public more analytical. But the mere presence of printing could not have been determinative; printing was in wider use in several Catholic countries than in England. Still, there can be no doubt that the state's spasmodic toleration of pamphleteering was important in making religion a matter of debate and therefore of doubt.

Aside from the advent of printing technology, it would make as much sense to speak of economic development as the result of secularization than as its cause, when one thinks of Henry's economic mobilization of the church lands and Edward's damage to gild solidarity. In general, urbanization and economic development hardly seem determinative to England's secularization. Other countries of Europe were more advanced in these respects, most of which retained far more of their religious cultures. Beyond that, most of the features of this secularization were not specific to an urban setting. The transformation of space and time, of language and education, power and personhood, and perhaps even of work, affected both rural and urban settings, though perhaps to different degrees. Only with respect to the arts, science, and scholarship—the more glamorous aspects of the process—does the urban setting seem significant. These tend to be later aspects, more result than cause. Even newspapers, whose contribution to the final stage of secularization has yet to be discussed, were important in the provinces as well as in London.

The paucity of psychological explanations of secularization may be explained by the fact that scholars do not seek psychological causes for what they consider to be rationality itself. Historians who have proposed psychological causes of Protestantism (which they may find uncongenial) have not shown the same interest in psychologizing secularization (which they may think of as self-evident). But the connection of the two has been striking. It is often observed that Protestantism encouraged the triumph of religious "transcendence" over cultural "immanence." In our terms, transcendence means a religion that does not expect to find entry points for the divine within the world of everyday life, or does not expect God to use them more than once. A religion of immanence builds a religious culture around the points of entry which seem in regular use. Transcendence has been interpreted in psychological terms as an objectification of the self. As such it is sometimes related to anxiety, depression, inadequacy, difficulties in self-completion, and social alienation.[11] Transcendence has also been linked to rationality. We have already mentioned the link which Tillich posited between monotheism and rationalist scepticism.[12] Thus, the same psychological explanations would be relevant to both Protestantism and secularism. Of course, they both had an aesthetic, ethical, metaphysical, and spiritual—as well as psychological—appeal. Assessing the relative weight of each of these would hardly be the job of objective scholarship.

Perhaps the simplest way to account for our story is to point out that no other country had a Henry VIII. The sequence of changes indicates the overriding importance of his state and his decisions. He dealt the first blows to religious culture before Protestantism was an issue and before a "print consciousness" could have taken hold. A secularization of sacred space and time both began in the 1530s. Monasteries and shrines were transferred to the king's account, changing England's geography. Holy days were eliminated, to be replaced with national holidays. Work time replaced sacred cycles as central to English culture.

Other changes, in later reigns, are less clear in their causes, but the order of chapters gives a rough idea of their sequence. Worship in a profane language (in the 1550s) led to the profanation of religious discussion, the rise of a vocabulary of scepticism (especially between 1560 and 1650), and rhetorical methods which lacked religious suggestiveness. There was also, apparently, some slow decline in oaths, curses, spells, and casual profanity. The state's influence was seen even in this area.

Evidence for the secularization of work patterns is too sparse to offer a sense of the timing involved. Technological development must have played some part, including the printing of occupational manuals of all types. Even here the state and Protestantism played their part, in secularizing gilds and disparaging occult aid. For religion had become less a technology and more a way of changing oneself, even as work became an autonomous activity.

Art lost its function as an aid to the glorification of God with the advent of notions of Protestant worship. The Church's architectural heritage constrained the change of worship that could be accommodated, but artists, architects, and writers who now lacked church patronage sought other outlets. Music, drama, and painting found new venues outside of church, and their subjects were humanized accordingly. At a humbler level, those with a collector's urge turned their attention from saints' relics to curios.

Henry's secularization of power in the early 1530s was an essential change and the source of other developments. By way of reaction, efforts to reintegrate political and religious authority persisted until about 1650. Ungenerous as it was, the legal toleration of religion in 1689 was the signal that English society had found a new and secular basis. The lag between legal toleration and social tolerance is another measure of the priority of state action over attitudes.

Many sacred social roles were lost in Henry's reformation, even before the English church took on a Protestant character. English nationalism was heir to a declining sense of religious solidarity. This hardly amounted to a sacralization of the nation, being so largely an expression of anticlericalism and antipapalism.

Finally, it was possible to speak of the secularization of scholarship and thought. The state's demonstrated power over society was a factor in the projection of more perfect societies and new theories of power. Scientists, curiously, resisted the secular tendencies within a mechanical philosophy and tried to leave room in their models for God and personal or vital principles. Hobbes and his libertine admirers were less like heroes to the reading public than an awful warning. On the other hand, England's experience with religious "enthusiasm" raised suspicions of any vital religion, encouraging naturalistic and reductionistic (and even pathological) explanations of the phenomenon.

The religious roots of secularization are not a new discovery. Max Weber sensed that Protestantism had been a major force in the "disenchantment" of this world. Friedrich Gogarten, Henri Frankfort, and others pushed that development back to ancient times by showing how poor the Jewish Scriptures are in mythic materials.[13] True, the medieval church had been inundated with the residual paganism of its converts, and the cults of certain shrines show the extent to which religion became polycentric once again. But Protestants likened their efforts to Jesus' campaign to cut through laws and rites to the more spiritual essence of religion. Weber also argued that forces within Christianity helped to create the state, science, and capitalism, which have traditionally been recognized as secularizing agents. Specifically, he related them all to a "Puritan" drive toward world mastery.[14]

What might be investigated further is how Catholic Recusants, who tried to remain true to the medieval religious heritage, reacted to this transformation of culture. Did the religion of Catholics also become more a matter of faith? If not, how did they maintain a religious subculture in defiance of secularizing trends?

One other factor, appearing at the very end of our period, must be mentioned for its solvent effect on religious culture and even on religious faith. The advent of journalism should not be considered simply as an aspect of the history of printing. The invention of newspapers is as important a milestone in the history of consciousness as is printing itself, for the dynamics of periodical publication created a new level of awareness.

Periodical publication suggests a new tempo and urgency in the world's affairs. Each issue fills up, somehow, with developments which clamor for our attention. Once a schedule of publication is announced, journalists will not admit that there is no news of importance. The very concept of "news" implies that each day brings a budget of information which we must master in order to consider ourselves informed. Being informed replaces the ideal of being wise, and the day or the week becomes the focus of attention, rather than eternity. Religion points to a reality beyond time, and therefore can hardly be a subject of the news. Only religious controversy or change could find its way into the news, as religion came to be a subject of politics.

Of course, everything was politicized by the news. That is, newspapers invited readers to connect all human affairs to society's instruments of decision and power. The news was a call for change, a single-minded concentration on the world's daily processes. The other important result of periodical publication was the undermining of all authority except that of polite society or the reading public. Selling tomorrow's issue depends upon flattering today's readers, and the techniques of doing this were learned very early. Newspapers appealed to their readers' judgment, feeling sure of what "the people" would think of this or that policy. They welcomed correspondence from their readers and gave them the thrill of seeing their contributions in print.

In short, writers of newspapers had a different relation to their readers than writers of books or pamphlets. There was no question of speaking down to those readers. Nothing was beyond the judgment of the "informed" public. Science, literature, politics, philosophy, theology were all presented for the verdict of the semieducated. The views of intellectual elites were discounted, while the judgment that mattered was that of Reason, which could mean the prejudices of the coffeehouse.

We might or might not sympathize with this "Enlightenment," depending on our view of the decadence of late-Renaissance scholarship, but we can hardly ignore the revolutionary character of the change. Newspapers completed what Protestant "lecturers" started—remembering how Laudians sneered at those lecturers as "the people's creatures," forced to flatter their audience and adopt their language in order to keep them coming back.[15]

Joseph Addison's famous statement from one of the first issues of the *Spectator* (12 March 1711) creates a different effect if viewed in this light: "I shall be ambitious to have it said of me, that I have brought Philosophy out of closets and Libraries, Schools and Colleges, to dwell in Clubs and Assemblies, at Tea-Tables and in Coffee-Houses." One's reaction depends on how one thinks philosophy fared in those new surroundings. Addison also suggested that every family should set aside an hour each morning for tea and bread and butter and the reading of the day's *Spectator*—his modern substitute for morning devotions.

In assessing a variety of possible explanations for the decline of the "magical" elements within English culture, Keith Thomas acknowledged that the change was "not so much technological as mental." He specifically mentions "general improvement in communications"—meaning newspapers—that helped to "break down local isolation and to disseminate sophisticated opinion" among those classes which could afford to keep current.[16]

Of course, an authoritarian state immediately recognized the threat from newspapers and tried to ban them. But with the loss of political control in the

1640s papers began to appear. In the excitement of the wars God was often on the front page. Joseph Frank observes that "almost every weekly gave some space to pious asides and exhortations, and God was often actively in the news." Editors could not resist assuming the mantle of the prophet, offering their observations from on high. It was not long, however, before these references became more conventional than authentic: in Frank's words, "Publicists used the deity as a slogan rather than a mystery." And the restlessness of the journalistic enterprise soon became apparent; the issue of toleration became the religious matter of greatest interest, as one would expect of editors attuned to political change.[17]

As early as the 1650s Cromwell's government concluded that there was no hope of stifling journalism and that the wisest thing would be to monopolize it. The Restoration regime agreed. But during the "Exclusion" crisis of 1678–81 the government's own papers abandoned the lofty tone of the authoritative publication and tried appealing to public judgment.[18] In the freer circumstances after the Revolution of 1688 there was no question of monopolizing the news. Minority parties which needed public support, like Robert Harley's Old Whigs, did not hesitate to create it through journalism.[19] Even Bishop Atterbury used the papers to promote his reactionary church policies, unwittingly encouraging this secularizing force.

A contemporary remembered the first flush of news mania:

> About 1695 the press was again set to work, and such a furious itch of novelty has ever since been the epidemical distemper, that it has proved fatal to many families, the meanest of shopkeepers and handicrafts spending whole days in coffee-houses to hear news and talk politics.[20]

By 1704 there were nine papers in London and three in the country, with a circulation of some 45,000 copies. At least three papers appeared every day except Sunday. (Newspapers profaning the Sabbath rest did not appear until 1780, although there was the compensation of six Saturday papers in London by 1704.) The number of London papers rose to eighteen by 1709. Even after the Stamp Tax of 1712 attempted to make the news too expensive for the lower classes, circulation hovered around 46,000.[21]

The provinces were very much a part of this development. Newsletters, the precursors of newspapers, were primarily to inform country readers of national concerns. Those papers which had "Post" as a prominent part of their titles were indicating that they appeared on the days that mail left London. By 1723 there were twenty-four provincial papers, and after 1737 there were never fewer than thirty. Ten million newspaper stamps were sold in 1760.[22]

Coffeehouses proliferated in country towns too, in imitation of the institution that had developed in London for the consumption of news. Like so many of the developments which have proved important to our account, coffeehouses owed something to puritanical Protestantism. They originated in the 1650s as a temperance institution—a rebuke to the inebriated fellowship of the tavern. Their early rules typically forbade swearing and gambling, they were democratically open to anyone with a penny for a first cup, and they were devoted to radical discussion of the issues of the day. By 1700 there were said to be more than 2,000 in London alone.[23]

From the beginning these establishments found the discussion as stimulating as the coffee. Anthony Wood complained that even in Oxford they eroded scholarly exchange, as news addiction spread.[24] Those of Wood's mind lamented the decline of standards which resulted from periodical publication of book abstracts, which began with the *Weekly Memorials for the Ingenious* in 1682. By 1692, with the first important miscellany, the *Gentleman's Journal*, the whole range of artistic and scholarly interests had been made into news and would therefore suffer the effects of fashion.[25] Religion was one such "interest."

Contemporaries shared an apprehension that religion was fading. They lamented the scoffing at particular doctrines, the neglect of certain religious practices, the heterodoxy or the sheer ignorance of so many. Of course it is hard to know what would have satisfied pious observers; complaints may only show more stringent standards. But by the Restoration, the issue did not seem to be Christian orthodoxy so much as the bare presence of religion in England. Bishop Sprat in 1667 observed that "the influence which Christianity once obtain'd on men's minds is now prodigiously decay'd."[26] Thomas Burnet, a bishop's son, wrote a friend in 1719, "I cannot but remind you with joy how the world's changed, since the time when, as we know, a word against the clergy passed for rank atheism, and now to speak tolerably of them passes for superstition."[27] His contemporary, Addison, thought that there was "less appearance of religion in England than in any neighboring state, Catholic or Protestant." Montesquieu's continental perspective did not differ: "In England there is no religion, and the subject, if mentioned in Society, excites nothing but laughter. Bishop Joseph Butler concluded early in the eighteenth century that "It has come to be taken for granted that Christianity is not so much a subject for inquiry, but that it is now at length discovered to be fictitious."[28] Such quotations, while always ambiguous, could be multiplied endlessly and may even have had a self-fulfilling effect.

Of course, the beginning of doubt increases the scope of faith. Richard Baxter sounded the new note in asserting that "Nothing is so firmly believed as that which hath been sometimes doubted of."[29] His clerical brethren never tired of casting scorn on what they called "implicit faith." Implicit faith would not have been a matter for reproach in an earlier period. It simply meant the sort of cloudless confidence that a saint might enjoy. That kind of assurance was rare by 1700, at least among the more articulate. They despised the blind religiosity they met on their continental travels.[30]

Even the commonest reader sensed that something was amiss in England. A content analysis of the most popular religious literature in the period 1660–1711 gives evidence of a shrinking confidence, narrowing interest, and a privatization of piety in both Anglican and Dissenting works. Within these books there was a statistically significant shift over time toward an image of a more benevolent deity, and from a decidedly anxious to a more confident tone. But this serenity was related to a declining attention to society, and to any possible growth of vice, heterodoxy, and indifference. In other words, the religious interest of the reading public was less engaged with the religious tone or welfare of the nation. Instead, we find a new devotionalism that was measureably more private, passive, and pietistic.[31]

This privatization of religion is the reverse side of institutional secularization. It is further demonstrated within the popular religious literature by a decline of appeals to various intellectual authorities or to arguments that had once been made as a matter of course. Appeals to reason, nature, and history all declined, leaving Scripture as the only safe authority for religious authors. This is a surprise in that the Latitudinarian apologists so popular with historians were using just such "sources" in appealing to a more philosophical audience. Apparently the reading public sensed that these sources were problematical. There had been a time when any argument would do because none was really necessary. Now readers sensed that one had to be wary, because the ground of discourse was shifting. What now seemed self-evident to society might be at odds with revealed truth. Even in citing Scripture there was a statistically significant change from using all parts of the Bible indiscriminately to concentrating on the New Testament as the heart of the faith. It shows a similar concern over what were safe arguments in a more critical environment.

By 1700 we have seen many of the marks of completed secularization: the appearance of religious movements as a reaction to the failure of religious establishment, reductionistic explanations of the religious sense, the state's power to define religion. A further sign of the times was that the enemy of religion was now seen, not as a spiritual opponent, Satan, but as simple indifference. Medieval religion envisioned God's enemies as fiendishly malevolent, from the dark side of a spiritual realm. By the Restoration the enemy was more likely to be recognized as society's lack of a religious response. Evangelists faced a new problem when the resistance came not from some flaw in human nature—pride, idolatry, sensuality, or stupidity—but from an indifference that might even seem natural.

It would not be long before religious horror was used for trivial literary effect. By 1760 the sense of the numinous had declined to the point that it became a toy for Gothic novelists and aestheticians of the sublime.[32] To play with religious dread in this way does not even pay religion the blasphemer's complement of disrespect.

It bears repeating that in 1700 religion was very much in the thoughts of English men and women. The good of their families and businesses, their nation and their souls depended on their faithfulness to particular doctrines and moral injunctions. But this was a narrower, more explicit matter than the culture which had enclosed their ancestors. In 1500 religion was hardly even a noun; it was more likely to be an adverb. One did things religiously. One did everything religiously, meaning piously, with due regard for the unseen forces that could aid you or trip you up. Clerics and heretics, witches and peasants, housewives and gildsmen vied with each other to elaborate the customs that would ensure good fortune in this world and the next. It would have surprised them enormously to foresee a time when Puritans and Latitudinarians, Deists and politicians and newspaper critics would be suggesting ways to simplify religion, in order to increase its appeal.

Historically, religion has sometimes been a constructive force within society, and sometimes a critical force. Some religions are congenial toward artistic efforts in organizing worship, while others are fearful of idolizing human creations. Some churches take a major responsibility for the political, social, and economic life of the community, bringing religious and moral values to bear. Other religious traditions see only the dangers of oppression here, and the promotion of ecclesiastical power in the place of divine demands. They may try to preserve the freedom to make right choices spontaneously. Some churches want to be recognized as partners with other institutions, while others see themselves primarily in a "prophetic" mode and expect hostility. It is essentially the difference between religious culture and religious faith.

Only in a situation of competing denominations can a paradoxical religion preserve both modes. Indeed, the Western tradition began in such a competition, as Jesus and the leaders of Israel found no compromise between prophetic and custodial roles. But we would misunderstand even Jesus's views if we remembered only his criticisms of the legalism of his day and imagined that he was offering a replacement rather than a corrective. It seems unlikely that a prophetic, critical emphasis can survive the entire absence of the priestly and creative one. In the end, English Reformers failed to agree on a blueprint for institutionalizing Jesus's teaching. In the eighteenth century they decided to make a virtue of this fact by equating the Protestant principle with the freedom of faith. As always, they found it easy to criticize that side of the religious dichotomy which had atrophied. In modern history that has been religious culture, which can barely be imagined in most countries of the West.

Notes

1. The Study of Secularization

1. Keith Thomas, *Religion and the Decline of Magic* (New York, 1971), 172.

2. See David Martin, "Towards Eliminating the Concept of Secularization," *Penguin Survey of the Social Sciences, 1965* (Baltimore, 1965) 169–82; but compare his *A General Theory of Secularization* (New York, 1978). On secularization generally, see Larry Shiner, "Toward a Theology of Secularization," *Journal of Religion*, 45 (1965), 279–95; idem, "The Meanings of Secularization," *International Yearbook for the Sociology of Religion*, 3 (1967), 51–59; Richard K. Fenn, "The Process of Secularization; A Post-Parsonian View," *Journal for the Scientific Study of Religion*, 9 (1970), 117–36; idem, *Toward a Theory of Secularization* (Society for the Scientific Study of Religion Monograph Series, 1, 1978).

3. See Peter L. Berger, *The Sacred Canopy; Elements of a Sociological Theory of Religion* (New York, 1967), 113f.

4. Thomas Luckmann, *The Invisible Religion; The Problem of Religion in Modern Society* (New York, 1967, orig. 1963), 61.

5. Hans Blumenberg, *The Legitimacy of the Modern Age* (Cambridge, Mass., 1983, orig. 1966), 4, 16.

6. John W. McKenna, "How God became an Englishman," in *Tudor Rule and Revolution*, ed. Delloyd J. Guth and John W. McKenna (New York, 1982), 25–43.

7. Harold J. Berman, *Law and Revolution; The Formation of the Western Legal Tradition* (Cambridge, Mass., 1983), 85–87, 273–76, 534.

8. See Robert N. Bellah, *International Encyclopedia of the Social Sciences* (New York, 1968), 13:406–13; Luckmann, *Invisible Religion*, 49. In his definition of religion, Clifford Geertz, *The Interpretation of Cultures* (New York, 1973), 90, does not prejudge the functions to be served but concentrates on the "unique realism" with which religious symbols are invested.

9. See William A. Christian, *Meaning and Truth in Religion* (Princeton, 1964), 60–72; and Ronald Robertson, "Sociologists and Secularisation," *Sociology*, 5 (1971), 297–312, for further discussion of these issues.

10. See Peter G. Foster, "Secularization in the English Context; Some Conceptual and Empirical Problems," *Sociological Review*, 20 (1972), 153–55; Bryan Wilson, *Religion in a Sociological Perspective* (New York, 1982), 36–42; Ernest Krausz, "Religion and Secularization; A Matter of Definitions," *Social Compass*, 18 (1971), 203–12; Robin Horton, "A Definition of Religion and Its Uses," *Journal of the Royal Anthropological Institute of*

Great Britain and Ireland, 90 (1961), 201–26; Jack Goody, "Religion and Ritual; The Definitional Problem," *British Journal of Sociology,* 12 (1961), 142–64.

11. Alan D. Gilbert, *The Making of Post-Christian Britain; A History of the Secularization of Modern Society* (London, 1980), 5.

12. Rudolf Otto, *The Idea of the Holy* (Harmondsworth, 1959, orig. 1917), 34–39; Gerardus Van Der Leeuw, *Religion in Essence and Manifestation* (New York, 1963, orig. 1933), 1:23f.; Mircea Eliade, *The Sacred and the Profane; The Nature of Religion* (New York, 1959), 8–13. Paul Tillich also proposed a definition of religious experience in terms of power, or the "power of being." While "being" is his ultimate term of analysis, he speaks evocatively of "the power of being" which overcomes the "non-being" which is human finitude. Faith and love are affirmations inspired by this sense of the power of being. The religious experience is "the feeling of being in the hand of a power which cannot be conquered by any other power . . . which is the infinite resistance against non-being and the eternal victory over it." Paul Tillich, *Love, Power and Justice* (New York, 1954), 35–53, 110f.

13. Victor Turner, *The Ritual Process; Structure and Anti-Structure* (Chicago, 1969), 4; Richard C. Trexler, "Reverence and Profanity in the Study of Early Modern Religion," in *Religion and Society in Early Modern Europe,* ed. Kaspar von Greyerz (London, 1984), 259; Bob Scribner, "Cosmic Order and Daily Life; Sacred and Secular in Pre-Industrial German Society," in von Greyerz, *Religion and Society,* 18.

14. Other understandings of religion are readily assimilable to ours. "Salvation," for example, can be analyzed as power over evil and death, and as the result of an exercise of power on our behalf, against contrary forces. On the other hand, recent definitions of religion as a way of understanding the world rather than acting upon it are evidence of exactly the process of secularization that this study will trace. See Catherine L. Albanese, *America; Religions and Religion* (Belmont, Cal., 1981), 2–9.

15. Larry Shiner, *The Secularization of History; An Introduction to the Theology of Friedrich Gogarten,* (Nashville, 1966); Henri Frankfort, et al., *Before Philosophy* (Chicago, 1946); Willis B. Glover, *Biblical Origins of Modern Secular Culture* (Macon, Ga., 1984).

16. Michel Vovelle, *Religion et Révolution: la déchristianisation de l'an II* (Paris, 1976); Timothy Tackett, *Religion, Revolution, and Regional Culture in Eighteenth-Century France* (Princeton, 1986).

17. Faith meets our definition of religion in its expectation of supernatural aid, though it lacks the technical means to ensure that aid. It is subject to a secularization of the last type—a disuse through failure of confidence.

18. Luckmann, *Invisible Religion,* 109.

19. Bellah, *Encyclopedia,* 13:413.

20. Claire Cross, *Church and People 1450–1660; The Triumph of the Laity in the English Church* (Glasgow, 1976).

21. J. J. Scarisbrick, *The Reformation and the English People* (Oxford, 1984), 42–44, 165–74.

22. David Berman, *A History of Atheism in Britain; From Hobbes to Russell* (London, 1988), 1–47.

23. Lucien Febvre, *The Problem of Unbelief in the Sixteenth Century* (Cambridge, Mass., 1982), 116, 141.

24. Frank E. Manuel, *The Eighteenth Century Confronts the Gods* (New York, 1967).

25. Joseph R. Strayer, "The Laicization of French and English Society in the Thirteenth Century," *Speculum,* 15 (1940), 76–86.

26. See Anne Hudson, *The Premature Reformation; Wycliffite Texts and Lollard History* (Oxford, 1988), and chapter 13 below.

27. G. R. Elton, *Policy and Police; The Enforcement of the Reformation in the Age of Thomas Cromwell* (Cambridge, 1972), 25, 197; J. J. Scarisbrick, *Henry VIII* (Berkeley, 1968), 339, 347f., 416–19.

28. George Macaulay Trevelyan, *England Under Queen Anne* (London 1965, orig. 1930–34), 3:146; Conrad Russell, *The Crisis of Parliaments; English History 1509–1660* (London, 1971), 180.

29. A. G. Dickens, *The English Reformation* (London, 1964), 249–51.

30. Ronald A. Marchant, *The Church Under the Law* (Cambridge, 1969), 227.

31. G. R. Elton, ed., *The Tudor Constitution; Documents and Commentary* (Cambridge, 1965), 242.

32. Ibid., 231f.

33. Christopher Haigh, "The Recent Historiography of the English Reformation," *Historical Journal*, 25 (1982), 995–1007; Thomas B. Macaulay, *Critical and Historical Essays* (London, 1907), 1:93.

34. Cross, *Church and People*, 226–29.

35. For example, see Peter Burke, "Religion and Secularisation," in *New Cambridge Modern History* (Cambridge, 1979), 13:293–317.

36. Wilfred Cantwell Smith, *The Meaning and End of Religion; A New Approach to the Religious Traditions of Mankind* (New York, 1962), 31–45, 72–77.

2. The Secularization of Space

1. Alexander Koyré, *From the Closed World to the Infinite Universe,* (New York, 1958), 155–89.

2. Bernard Manning, *The People's Faith in the Time of Wyclif* (Cambridge, 1919), 137.

3. Ibid., 175.

4. Desiderius Erasmus, *Ten Colloquies of Erasmus* (New York, 1957), 64, 76.

5. Geoffrey Baskerville, *English Monks and the Suppression of the Monasteries* (London, 1965, orig. 1937), 20, 48.

6. Scarisbrick, *Reformation and the English People*, 164.

7. Peter Clark, *English Provincial Society from the Reformation to the Revolution* (Rutherford, N.J., 1977), 6.

8. G. W. O. Woodward, *The Dissolution of the Monasteries* (London, 1966), 4.

9. Elton, *Tudor Constitution*, 369.

10. Timothy Baker, *Medieval England* (New York, 1970), 212.

11. Baskerville, *English Monks*, 233.

12. Lawrence Stone, *The Crisis of the Aristocracy, 1558–1641* (London, 1965), 395; Christopher Hill, *Economic Problems of the Church; From Archbishop Whitgift to the Long Parliament* (London, 1971, orig. 1956), 14–18.

13. *The Lisle Letters*, ed. Muriel St.Clare Byrne (Chicago, 1981), 3:283, 289, 300, 296.

14. Woodward, *Dissolution of the Monasteries*, 133.

15. Baskerville, *English Monks*, 98, 109.

16. David Knowles, *The Religious Orders in England* (Cambridge, 1961), 3:384–87; John Stow, *Survey of London* (London, 1956, orig. 1598), 387.

17. Knowles, *Religious Orders*, 3:23, 69f.

18. Margaret Bowker, *Henrician Reformation; the Diocese of Lincoln Under John*

Longland, 1521–1547 (Cambridge, 1981), 153; Francis A. Gasquet, *Henry VIII and the English Monasteries* (London, 1889), passim; Robert Whiting, "Abominable Idols; Images and Image-breaking under Henry VIII," *Journal of Ecclesiastical History,* 33 (1982), 30–47.

19. Joyce Youings, *The Dissolution of the Monasteries* (London, 1971), 164f. Robert Whiting, *The Blind Devotion of the People; Popular Religion and the English Reformation* (Cambridge, 1989), 75, calls this episode exceptional, even for the conservative southwestern counties.

20. Stow, *Survey,* 115, 285, 387.

21. Scarisbrick, *Reformation and the English People,* 106.

22. Ibid., 74, 81; G. H. Cook, ed., *Letters to Cromwell and Others on the Suppression of the Monasteries* (London, 1965), 200–202, 212.

23. Scarisbrick, *Reformation and the English People,* 107.

24. Dr. Elizabeth Monroe counted only six, on the basis of Stow's *Survey* and Francis Drake, *Eboracum: or, The History and Antiquities of the City of York* (London, 1736).

25. Stone, *Crisis of the Aristocracy,* 549f.

26. D. W. Robertson, *Chaucer's London* (New York, 1968), 26; J. G. Davies, *The Secular Use of Church Buildings* (London, 1968), 144.

27. Scarisbrick, *Reformation and the English People,* 134, 168.

28. Ibid., 91.

29. Thomas, *Religion and the Decline of Magic,* 96–104.

30. Cook, *Letters to Cromwell,* 100, see also 86, 148, 152, 166.

31. Ibid., 86f.

32. Mary Lee and Sidney Nolan, *Christian Pilgrimage in Modern Western Europe* (Chapel Hill, 1989), 85–100.

33. Stanford E. Lehmberg, *The Reformation of Cathedrals; Cathedrals in English Society, 1485–1603* (Princeton, 1988), 31, 52.

34. Peter Iver Kaufman, *The 'Polytyque Churche'; Religion and Early Tudor Political Culture, 1485–1516* (Macon, Ga., 1986), 82f.; John N. King, *Tudor Royal Iconography; Literature and Art in an Age of Religious Crisis* (Princeton, 1989), 25.

35. Ronald C. Finucane, *Miracles and Pilgrims; Popular Beliefs in Medieval England* (Totowa, N.J., 1977), 201f.; cf. 193–95.

36. Arthur P. Stanley, *Historical Memorials of Canterbury* (London, 1912), 231f.

37. Erasmus, *Ten Colloquies,* 86; William Townsend, *Canterbury* (London, 1950), 36; E. F. Lincoln, *The Story of Canterbury* (London, 1955), 88f., 102f.

38. Stanley, *Historical Memorials of Canterbury,* 241–44.

39. Cook, *Letters to Cromwell,* 189, 198.

40. Ibid., 144f.

41. Ibid., 113.

42. Glanmor Williams, *The Welsh Church from Conquest to Reformation* (Cardiff, 1976), 481; Finucane, *Miracles and Pilgrims,* 213–15.

43. Whiting, *Blind Devotion,* 74.

44. Tackett, *Religion, Revolution, and Regional Culture,* 230, makes the same point.

45. Ibid., 53f.; Jonathan Sumption, *Pilgrimage; An Image of Medieval Religion* (Totowa, N.J., 1975), 277f.; Williams, *Welsh Church,* 478–85.

46. Stow, *Survey,* 188.

47. Erasmus, *Ten Colloquies,* 62f.

48. Paul Tillich, *Theology of Culture* (London, 1959), 25, 31–33.

49. Cross, *Church and People,* 91; Felicity Heal, *Of Prelates and Princes; A Study of*

the *Economic and Social Position of the Tudor Episcopate* (Cambridge, 1980), 107–15, 320; Hill, *Economic Problems of the Church*, 17.

50. Woodward, *Dissolution of the Monasteries*, 20f.

51. Victor Morgan, "The Cartographic Image of 'The Country' in Early Modern England," *Transactions of the Royal Historical Society*, 29 (1979), 129–54; R. A. Skelton, *Saxton's Survey of England and Wales* (Amsterdam, 1974).

52. Margaret Aston, "English Ruins and English History; the Dissolution and the Sense of the Past," *Journal of the Warburg and Courtauld Institute*, 36 (1973), 231–55.

53. Christopher Haigh, *Reformation and Resistance in Tudor Lancashire* (Cambridge, 1975), 118.

54. See the debate in Dickens, *English Reformation*, 124–28; Knowles, *Religious Orders in England*, 3:327; Scarisbrick, *Henry VIII*, 338–48; G. R. Elton, *Reform and Reformation; England, 1509–1558* (Cambridge, Mass., 1977), 260–72; C. S. L. Davies, "The Pilgrimage of Grace Reconsidered," *Past and Present*, 41 (1968), 54–76; B. W. Beckingsale, *Thomas Cromwell* (Totowa, N.J., 1978), 61–65; Anthony Fletcher, *Tudor Rebellions* (London, 1968), 21, 33–35.

55. Fletcher, *Tudor Rebellions*, 120, 128–30. See also Richard Morison, *Humanist Scholarship and Public Order; Two Tracts Against the Pilgrimage of Grace*, ed. David Sandler Berkowitz (Washington, 1984), 178f.

56. Fletcher, *Tudor Rebellions*, 133f.

57. Woodward, *Dissolution of the Monasteries*, 101, 110.

58. Ibid., 100, 114.

59. Henry Spelman, *De non temerandis Ecclesiis; Churches not to be Violated*, fourth edition (Oxford, 1668), 54–72.

60. Henry Spelman, *An Apology of the Treatise De non temerandis Ecclesiis* (London, 1646), sigs. A4v, B4.

61. Davies, *Secular Use of Church Buildings*, 115f.

62. Spelman, *De non temerandis Ecclesiis*, 117–28, 88.

63. Ibid., 20–38, 91.

64. Ibid., 41–44, 50; Henry Spelman, *The History and Fate of Sacrilege* (London, 1698, written 1632), 188–90, 225–27.

65. See C. John Sommerville, "On the Distribution of Religious and Occult Literature in Seventeenth-Century England," *The Library*, 29 (1974), 221–25.

66. Spelman, *De non temerandis Ecclesiis*, sigs. A5–A8.

67. Spelman, *History and Fate of Sacrilege*, sig. A3.

68. Spelman, *De non temerandis Ecclesiis*, 42–45.

69. Spelman, *History and Fate of Sacrilege*, 243.

70. Ibid., 244f., 268.

71. Spelman, *De non temerandis Ecclesiis*, 284–88.

72. E. Lipson, *The Economic History of England*, tenth edition (London, 1949), 1:151–53; Christopher Kitching, "The Disposal of Monastic and Chantry Lands," in *Church and Society in England; Henry VIII to James I* ed. Felicity Heal and Rosemary O'Day (Hamden, Conn., 1977), 127.

73. Davies, *Secular Use of Church Buildings*, passim.

74. Kaufman, *Polytyque Churche*, 143–50; Lehmberg, *Reformation of Cathedrals*, 291.

75. John A. F. Thomson, *The Transformation of Medieval England, 1370–1529* (London, 1983), 328f.; Paul Murray Kendall, *Warwick the Kingmaker* (New York, 1957), 315f., 324.

76. Peter Iver Kaufman, "Henry VII and Sanctuary," *Church History*, 53 (1984), 468–72; Charles Ross, *Richard III* (Berkeley, 1981), 56, 80, 86, 100, 198.

77. Thomson, *Transformation of Medieval England*, 329.

78. Stow, *Survey*, 275; Davies, *Secular Use of Church Buildings*, 158; I. D. Thornley, "The Destruction of Sanctuary," in *Tudor Studies*, ed. R. W. Seton-Watson (London, 1924), 182–207.

79. Stow, *Survey*, 16, 86.

80. Ibid., 437f.; Roger Finlay, *Population and Metropolis; the Demography of London, 1580–1650* (New York, 1981), 51; E. S. deBeer, "Places of Worship in London About 1738," in *Studies in London History*, ed. A. E. J. Hollaender and William Kellaway (London, 1969), 393–400.

81. Lehmberg, *Reformation of Cathedrals*, 11, 271, 154.

82. W. K. Jordan, *Philanthropy in England 1480–1660; A Study of the Changing Patterns of English Social Aspirations* (London, 1959), 319f.; idem, *The Charities of London, 1480–1660; The Aspirations and the Achievements of the Urban Society* (London, 1960), 297–307.

83. Lehmberg, *Reformation of Cathedrals*, 150, 276.

3. The Secularization of Time and Play

1. Peter Burke, *Popular Culture in Early Modern Europe* (New York, 1978), 179.

2. Edmund R. Leach, "Two Essays Concerning the Symbolic Representation of Time," in *Reader in Comparative Religion*, ed. William A. Lessa and Evon Z. Vogt, second edition (New York, 1965), 241–49.

3. A. J. Gurevich, *Categories of Medieval Culture* (London, 1985, orig. 1972), 118–21.

4. Howard J. Happ, "Calendary Conflicts; The Religious Significance of Time in Renaissance England" (Ph.D. dissertation, Princeton University, 1974), 77. I owe this reference to Gary Gibbs.

5. John P. Dolan, "Religious Festivities During the Reformation and Counter-Reformation," *Societas*, 2 (1972), 104; Edith Cooperrider Rodgers, *Discussion of Holidays in the Later Middle Ages* (New York, 1967), 118f.

6. Thomas More, *The Confutation of Tyndale's Answer*, in *The Complete Works of St. Thomas More* (New Haven, 1973), 8:321, 76.

7. Henry Gee and William John Hardy, eds., *Documents Illustrative of English Church History* (New York, 1921), 150, 173.

8. Happ, "Calendary Conflicts," 67–69, 79.

9. Jasper Ridley, *Thomas Cranmer* (Oxford, 1962), 247.

10. For examples, see Elton, *Tudor Constitution*, 55f., 135f., 141, 384, 395–97, 401, 424.

11. Sydney Anglo, "An Early Tudor Programme for Plays and Other Demonstrations Against the Pope," *Journal of the Warburg and Courtauld Institutes*, 20 (1957), 176–79.

12. Ibid.

13. Jasper Ridley, *Elizabeth I; The Shrewdness of Virtue* (New York, 1989), 69.

14. Winthrop S. Hudson, "Fast Days and Civil Religion," in *Theology in Sixteenth-and Seventeenth-Century England* (Los Angeles, 1971), 7–11.

15. Christopher Hill, *Society and Puritanism in Pre-Revolutionary England*, second edition (New York, 1967), 216, quoting John Evelyn.

16. John Walter Stoye, *English Travellers Abroad, 1604–1667* (London, 1952), 243, 424; Jeremy Black, *The British and the Grand Tour* (London, 1985), 191.

17. Hill, *Society and Puritanism*, 145–218.

18. Happ, "Calendary Conflicts," 80.

19. See Johan Huizinga, *Homo Ludens; A Study of the Play-Element in Culture* (Boston, 1955).

20. Phillip Stubbes, *The Anatomie of Abuses* (London, 1583), sig. P5.

21. Manning, *People's Faith*, 138.

22. Burke, *Popular Culture*, 210.

23. Stubbes, *Anatomie of Abuses*, sigs. M2–M4.

24. J. A. R. Pimlott, *The Englishman's Christmas; A Social History* (Hassocks, 1978), 35–38; Dennis Brailsford, *Sport and Society; Elizabeth to Anne* (London, 1969), 205.

25. Pimlott, *Englishman's Christmas*, 46–50.

26. See Kenneth L. Parker, *The English Sabbath; A Study of the Doctrine and Discipline from the Reformation to the Civil War* (Cambridge, 1988).

27. Ibid., 52; Chris Durston, "Lords of Misrule: The Puritan War on Christmas 1642–60," *History Today*, 35 (1985), 13f.

28. *Acts and Ordinances of the Interregnum, 1642–1660*, eds. C. H. Firth and R. S. Rait (London, 1911), 1:22, 580, 954.

29. Hudson, "Fast Days and Civil Religion," 14f.; Happ, "Calendary Conflicts," 145, 158, 186.

30. *Acts and Ordinances*, 2:79–81, 1:606.

31. Brailsford, *Sport and Society*, 206.

32. Bernard Capp, *English Almanacs, 1500–1800; Astrology and the Popular Press* (Ithaca, 1979), 57, 210f., 223; [Himbert de Billy], *A Wonderfull Prognostication: Or, a prediction, for these seven years insuing* (London, 1604), 27.

33. Roy Strong, *The Cult of Elizabeth; Elizabethan Portraiture and Pageantry* (London, 1977), 16, 114–26.

34. Thomas Holland, *A Sermon Preached at Pauls in London the 17. of November Ann. Dom. 1599* (Oxford, 1601), sigs. L3, R1; cf. H2v.

35. John Howson, *A sermon preached at St. Maries in Oxford, the 17. Day of November, 1602 in defence of the festivities of the Church of England, and namely that of her majesties coronation* (Oxford, 1602), sigs. D1v–D2v.

36. Horton Davies, *Worship and Theology in England* (Princeton, 1961–75), 2:230–34; David Cressy, *Bonfires and Bells; National Memory and the Protestant Calendar in Elizabethan and Stuart England* (London, 1989), 59, 134–38.

37. John Miller, *Popery and Politics in England, 1660–1688* (Cambridge, 1973), 74, 183–87; Sheila Williams, "The Pope-burning Processions of 1679, 1680 and 1681," *Journal of the Warburg and Courtauld Institutes*, 21 (1958), 104–18; O. W. Furley, "The Pope-Burning Processions of the Late Seventeenth Century," *History*, 44 (1959), 16–23.

38. Ibid.

39. Cressy, *Bonfires and Bells*, 21.

40. Helen W. Randall, "The Rise and Fall of a Martyrology; Sermons on Charles I," *Huntington Library Quarterly*, 10 (1947), 135–67; Byron S. Stewart, "The Cult of the Royal Martyr," *Church History*, 38 (1969), 174–87.

41. J. G. A. Pocock, "England," in *National Consciousness, History, and Political Culture in Early Modern Europe*, ed. Orest Ranum (Baltimore, 1975), 108–12; see also J. G. A. Pocock, "Time, History and Eschatology in the Thought of Thomas Hobbes," in *The Diversity of History*, ed. J. H. Elliott and H. G. Koenigsberger (Ithaca, 1970), 179.

42. Eric Bruton, *The History of Clocks and Watches* (New York, 1979), 63; David S.

Landes, *Revolution in Time; Clocks and the Making of the Modern World* (Cambridge, Mass., 1983), 92f., 219.

43. Landes, *Revolution in Time*, 71f.

44. Ibid., 78f., 220; Bruton, *History of Clocks*, 113, 121.

45. Robert W. Malcolmson, *Popular Recreations in English Society, 1700–1850* (Cambridge, 1973), 74.

46. E. P. Thompson, "Patrician Society, Plebian Culture," *Journal of Social History*, 7 (1974), 392.

47. Thomas L. Haskell, "Capitalism and the Origins of the Humanitarian Sensibility," *American Historical Review*, 90 (1985), 560.

48. Gabor Klaniczay, *The Uses of Supernatural Power; The Transformation of Popular Religion in Medieval and Early-Modern Europe* (Princeton, 1990), 34, 13.

49. Owen Barfield, *History in English Words* (Grand Rapids, Mich., 1967), 166.

50. Lynn Thorndike, *A History of Magic and Experimental Science* (New York, 1923–58), 7:10.

4. The Secularization of Language

1. Keith Wrightson, *English Society, 1580–1680* (New Brunswick, N.J., 1982), 181; Frances A. Shirley, *Swearing and Perjury in Shakespeare's Plays* (London, 1979), 126–30.

2. *Dictionary of National Biography* (London, 1921–22), 15:646, art. "Pecock, Reginald."

3. George Philip Krapp, *The Rise of English Literary Prose* (New York, 1963), 64–75.

4. Anne Hudson, "Lollardy; The English Heresy?" *Studies in Church History*, 18 (1982), 261–83.

5. Scarisbrick, *Henry VIII*, 253.

6. Dickens, *English Reformation*, 132.

7. Otto, *Idea of the Holy*, 80.

8. Richard Foster Jones, *The Triumph of the English Language* (Stanford, 1953), 63.

9. Whiting, *Blind Devotion*, 195.

10. Dickens, *English Reformation*, 71.

11. Barfield, *History in English Words*, 65f.

12. Jones, *Triumph of the English Language*, 55–59.

13. More, *Confutation of Tyndale's Answer*, 270.

14. Ibid., 339.

15. Ronald Ralph Williams, *Religion and the English Vernacular; A Historical Study Concentrating upon the Years 1526–53* (London, 1940), 96, 78.

16. Dickens, *English Reformation*, 220f. Whiting, *Blind Devotion*, does not think the rebellion represents majority opinion even in Devon and Cornwall (36f., 74, 117f.).

17. Sommerville, "Religious and Occult Literature," 221–25.

18. John Standish, *A discourse wherein is debated whether it be expedient that the Scriptures should be in English* (London, 1554), sigs. A4v–A7.

19. Ibid., sigs. C5v, E8v.

20. Ibid., sigs. F5, F2, G4, H3, L2, J1–J2.

21. George Herbert, *The Temple and A Priest to the Temple* (London, n.d.), 288.

22. Thomas, *Religion and the Decline of Magic*, 224f.; Elizabeth Eisenstein, *The Printing Press as an Agent of Change* (Cambridge, 1980), 77, 274.

23. Thomas, *Religion and the Decline of Magic*, 68, 275, and passim.

24. Watson E. Mills, *Speaking in Tongues: A Guide to Research in Glossolalia* (Grand

Rapids, Mich., 1986), 186; Richard Bauman, *Let Your Words Be Few; Symbolism of Speaking and Silence Among Seventeenth-Century Quakers* (New York, 1983), 82 n.2.

25. Ibid., 109–19.

26. Robert Adolph, *The Rise of Modern Prose Style* (Cambridge, Mass., 1968), 190–210.

27. Ibid., 116, 198–203.

28. Works like Richard Allestree's *The Gentleman's Calling* (1659) and *The Causes of the Decay of Christian Piety* (1667); and William Stanley's *The Faith and Practice of a Church of England Man* (1688) make this point explicitly. See below, chapter 12.

29. James Knowlson, *Universal Language Schemes in England and France, 1600–1800* (Toronto, 1975).

30. James H. Cassedy, "Medicine and the Rise of Statistics," in *Medicine in Seventeenth Century England,* ed. Allen G. Debus (Berkeley, 1974), 294f.

31. Ian Hacking, *The Emergence of Probability* (New York, 1975), 102.

32. John U. Nef, *Cultural Foundations of Industrial Civilization* (New York, 1960), 8–10.

33. Margreta deGrazia, "The Secularization of Language in the Seventeenth Century," *Journal of the History of Ideas,* 41 (1980), 319–29.

34. Richard Foster Jones, ed., *The Seventeenth Century; Studies in the History of English Thought and Literature from Bacon to Pope* (Stanford, 1951).

35. Jack Goody, ed., *Literacy in Traditional Societies* (Cambridge, 1968), 67; see also 2f. Walter Ong, *The Presence of the Word; Some Prolegomena for Cultural and Religious History* (New Haven, 1967), 272–75.

36. David Cressy, *Literacy and the Social Order* (Cambridge, 1980).

37. Thomas Elyot, *The Dictionary* (London, 1538).

38. Randle Cotgrave, *A Dictionarie of the French and English Tongues* (London, 1611).

39. John Florio, *Queen Anna's New World of Words* (London, 1611).

40. Edward Phillips, *The New World of Words, or, Universal English Dictionary* (London, 1658).

41. Abel Boyer, *The Royal Dictionary Abridged* (London, 1700).

42. Thomas Dyche, *A New General English Dictionary* (London 1735). See John Bossy, "Some Elementary Forms of Durkheim," *Past and Present,* 95 (1982), 3–18; and idem, *Christianity in the West, 1400–1700* (New York, 1985), 168–70, for similar conclusions.

43. Barfield, *History in English Words,* 151, 164, 203.

44. Whiting, *Blind Devotion,* 140f.

45. C. S. Lewis, "The Literary Impact of the Authorized Version," in *They Asked for a Paper* (London, 1962), 44–46.

5. The Politics of Secularization (1529–1603)

1. Ronald Hutton, "The Local Impact of the Tudor Reformation," in *The English Reformation Revised,* ed. Christopher Haigh (Cambridge, 1987), 116; Haigh, *Reformation and Resistance,* 71; cf. Peter Clark, *English Provincial Society,* 26; Alan Kreider, *English Chantries; the Road to Dissolution* (Cambridge, Mass., 1979), 72f., 88–90. Whiting, *Blind Devotion,* reviews this evidence (50f., 89, 262–68).

2. For example, see James Oxley, *The Reformation in Essex to the Death of Mary* (Manchester, 1965), 63.

3. J. H. M. Beattie, "On Understanding Ritual," in *Rationality*, ed. Bryan Wilson (Oxford, 1970), 261.

4. W. K. Jordan, *Edward VI: The Young King; The Protectorship of the Duke of Somerset* (Cambridge, Mass., 1968), 28; Knowles, *Religious Orders in England*, 3:318; Scarisbrick, *Henry VIII*, 473.

5. *Lisle Letters*, 5:478.

6. Bernard J. Verkamp, *The Indifferent Mean; Adiaphorism in the English Reformation to 1554* (Athens, Ohio, 1977), 7–12.

7. W. Gordon Zeeveld, *Foundations of Tudor Policy* (London, 1969, orig. 1948), 128f., 138–41. Cf. Arthur J. Slavin, ed., *Thomas Cromwell on Church and Commonwealth; Selected Letters, 1523–1540* (New York, 1969), 158; and Thomas Mayer, *Thomas Starkey and the Commonweal; Humanist Politics and Religion in the Reign of Henry VIII* (Cambridge, 1989), 220–22.

8. Gee and Hardy, *Documents Illustrative of English Church History*, 270.

9. Ibid., 173.

10. Paul Elmer More and Frank Cross, eds., *Anglicanism; The Thought and Practice of the Church of England* (Milwaukee, 1935), xxiv.

11. Verkamp, *Indifferent Mean*, 41, 171, 62–107, 163–67.

12. Ibid., 72–78.

13. Ibid., 116–22; Jordan, *Edward VI; The Young King*, 219, 340.

14. Manning, *People's Faith*, 6, 66f.

15. Jordan, *Edward VI; The Young King*, 142, 189.

16. 1 Edw. VI, c. 1, and Proclamations of 27 December 1547, 8 March 1548, 23 September 1548.

17. Jordan, *Edward VI; The Young King*, 139f.

18. Ibid., 312–25.

19. Margaret Aston, *England's Iconoclasts*, vol. 1: *Laws Against Images* (Oxford, 1988), 10, 105, 343.

20. Ibid., 5, 86, 212–17.

21. Gee and Hardy, *Documents Illustrative of English Church History*, 271, 277f.

22. Aston, *England's Iconoclasts*, 223.

23. Ibid., 234; Thomas, *Religion and the Decline of Magic*, 74f.; Oxley, *Reformation in Essex*, 89; Carlos M. N. Eire, *War Against the Idols; The Reformation of Worship from Erasmus to Calvin* (New York, 1986), 28; Sydney Anglo, *Spectacle, Pageantry and Early Tudor Policy* (Oxford, 1969), 273f.

24. Jordan, *Edward VI; The Young King*, 148.

25. Aston, *England's Iconoclasts*, 86.

26. Hutton, "Local Impact of the Tudor Reformation," 124; Cross, *Church and People*, 76.

27. Cross, *Church and People*, 92.

28. Michael Sherbrook, "The Fall of Religious Houses," in *Tudor Treatises*, ed. A. G. Dickens, *Yorkshire Archaeological Society Record Series*, 125 (1959), 124f.

29. Gasquet, *Henry VIII and the English Monasteries*, 414; Baskerville, *English Monks*, 260.

30. W. K. Jordan, *Edward VI: The Threshold of Power; The Dominance of the Duke of Northumberland* (Cambridge, Mass., 1970), 392–400; Oxley, *Reformation in Essex*, 167–73.

31. Scarisbrick, *Reformation and the English People*, 42–44, 74, 102, 106f.

32. Whiting, "Abominable Idols," 44–46.

33. Aston, *England's Iconoclasts*, 232, 262.

34. Hutton, "Local Impact of the Tudor Reformation," 120–26; Jordan, *Edward VI; The Young King*, 146f., 165f., 186.

35. Jordan, *Philanthropy in England*, 374f., 16, 19f., 57f., 111f., 147. Jordan's figures are here corrected by reference to William G. Bittle and R. Todd Lane, "Inflation and Philanthropy in England: A Re-Assessment of W. K. Jordan's Data," *Economic History Review*, 29 (1976), 209.

36. Jordan, *Philanthropy in England*, 297–320.

37. Ibid., 51, 247.

38. Kreider, *English Chantries*, 115.

39. Ibid., 123, 127, 151.

40. Ibid., 176, 205.

41. Paul S. Seaver, *The Puritan Lectureships; The Politics of Religious Dissent, 1560–1662* (Stanford, 1970).

42. Cross, *Church and People*, 88.

43. Fletcher, *Tudor Rebellions*, 50–53. See above, chapter 4, note 16.

44. Fletcher, *Tudor Rebellions*, 135f.

45. Ibid., 55f.; Scarisbrick, *Reformation and the English People*, 83f.

46. Whiting, *Blind Devotion*, 255.

47. Haigh, *Reformation and Resistance*, 207; Hutton, "Local Impact of the Tudor Reformation," 130f.

48. A. G. Dickens, *The Marian Reaction in the Diocese of York* (London, 1957), 2:21; also idem, *English Reformation*, 279f.

49. Rex Pogson, "Reginald Pole and the Priorities of Government in Mary Tudor's Church," *Historical Journal*, 18 (1975), 3–20.

50. Scarisbrick, *Reformation and the English People*, 89; D. M. Loades, *The Reign of Mary Tudor; Politics, Government, and Religion in England, 1553–1558* (New York, 1979), 153; Claire Cross, *The Royal Supremacy in the Elizabethan Church* (London, 1969), 70.

51. Gee and Hardy, *Documents Illustrative of English Church History*, 381f.; Oxley, *Reformation in Essex*, 179–91, 229; Aston, *England's Iconoclasts*, 292.

52. 1 & 2 Philip and Mary, c. 8.

53. Knowles, *Religious Orders in England*, 3:424, 440, 456.

54. Cross, *Church and People*, 108.

55. Whiting, *Blind Devotion*, 68f., 80, 96, 108, 111.

56. D. M. Loades, "The Enforcement of Reaction, 1553–1558," *Journal of Ecclesiastical History*, 16 (1965), 54–66.

57. Cross, *Church and People*, 105; Loades, *Reign of Mary Tudor*, 152.

58. Cross, *Church and People*, 123.

59. Fletcher, *Tudor Rebellions*, 81.

60. Haigh, *Reformation and Resistance*, 220f.

61. Cross, *Church and People*, 137; Aston, *England's Iconoclasts*, 312f., 302.

62. Roger B. Manning, *Religion and Society in Elizabethan Sussex* (Leicester, 1969), 46.

63. Haigh, *Reformation and Resistance*, 219–21; Cross, *Church and People*, 135.

64. Gee and Hardy, *Documents Illustrative of English Church History*, 435f.

65. *Certain Sermons or Homilies, appointed to be read in Churches* (1623), 2:231.

66. Thomas Beard, *The Theatre of Gods Judgements* (London, 1597), 157–92.

67. Scarisbrick, *Reformation and the English People*, 163.

6. The Secularization of Technology and Work

1. Thomas, *Religion and the Decline of Magic*, 25–50, 255, 266f.

2. Godfrid Storms, *Anglo-Saxon Magic* (The Hague, 1948), 6.

3. Thomas, *Religion and the Decline of Magic*, 278.

4. Storms, *Anglo-Saxon Magic*, 6f.

5. Thomas, *Religion and the Decline of Magic*, 178–81, 214f., 236.

6. Ibid., 185, 231, 267–75, 245, 253–63.

7. *Certain Sermons or Homilies*, 2:225.

8. Katherine M. Briggs, *A Dictionary of British Folk-Lore in the English Language* (Bloomington, Ind., 1971), A1:167, 211, 217, 221, 407, 428, 493; B1:241, 334, 336, 343, 348, 374. See also Jeffrey Burton Russell, *Lucifer; The Devil in the Middle Ages* (Ithaca, 1984), 76–84, 259–63.

9. II Corinthians 4:4; Ephesians 2:2; John 12:31, 14:30, 16:11; Revelation 12:9.

10. Matthew 4:8–9; Luke 4:5–7.

11. *Certain Sermons or Homilies*, 2:222f.

12. Laura Caroline Stevenson, *Praise and Paradox; Merchants and Craftsmen in Elizabethan Popular Literature* (Cambridge, 1984), 131–58. See also Charles W. Camp, *The Artisan in Elizabethan Literature* (New York, 1924).

13. Keith Thomas, "Work and Leisure in Pre-Industrial Society," *Past and Present*, 29 (1964), 56–59; Jacques LeGoff, *Time, Work, and Culture in the Middle Ages* (Chicago, 1980), 107–21; Sebastian deGrazia, *Of Time, Work and Leisure* (Garden City, N.Y., 1962), 26–29; Gurevich, *Categories of Medieval Culture*, 260f.

14. Ibid., 264f.

15. P. D. Anthony, *The Ideology of Work* (London, 1977), 37.

16. T. F. Thiselton Dyer, *British Popular Customs* (London, 1911), 37.

17. Thomas, *Religion and the Decline of Magic*, 62f., 648f.

18. John Brand, *Observations on the Popular Antiquities of Great Britain* (London, 1908), 3:309–19.

19. Lipson, *Economic History of England*, 37.

20. G. F. Northall, *English Folk-Rhymes* (London, 1892), 452.

21. John Aubrey, *Remaines of Gentilisme and Judaisme*, ed. John Buchanan-Brown (Carbondale, Il., 1972), 157.

22. Brand, *Popular Antiquities*, 3:31–33.

23. Thomas, *Religion and the Decline of Magic*, 64.

24. H. S. Bennett, *Life on the English Manor* (Cambridge, 1960, orig. 1937), 36.

25. Whiting, *Blind Devotion*, 20.

26. Stow, *Survey of London*, 55f., 42; Thomas, *Religion and the Decline of Magic*, 664, 649.

27. W. Carew Hazlett, *Faiths and Folklore of the British Isles* (New York, 1965, orig. 1905), 1:72.

28. J. Aubrey Rees, *The Worshipful Company of Grocers; An Historical Retrospect, 1345–1923* (London, 1923), 47; Walter M. Stern, *The Porters of London* (London, 1960), 54; Charles Welch, *History of the Cutlers' Company of London* (London, 1916–23), 2:338–40; W. Carew Hazlett, *The Livery Companies of the City of London* (London, 1892), 104; Francis W. Steer, *A History of the Worshipful Company of Scriveners of London* (London, 1973), 30–33.

29. Thomas Girtin, *The Golden Ram; A Narrative History of the Clothworkers' Company, 1528–1958* ([London], 1958), 24f.

30. Charles Clode, *The Early History of the Guild of Merchant Taylors, of the Fraternity of St. John the Baptist, London* (London, 1888), 1:149, 152, 88f., 172, 237, 4.

31. John Dummelow, *The Wax Chandlers of London* (London, 1973), 10, 33f., 39.

32. Lehmberg, *Reformation of Cathedrals*, 216; Hazlett, *Livery Companies*, 574.

33. T. F. Reddaway and Lorna E. M. Walker, *The Early History of the Goldsmiths' Company, 1327–1509* (London, 1975), 186; George Unwin, *The Gilds and Companies of London* (London, 1938, orig. 1908), 207.

34. T. C. Mendenhall, *The Shrewsbury Drapers and the Welsh Wool Trade in the XVI and XVII Centuries* (London, 1953), 82–84.

35. Girtin, *Golden Ram*, 1.

36. Clode, *Merchant Taylors*, 111–16.

37. Harold C. Gardiner, *Mysteries' End; An Investigation of the Last Days of the Medieval Religious Stage* (New Haven, 1946), 29–45.

38. Unwin, *Gilds and Companies of London*, 108.

39. Ibid., 212; Reddaway and Walker, *Goldsmiths' Company*, 239, 242, 272; Clode, *Merchant Taylors*, 110.

40. Unwin, *Gilds and Companies of London*, 209.

41. Mendenhall, *Shrewsbury Drapers*, 82–84.

42. Gee and Hardy, *Documents Illustrative of English Church History*, 427; Thomas, *Religion and the Decline of Magic*, 71.

43. Harold J. Cook, *The Decline of the Old Medical Regime in Stuart England* (Ithaca, 1986), 31f.

44. Lucinda McCray Beier, *Sufferers and Healers; The Experience of Illness in Seventeenth-Century England* (London, 1987), 18.

45. Donald Caton, "The Secularization of Pain," *Anesthesiology*, 62 (1985), 493–501.

46. Northall, *English Folk-Rhymes*, 128.

47. Thomas, *Religion and the Decline of Magic*, 204–11, 656–60; Paul Slack, *The Impact of Plague in Tudor and Stuart England* (London, 1985), 33.

48. Richard Baxter, *A Christian Directory*, in *The Practical Works of Richard Baxter* (London, 1854), 1:378.

49. Ibid., 382, citing Ephesians 6:7 and Colossians 3:23.

50. Ibid., 386.

51. Ibid., 115, 377.

52. Paul S. Seaver, *Wallington's World; A Puritan Artisan in Seventeenth-Century London* (Stanford, 1985), 124–27, 138.

53. Sebastian deGrazia, *Of Time, Work and Leisure*, 29, 39–46.

7. The Secularization of Art

1. Jordan, *Philanthropy in England*, 375.

2. By Bittle and Lane's calculations ("Inflation and Philanthropy," 203–10) the fall in constant pounds was from £19,520 to 181.

3. Jordan, *Philanthropy in England*, 315.

4. Mark Girouard, *Robert Smythson and the Architecture of the Elizabethan Era* (New York, 1966), 18.

5. Sumption, *Pilgrimage*, 29; Harold W. Turner, *From Temple to Meeting House; The Phenomenology and Theology of Places of Worship* (The Hague, 1979), 17, 169.

6. Richard D. Altick, *The Shows of London* (Cambridge, Mass., 1978), 6.

7. Turner, *From Temple to Meeting House*, 207–9, references to John 2:19–22 and I Corinthians 3:16–17.

8. G. G. Coulton, *Art and the Reformation* (Cambridge, 1953, orig. 1928), 323f.

9. Davies, *Worship and Theology in England*, 1:362–64.

10. Turner, *From Temple to Meeting House,* 215f.

11. Davies, *Worship and Theology in England,* 1:371.

12. Ibid., 1:357–59; Oliver Millar and Margaret Whinney, *English Art, 1625–1714* (Oxford, 1957), 54–59.

13. Graham Parry, *The Golden Age restor'd; The Culture of the Stuart Court, 1603–42* (New York, 1981), 248; John M. Schnorrenberg, "Early Anglican Architecture, 1558–1662; Its Theological Implications and Its Relation to the Continental Background" (Ph.D. dissertation, Princeton, 1964).

14. Millar and Whinney, *English Art,* 154f.

15. Turner, *From Temple to Meeting House,* 199.

16. Ibid., 229–39.

17. Davies, *Worship and Theology in England,* 3:38.

18. W. R. Jones, "Lollards and Images; The Defense of Religious Art in Later Medieval England," *Journal of the History of Ideas,* 34 (1973), 27–50.

19. Aston, *England's Iconoclasts,* 179–81.

20. John Phillips, *The Reformation of Images; Destruction of Art in England, 1535–1660* (Berkeley, 1973), 51.

21. Aston, *England's Iconoclasts,* 432, 436f., 452.

22. Whiting, "Abominable Idols," 30–47; Phillips, *Reformation of Images,* 52–56; Gee and Hardy, *Documents Illustrative of English Church History,* 271, 277f.; Roy Strong, *The English Icon; Elizabethan and Jacobean Portraiture* (New Haven, 1969), 2.

23. Phillips, *Reformation of Images,* 94f., 117.

24. *Certain Sermons or Homilies,* 2:20, 27, 72f.

25. Ibid., 2:20, 46, 56, 62, 68.

26. Aston, *England's Iconoclasts,* 267.

27. Janet Mayo, *A History of Ecclesiastical Dress* (New York, 1984), 75.

28. Jordan, *Edward VI; The Threshold of Power,* 388–400; Margaret Spufford, *Contrasting Communities; English Villagers in the Sixteenth and Seventeenth Centuries* (Cambridge, 1974), 243.

29. Aston, *England's Iconoclasts,* 289.

30. Whiting, *Blind Devotion,* 206.

31. Eric Mercer, *English Art, 1553–1625* (Oxford, 1962), 124–28, 143–50.

32. Strong, *English Icon,* 52.

33. Davies, *Worship and Theology in England,* 1:375f.; Parry, *Golden Age restor'd,* 131.

34. William Gaunt, *A Concise History of English Painting* (New York, 1964), 57.

35. Tessa Watt, *Cheap Print and Popular Piety; 1550–1640* (Cambridge, 1991), 181–91, 202, 214.

36. John N. King, *English Reformation Literature; The Tudor Origins of the Protestant Tradition* (Princeton, 1982), 147f.

37. Edward Hodnett, *English Woodcuts, 1480–1535* (Oxford, 1973), vi.

38. Patrick Collinson, *The Birthpangs of Protestant England; Religious and Cultural Changes in the Sixteenth and Seventeenth Centuries* (New York, 1988), 122f.

39. Mercer, *English Art,* 220–22, 244–47; Davies, *Worship and Theology in England,* 1:372f.

40. Lawrence E. Tanner, *The History and Treasures of Westminster Abbey* (London, 1953), 65f.

41. Erasmus, *Ten Colloquies,* 81f.

42. Altick, *Shows of London,* 5–10, 101; Michael Foss, *The Age of Patronage; The Arts in England, 1660–1750* (Ithaca, 1971), 170.

43. King, *Tudor Royal Iconography,* 17, 233; Frances A. Yates, *Astraea; The Imperial Theme in the Sixteenth Century* (London, 1975), 78, 33–39, 59f.

44. Louise Cuyler, "The Imperial Motet; Barometer of Relations between Church and State," in *The Pursuit of Holiness in Late Medieval and Renaissance Religion,* ed. Charles Trinkaus and Heiko Oberman (Leiden, 1974), 483–502.

45. Peter LeHuray, *Music and the Reformation in England, 1549–1660* (New York, 1967), 2–17.

46. Davies, *Worship and Theology in England,* 1:383, 393.

47. Percy M. Young, *The Concert Tradition; From the Middle Ages to the Twentieth Century* (London, 1965), 34–40; David C. Price, *Patrons and Musicians of the English Renaissance* (New York, 1981), 40–62, 169–77; Henry Raynor, *A Social History of Music* (London, 1972), 132–49.

48. LeHuray, *Music and Reformation,* 36, 83.

49. Davies, *Worship and Theology in England,* 1:386.

50. Ibid.

51. Ibid., 1:387; LeHuray, *Music and Reformation,* 374–76; Lehmberg, *Reformation of Cathedrals,* 154, 271.

52. LeHuray, *Music and Reformation,* 370, 384–94; Davies, *Worship and Theology in England,* 1:389–91.

53. J. A. Westrup, *Purcell* (New York, 1962), 126–28.

54. Robert Elkin, *The Old Concert Rooms of London* (London, 1955), 15–42; Young, *Concert Tradition,* 34–40; William Weber, *Music and the Middle Class; The Structure of Concert Life in London, Paris and Vienna* (New York, 1975), 3.

55. Westrup, *Purcell,* 221–33.

56. Raynor, *Social History of Music,* 253f.

57. Westrup, *Purcell,* 231f.

58. Young, *Concert Tradition,* 18; Paul Henry Lang, *George Frideric Handel* (New York, 1966), 114f.

59. Westrup, *Purcell,* 128.

60. Young, *Concert Tradition,* 43.

61. Lang, *Handel,* 213f., 372, 342.

62. Ibid., 279f.

63. John Newton, *Messiah. Fifty Expository Discourses, on the series of Scriptural Passages, which form the Subject of the celebrated Oratorio of Handel, Preached in the Years 1784 and 1785* (London, 1786).

64. Edith L. Klotz, "A Subject Analysis of English Imprints for Every Tenth Year from 1480 to 1640," *Huntington Library Quarterly,* 1 (1938), 417–19.

65. King, *English Reformation Literature,* 275.

66. Proclamation of October 1544.

67. Glynne Wickham, *A History of the Theatre* (Cambridge, 1985), 113–16.

68. Proclamation of 16 May 1559.

69. Gardiner, *Mysteries' End,* 65–72.

70. Ibid., xii.

71. Ibid., 73.

72. Burke, *Popular Culture,* 219; Gardiner, *Mysteries' End,* 77–79, 88.

73. Collinson, *Birthpangs of Protestant England,* 98–121.

74. Ibid., 92f., 117.

75. Wickham, *History of the Theatre,* 116, 128–30.

76. Stephen Orgel, *The Illusion of Power; Political Theater in the English Renaissance* (Berkeley, 1975), 52, 75.

77. Roy Strong, *Art and Power; Renaissance Festivals, 1450–1650* (Berkeley, 1984), 159–73.

78. Basil Willey, *The Seventeenth Century Background* (Garden City, N.Y., 1953), 263.

79. Ibid., 50; T. S. Eliot, *Selected Essays*, new edition (New York, 1950), 241–50.

80. S. L. Bethell, *The Cultural Revolution of the Seventeenth Century* (London, 1951), 12–57, 65.

81. James Sutherland, *A Preface to Eighteenth Century Poetry* (Oxford, 1948), 2.

82. Douglas Bush, *English Literature in the Earlier Seventeenth Century, 1600–1660*, second edition (Oxford, 1962), 422f.

83. Barbara Kiefer Lewalski, *Protestant Poetics and the Seventeenth-Century Religious Lyric* (Princeton, 1979), 425.

84. Ian Watt, *The Rise of the Novel; Studies in Defoe, Richardson and Fielding* (Berkeley, 1967), 82–85, 50; see also John Richetti, *Popular Fiction Before Richardson; Narrative Patterns, 1700–1739* (Oxford, 1969), 13–116, 118, 216, 264.

85. Leopold Damrosch, Jr., *God's Plot and Man's Stories* (Chicago, 1985), 11–13, 302.

86. Ibid., 213.

87. Aubrey Williams, *An Approach to Congreve* (New Haven, 1979), 18, 28, 38, 68.

8. The Politics of Reaction (1603–1659)

1. Anglo, *Spectacle, Pageantry and Early Tudor Policy*, 344–357.

2. Cross, *Royal Supremacy*, 72f.

3. Hugh Trevor-Roper, *Catholics, Anglicans and Puritans; Seventeenth Century Essays* (Chicago, 1987), xi, 43.

4. J. E. Neale, *Elizabeth I and Her Parliaments, 1559–1581* (New York, 1958), 54.

5. J. P. Sommerville, "The Royal Supremacy and Episcopacy *Jure Divino*, 1603–1640," *Journal of Ecclesiastical History*, 34 (1983), 548–58; Claire Cross, "Churchmen and the Royal Supremacy," in *Church and Society in England* ed. Heal and O'Day, 28–33; W. D. J. Cargill Thompson, "Sir Francis Knollys's Campaign against the *Jure Divino* Theory of Episcopacy," in *Studies in the Reformation; Luther to Hooker* (London, 1980), 101–26.

6. Gee and Hardy, *Documents Illustrative of English Church History*, 516–18.

7. Cross, *Church and People*, 72.

8. W. H. Hutton, *William Laud* (London, 1895), 32.

9. David Underdown, *Revel, Riot and Rebellion; Popular Politics and Culture in England, 1603–1660* (Oxford, 1985), 65f.

10. Spufford, *Contrasting Communities*, 231.

11. Hill, *Economic Problems of the Church*, 134, 155.

12. John Selden, *The Historie of Tythes* (London, 1618), xvi.

13. George William Johnson, *Memoirs of John Selden* (London, 1835), 64–70.

14. Thomas Mason, *Serving God and Mammon; William Juxon, 1582–1663* (Newark, Del., 1985), 77.

15. Henry Spelman, *The English Works of Sir Henry Spelman* (London, 1723), lxi, 69, 99.

16. Margaret James, "The Political Importance of the Tithes Controversy in the English Revolution, 1640–1660," *History*, 26 (1942), 4.

17. Hutton, *William Laud*, 149.

18. Hugh Trevor-Roper, *Archbishop Laud, 1573–1645*, second edition (London, 1963), 95f.

19. Cross, *Church and People*, 185; Hill, *Economic Problems of the Church*, 324–30.

20. Trevor-Roper, *Archbishop Laud*, 5.

21. Ibid., 166, 5.

22. Ibid., 271 n., Mason, *Serving God and Mammon*, 56; Elton, *Tudor Constitution*, 92.

23. Trevor-Roper, *Archbishop Laud*, 234, 338f.

24. Hill, *Economic Problems of the Church*, 282.

25. Mason, *Serving God and Mammon*, 117, 53.

26. Margaret Stieg, *Laud's Laboratory; The Diocese of Bath and Wells in the Early Seventeenth Century* (London, 1982), 287.

27. Trevor-Roper, *Archbishop Laud*, 112.

28. Hutton, *William Laud*, 32.

29. Russell, *Crisis of Parliaments*, 216.

30. Hutton, *William Laud*, 77.

31. Phillips, *Reformation of Images*, 172–74.

32. Russell, *Crisis of Parliaments*, 315.

33. William Chillingworth, *The Works of William Chillingworth* (Oxford, 1838), 3:171.

34. G.W.O. Addleshaw and Frederick Etchells, *The Architectural Setting of Anglican Worship* (London, 1948), 24–29, 119–37.

35. More and Cross, *Anglicanism*, 609.

36. Phillips, *Reformation of Images*, 164–67; Cross, *Church and People*, 180, 189.

37. Nicholas Tyacke, *Anti-Calvinists; The Rise of English Arminianism, c.1590–1640* (Oxford, 1987), 187, 221, 201f.

38. Mason, *Serving God and Mammon*, 61.

39. LeHuray, *Music and Reformation*, 51f.

40. Tyacke, *Anti-Calvinists*, 204.

41. Trevor-Roper, *Catholics, Anglicans and Puritans*, 72–87, 107; Millar and Whinney, *English Art*, 55.

42. Tyacke, *Anti-Calvinists*, 192, 198, 219, 202, 118, 206, 216, 221, 223.

43. Trevor-Roper, *Archbishop Laud*, 123.

44. Davies, *Secular Use of Church Buildings*, 142–44; Charles Carlton, *Charles I; The Personal Monarch* (London, 1983), 166.

45. Mason, *Serving God and Mammon*, 80; Millar and Whinney, *English Art*, 30.

46. Richard Mountagu, *Appello Caesarem. A Just Appeale from two Unjust Informers* (London, 1625).

47. Peter Heylen, *The Historie of That most famous Saint and Souldier of Christ Iesus; St. George of Cappadocia* (London, 1633), 227.

48. *The Kings Majesties Declaration to His Subjects, Concerning lawfull Sports to bee used* (London, 1633), sig. C2.

49. Cf. Leah S. Marcus, *The Politics of Mirth* (Chicago, 1986), 3–8.

50. Peter Heylyn, *The History of the Sabbath*, second edition (London, 1636).

51. Addleshaw and Etchells, *Architectural Setting*, 145.

52. Raynor, *Social History of Music*, 243.

53. Phillips, *Reformation of Images*, 184f.

54. Ibid., 187–97; Anon., *One More Argument against the Cavaliers; taken from their Violation of Churches* ([London], 1643]).

55. Mason, *Serving God and Mammon*, 139–41.

56. Trevor-Roper, *Archbishop Laud*, 416, 429.

57. Ronald Hutton, *The Restoration* (Oxford, 1985), 143.

58. Quoted in Aston, *England's Iconoclasts*, 69.

59. Gee and Hardy, *Documents Illustrative of English Church History*, 540–43.

60. Ibid., 551f.

61. Aston, *England's Iconoclasts*, 62–95; Underdown, *Revel, Riot and Rebellion*, 177 and plate 5.

62. Gilman, *Iconoclasm and Poetry*, 40.

63. J. P. Kenyon, ed., *The Stuart Constitution* (Cambridge, 1966), 246.

64. Ibid., 264.

65. William A. Shaw, *A History of the English Church During the Civil Wars and Under the Commonwealth, 1640–1660* (London, 1900), 1:122, 298–316.

66. *Acts and Ordinances*, 1:81.

67. Kenyon, *Stuart Constitution*, 305.

68. Underdown, *Revel, Riot and Rebellion*, 256.

69. Robert S. Bosher, *The Making of the Restoration Settlement; The Influence of the Laudians, 1649–1662* (Oxford, 1951), 6.

70. Kenyon, *Stuart Constitution*, 309.

71. Ibid., 347.

72. Barry Reay, *The Quakers and the English Revolution* (New York, 1985), 38f.

73. Hutton, *Restoration*, 47, 70–72; James, "Tithe Controversy," 15–18.

74. Cross, *Church and People*, 179f.; Hill, *Economic Problems of the Church*, 340–51. Hill holds that Laud's failure was due to capitalist developments which he failed to recognize or accept. It might be added that those developments had been greatly accelerated by prior secularization, most notably the sale of monasteries.

75. Gee and Hardy, *Documents Illustrative of English Church History*, 519.

76. Kenyon, *Stuart Constitution*, 85.

77. William Beveridge, *The Excellency and Usefulness of the Common-Prayer* (1682), in *The Works of the Right Reverend Father in God, Dr. William Beveridge* (London, 1720) 2:559. See also Addleshaw and Etchells, *Architectural Setting*, 50.

9. The Secularization of Power

1. Lacey Baldwin Smith, *Tudor Prelates and Politics, 1536–1558* (Princeton, 1953), 40–47, 305–8.

2. Ibid., 100f., 220–28.

3. Berman, *Law and Revolution*, 85–87, 436f.

4. Ibid., 113, 521, 529.

5. Kaufman, *Polytyque Churche*, 121–30, 76.

6. Ralph Houlbrooke, "The Decline of Ecclesiastical Jurisdiction under the Tudors," in *Continuity and Change; Personnel and Administration of the Church in England, 1500–1642*, ed. Rosemary O'Day and Felicity Heal (Leicester, 1976), 243; Marchant, *Church Under the Law*, 4–6, 283.

7. Richard M. Wunderli, *London Church Courts and Society on the Eve of the Reformation* (Cambridge, Mass., 1981), 137–39.

8. Ralph Houlbrooke, *Church Courts and the People During the English Reformation, 1520–1570* (Oxford, 1979), 8–10.

9. Dickens, *English Reformation*, 93f.

10. Stanford Lehmberg, *The Reformation Parliament, 1529–1536* (Cambridge, 1970), 36, 46.

11. Ibid., 64–75.

12. Ibid., 112–16.

13. Ibid., 150–53.

14. Ibid., 46, 137f. There were other such instances in later ecclesiastical legislation, including the Elizabethan Act of Supremacy. See Neale, *Elizabeth I and her Parliaments*, 65; Scarisbrick, *Henry VIII*, 301 n. 3.

15. Scarisbrick, *Reformation and the English People*, 63–65.

16. Lehmberg, *Reformation Parliament*, 48.

17. Ibid., 83, 92; cf. Woodward, *Dissolution of the Monasteries*, 6.

18. Lehmberg, *Reformation Parliament*, 38, 161, 185.

19. Ibid., 164–69, 191–93.

20. Ibid., 213–15, 253.

21. Ibid., 219, 242, 197f.

22. Margaret Bowker, "The Supremacy and the Episcopate; the Struggle for Control, 1534–1540," *Historical Journal*, 18 (1975), 227–43.

23. Dickens, *English Reformation*, 175; Smith, *Tudor Prelates and Politics*, 209f.

24. Smith, *Tudor Prelates and Politics*, 82f.

25. Ibid., 146–49, 256; Norman L. Jones, "Profiting from Religious Reform; The Land Rush of 1559," *Historical Journal*, 22 (1979), 279.

26. Smith, *Tudor Prelates and Politics*, 282–84, 290–92, 308.

27. Neale, *Elizabeth I and her Parliaments 1559–1581*, 54, 166.

28. Elton, *Tudor Constitution*, 92.

29. Heal, *Prelates and Princes*, 107–15.

30. Mason, *Serving God and Mammon*, 14; William M. Lamont, *Godly Rule; Politics and Religion, 1603–60* (London, 1969), 36–68.

31. Houlbrooke, "Decline of Ecclesiastical Jurisdiction," 243; idem, *Church Courts*, 14.

32. Houlbrooke, *Church Courts*, 17; Jordan, *Edward VI: The Threshold of Power*, 359–61.

33. Mark H. Curtis, *Oxford and Cambridge in Transition, 1558–1642; An Essay on Changing Relations Between the English Universities and English Society* (Oxford, 1959), 158.

34. Houlbrooke, "Decline of Ecclesiastical Jurisdiction," 249.

35. Ibid., 245, 255; idem, *Church Courts*, 146; John H. Pruett, *The Parish Clergy Under the Later Stuarts; The Leicestershire Experience* (Urbana, 1978), 91.

36. Houlbrooke, *Church Courts*, 15f.

37. Ibid., 266; Hill, *Economic Problems of the Church*, 66.

38. Hill, *Economic Problems of the Church*, 84–90, 123f., 165.

39. Haigh, *Reformation and Resistance*, 229–36.

40. Marchant, *Church Under the Law*, 4.

41. Elton, *Tudor Constitution*, 217–21; Houlbrooke, "Decline of Ecclesiastical Jurisdiction," 251.

42. Oxley, *Reformation in Essex*, 263f.; Guy Fitch Lytle, "Religion and the Lay Patron in Reformation England," in *Patronage in the Renaissance*, ed. Guy Fitch Lytle and Stephen Orgel (Princeton, 1982), 65–114.

43. Scarisbrick, *Henry VIII*, 29–32.

44. William Laird Clowes, *The Royal Navy; A History from the Earliest Times to the Present* (London, 1897), 1:419f., 588–603. Elizabeth's navy did contain the *Sts. Andrew* and *Mathew*, captured from the Spanish and not renamed.

45. *Encyclopedia Britannica*, eleventh edition (New York, 1910–11), 10:455–58; Michael Packe, *King Edward III* (London, 1985), 160, 166; Glanmor Williams, *Welsh Church*, 491.

46. Whitney Smith, *Flags Through the Ages and Across the World* (New York, 1975), 182–86.

47. Leonard Smith, "The Canonization of King Henry VI," *Dublin Review*, 168 (1921), 41–53.

48. J. H. Shennan, *The Origins of the Modern European State 1450–1725* (London, 1974), 61.

49. Ernst H. Kantorowicz, *The King's Two Bodies; A Study in Medieval Political Theology* (Princeton, 1957), 191f., 229.

50. Berman, *Law and Revolution*, 532–34.

51. Philip Corrigan and Derek Sayer, *The Great Arch; English State Formation as Cultural Revolution* (Oxford, 1985), 45–47; Kantorowicz, *King's Two Bodies*, 227.

52. John Neville Figgis, *The Divine Right of Kings* (New York, 1965), 145–54; Thomas Molnar, *Twin Powers; Politics and the Sacred* (Grand Rapids, Mich., 1988), 44 n.16.

53. Bossy, *Christianity in the West*, 158.

54. Yeats, *Astraea*, 60f., 101–9.

55. King, *Tudor Royal Iconography*, 99.

56. Ibid., 42, 78–81.

57. Ibid., 233.

58. Strong, *Art and Power*, 19–22, 154–73.

59. R. E. Head, *Royal Supremacy and the Trials of Bishops, 1558–1725* (London, 1962), 137; Russell, *Crisis of Parliaments*, 216.

60. Darrett Rutman, *Winthrop's Boston; Portrait of a Puritan Town, 1630–1649* (Chapel Hill, N.C., 1965), 65, 155, 232–34, 237, 257f.

61. Herschel Baker, *The Wars of Truth* (Cambridge, Mass., 1952), 299.

62. J. R. Jones, *Country and Court; England, 1658–1714* (Cambridge, Mass., 1979), 146f.; Cross, *Church and People*, 226–29.

63. Bertie Wilkinson, *The Coronation in History* (London, 1953), 25; David Ogg, *England in the Reigns of James II and William III* (London, 1955), 235f.

64. Head, *Royal Supremacy*, 114, 138.

65. F. G. James, "The Bishops in Politics, 1688–1714," in *Conflict in Stuart England*, ed. W. A. Aiken (London, 1960), 230–48.

66. Mark Goldie, "The Roots of True Whiggism, 1688–94," *History of Political Thought*, 1 (1980), 207–9.

67. G. V. Bennett, *White Kennett, 1660–1728, Bishop of Peterborough* (London, 1957), 31, 63–73; R. J. Smith, *The Gothic Bequest; Medieval Institutions in British Thought, 1688–1863* (New York, 1987), 28–38.

68. J. C. D. Clark, *English Society, 1688–1832* (Cambridge, 1985).

69. Ibid., 124.

70. Ibid., 69, 366–83.

71. Ibid., 87.

72. Clark describes a widening gulf between aristocratic and Christian values, most noticeably in the eclipse of duelling (Ibid., 94–116). To him that suggests a triumph of religion, and certainly it does represent a deeper understanding of Christianity. But in our terms of reference it shows a secularization of values by differentiation. Aristocratic honor was finally recognized to have no relation (or a negative relation) to a Christian value

system based on charity. Up until then, however, aristocratic honor was somehow a part of England's religion, which even imagined God to be concerned with divine honor. See Clark's further discussion in "England's Ancien Regime as a Confessional State," *Albion,* 21 (1989), 450–74.

73. Brian W. Hill, *Robert Harley; Speaker, Secretary of State and Premier Minister* (New Haven, 1988), 35, 172, 238f.

74. G. V. Bennett, *The Tory Crisis in Church and State, 1688–1730; The Career of Francis Atterbury, Bishop of Rochester* (Oxford, 1975), 137–44, 220f.

75. N. C. Hunt, *Two Early Political Associations; The Quakers and the Dissenting Deputies in the Age of Sir Robert Walpole* (Oxford, 1961).

76. W. K. Jordan, *The Development of Religious Toleration in England* (Gloucester, Mass., 1965), 1:42–44.

77. Leonard W. Levy, *Treason Against God; A History of the Offense of Blasphemy* (New York, 1981), 170.

78. Jordan, *Religious Toleration,* 2:43, 1:233–36, 295f.

79. Ibid., 2:472, 479, 1:25, 260.

80. Ibid., 2:44–51, 90, 4:478; G. D. Nokes, *A History of the Crime of Blasphemy* (London, 1928), 20.

81. Jordan, *Religious Toleration,* 3:91–138.

82. See Geoffrey F. Nuttall, *The Holy Spirit in Puritan Faith and Experience* (Oxford, 1947), 113–30.

83. *The Instrument of Government* (1653), in Kenyon, *Stuart Constitution,* 347.

84. Ivan Roots, *The Great Rebellion, 1642–1660* (London, 1966), 179.

85. Jordan, *Religious Toleration,* 4:22; Raymond C. Mensing, Jr., *Toleration and Parliament, 1660–1719* (Washington, 1979), 23; Nokes, *Crime of Blasphemy,* 43, 53. A fresh survey of the issue of religious freedom in the Restoration and eighteenth century will be found in essays by Gordon Schochet and Robert K. Webb, in the forthcoming *Making of Modern Freedom.*

86. Charles F. Mullett, "The Legal Position of English Protestant Dissenters, 1660–89," *Virginia Law Review,* 22 (1936), 495–526.

87. Roger Thomas, "Comprehension and Indulgence," in *From Uniformity to Unity, 1662–1962,* ed. Geoffrey F. Nuttall and Owen Chadwick (London, 1962), 191–253; Richard B. Barlow, "The Struggle for Religious Toleration in England, 1685–1719," *The Historian,* 22 (1960), 361–77.

88. Edward Carpenter, "Toleration and Establishment; 2: Studies in a Relationship," in *Uniformity to Unity,* ed. Nuttall and Chadwick, 295.

89. Nokes, *Crime of Blasphemy,* 49–59.

90. Norman Sykes, *William Wake; Archbishop of Canterbury, 1657–1737* (Cambridge, 1957), 2:135–39.

91. 2 Henry IV, c. 15; 2 Henry V, st. 1, c. 7.

92. 21 James I, c. 20; 6 & 7 Will. III, c. 11.

93. Courtney Kenny, "The Evolution of the Law of Blasphemy," *Cambridge Law Journal,* 1 (1922), 132. Clark cites several prosecutions for blasphemous libel at common law in the eighteenth century: *English Society,* 286–89.

10. The Secularization of Personhood and Association

1. Smith, *Tudor Prelates and Politics,* 119–25.

2. J. Charles Wall, *Shrines of British Saints* (London, 1905), 169.

3. Stephen Wilson, ed., *Saints and their Cults; Studies in Religious Sociology, Folklore and History* (Cambridge, 1983), 26–40.

4. Whiting, *Blind Devotion*, 59, 72.

5. Knowles, *Religious Orders in England*, 3:369.

6. Marc Bloch, *The Royal Touch; Sacred Monarchy and Scrofula in England and France* (London, 1973, orig. 1923),185, 65f.

7. Ibid., 105, 189f.

8. Ibid., 188–91, 170; Thomas, *Religion and the Decline of Magic*, 197.

9. Roots, *Great Rebellion*, 231.

10. Bloch, *Royal Touch*, 212, 219–21; Edward Gregg, "Was Queen Anne a Jacobite?", *History*, 57 (1972), 371; Ragnhild Hatton, *George I, Elector and King* (Cambridge, Mass., 1978), 165.

11. Elton, *Tudor Constitution*, 335f.

12. Cross, *Royal Supremacy*, 20.

13. Bloch, *Royal Touch*, 210; Stewart, "Cult of the Royal Martyr," 177.

14. David Starkey, "Representation Through Intimacy; A Study in the Symbolism of Monarchy and Court Office in Early-Modern England," in *Symbols and Sentiments*, ed. Ioan Lewis (London, 1977), 187–224.

15. Lehmberg, *Reformation of Cathedrals*, 138.

16. Stow, *Survey of London*, 13, 98f., 420, 104f, 134.

17. Gee and Hardy, *Documents Illustrative of English Church History*, 273.

18. Baskerville, *English Monks*, 233.

19. Bossy, *Christianity in the West*, 146; A. N. Galpern, *The Religions of the People in Sixteenth-Century Champagne* (Cambridge, Mass., 1976), 17, 36–38, 103.

20. Knowles, *Religious Orders in England*, 3:69f., 52; 2:261f.; Woodward, *Dissolution of the Monasteries*, 2, 16; E. A. Wrigley and R. S. Schofield, *The Population History of England 1541–1871* (Cambridge, Mass., 1981), 528.

21. Margaret Bowker, "The Henrician Reformation and the Parish Clergy," *Bulletin of the Institute of Historical Research*, 50 (1977), 33, 47.

22. Rosemary O'Day, "The Reformation of the Ministry, 1558–1642," in *Continuity and Change*, ed. O'Day and Heal, 59.

23. Russell, *Crisis of Parliaments*, 180.

24. Ian Green, "Career Prospects and Clerical Conformity in the Early Stuart Church," *Past and Present*, 90 (1981), 95.

25. Wrigley and Schofield, *Population History*, 528.

26. Jean Delumeau, *Catholicism Between Luther and Voltaire* (Philadelphia, 1977, orig. 1971), 38f., assuming that his population figures include children.

27. Thomas, *Religion and the Decline of Magic*, 449.

28. D. P. Walker, *Unclean Spirits; Possession and Exorcism in France and England in the Late Sixteenth and Early Seventeenth Centuries* (Philadelphia, 1981), 79–82.

29. Alan Macfarlane, *Witchcraft in Tudor and Stuart England* (New York, 1970), 200f.

30. Thomas, *Religion and the Decline of Magic*, 442, 452; Christina Larner, *Witchcraft in England* (Totowa, N.J., 1977), 167f.

31. Rosemary O'Day, *The English Clergy; The Emergence and Consolidation of a Profession, 1558–1642* (Leicester, 1979), 126, 143, 190, 210–19.

32. Patrick Collinson, *The Elizabethan Puritan Movement* (London, 1967), 60f., 73.

33. Stubbes, *Anatomie of Abuses*, 110–15.

34. Mayo, *History of Ecclesiastical Dress*, 71–77.

35. Baskerville, *English Monks*, 263.

36. John K. Yost, "The Reformation Defense of Clerical Marriage in the Reigns of Henry VIII and Edward VI," *Church History*, 50 (1981), 152–65; Richard M. Spielmann, "The Beginning of Clerical Marriage in the English Reformation; The Reigns of Edward and Mary," *Anglican and Episcopal History*, 56 (1987), 256.

37. Anne Llewellyn Barstow, "The First Generation of Anglican Clergy Wives," *Historical Magazine of the Protestant Episcopal Church*, 52 (1983), 3–16; Dickens, *English Reformation*, 245f.

38. Russell, *Crisis of Parliaments*, 140; D. M. Palliser, "Popular Reactions to the Reformation During the Years of Uncertainty, 1530–70," in *Church and Society in England*, ed. Heal and O'Day, 42.

39. Barstow, "Anglican Clergy Wives," 3–16.

40. Spielmann, "Beginning of Clerical Marriage," 252f.

41. Geoffrey Holmes, *Augustan England; Professions, State and Society, 1680–1730* (London, 1982), 87.

42. Leona C. Gabel, *Benefit of Clergy in England in the Later Middle Ages* (Northampton, Mass., 1929), 126f.

43. Elton, *Tudor Constitution*, 319f.; John G. Bellamy, *Criminal Law and Society in Late Medieval and Tudor England* (New York, 1984), 132–64.

44. George Buckley, *Atheism in the English Renaissance* (Chicago, 1932), 47–51; Leonard W. Levy, *Treason Against God; A History of the Offense of Blasphemy* (New York, 1981), 170–78.

45. Buckley, *Atheism in the English Renaissance*, 50, 136.

46. Levy, *Treason Against God*, 183–88.

47. Conrad Russell, "Arguments for Religious Unity in England, 1530–1650," *Journal of Ecclesiastical History*, 18 (1967), 201–26.

48. Levy, *Treason Against God*, 300f.

49. Christopher Hill, *Antichrist in Seventeenth-Century England* (London, 1971), 68–84.

50. Ibid., 52–59, 40, 91, 122, 34–50.

51. William Haller, *Foxe's Book of Martyrs and the Elect Nation* (London, 1963), 143–45, 152–55, 19, 69, 88, 121, 130, 136.

52. David Loades, "The Origins of English Protestant Nationalism," *Studies in Church History*, 18 (1982), 297–307.

53. Caroline M. Hibbard, *Charles I and the Popish Plot* (Chapel Hill, N.C., 1983).

54. William S. Maltby, *The Black Legend in England; The Development of Anti-Spanish Sentiment, 1558–1660* (Durham, N.C., 1971).

55. Miller, *Popery and Politics*, 69, 75.

56. John Lough, *France Observed in the Seventeenth Century by British Travellers* (Boston, 1985), 188–90, 218–31, 247–65.

57. J. R. Jones, *Britain and Europe in the Seventeenth Century* (New York, 1966), 11.

58. J. R. Jones, *The Revolution of 1688 in England* (New York, 1972), 76.

59. Miller, *Popery and Politics*, 183–87; Sheila Williams, "The Pope-burning processions of 1679, 1680 and 1681," *Journal of the Warburg and Courtauld Institutes*, 21 (1958), 104–18; Tim Harris, *London Crowds in the Reign of Charles II* (Cambridge, 1987), 93.

60. Hans Kohn, *The Idea of Nationalism; A Study of Its Origin and Background* (New York, 1961), 164f.

61. Scarisbrick, *Reformation and the English People*, 22–31.

62. Susan Brigden, "Religion and Social Obligation in Early Sixteenth Century London," *Past and Present*, 103 (1984), 94.

63. Charles Phythian-Adams, "Ceremony and the Citizen; The Communal Year at Coventry, 1450–1550," in *The Early Modern Town*, ed. Peter Clark (London, 1976), 106–11.

64. Merwyn James, *Society, Politics and Culture; Studies in Early Modern England* (Cambridge, 1986), 17, 38–41.

65. Phythian-Adams, "Ceremony and the Citizen," 123.

66. Peter Clark, "The Alehouse and the Alternative Society," in *Puritans and Revolutionaries*, ed. Donald Pennington and Keith Thomas (Oxford, 1978), 47–72; idem, *The English Alehouse; A Social History, 1200–1830* (London, 1983), 152–56.

67. Bossy, *Christianity in the West*, 48, 142, 168f., 25f.

68. Chilton Latham Powell, *English Domestic Relations, 1487–1653* (New York, 1917), 36–70, 93–99.

69. Lawrence Stone, *The Family, Sex and Marriage in England, 1500–1800* (London, 1977), 35f.

70. Shirley, *Swearing and Perjury*, 130, 16; Anon., *The History of Publick and Solemn State Oaths* (London, 1716), 4–8.

71. Shirley, *Swearing and Perjury*, 98, 10, 64.

72. Russell, *Crisis of Parliaments*, 38.

73. William Holdsworth, *A History of English Law*, sixth edition (Boston, 1934), 3:400, 4:273, 515f.

74. Hill, *Society and Puritanism*, 400f.

75. Elton, *Policy and Police*, 222.

76. 35 Henry VIII, c. 1. See the discussion of these statutes in Richard W. Stewart, "Statutory Oaths and English Constitutional Law (1509–1610)" (M.A. thesis, University of Florida, 1980), 32–44.

77. Kenyon, *Stuart Constitution*, 176–80.

78. Stewart, "Statutory Oaths," 133, 104, 118.

79. Shirley, *Swearing and Perjury*, xiii, 130, 16.

80. Edmund Calamy, *The Non-Conformist's Memorial*, ed. Samuel Palmer, second edition (London, 1802–3), 2:89f.

81. Hill, *Society and Puritanism*, 409.

82. Ibid., 418f.

83. Ibid., 416.

84. Clark, *English Society*, 303.

85. Smith, *Tudor Prelates and Politics*, 136, 120f.

86. Ibid., 120.

87. Steven Lukes, *Individualism* (Oxford, 1973), 76–80, 107–10, 32–35; Bossy, *Christianity in the West*, 161; idem, "Some Elementary Forms of Durkheim," 3–18.

11. The Secularization of Scholarship and Science

1. Christine Nasie Wilkins, "Secularization in Sixteenth-Century England" (M.A. thesis, University of Florida, 1981), 116–36.

2. Klotz, "Subject Analysis of English Imprints," 417–19.

3. May McKisack, *Medieval History in the Tudor Age* (Oxford, 1971), 96, 75.

4. F. J. Levy, *Tudor Historical Thought* (San Marino, Cal., 1967), 12, 86–89.

5. Haller, *Foxe's Book of Martyrs*, 58–69, 119–44.

6. Levy, *Tudor Historical Thought*, 287–89, 200, 211f., 33, 234, 8.

7. McKisack, *Medieval History*, 122f.; F. Smith Fussner, *The Historical Revolution; English Historical Writing and Thought, 1580–1640* (New York, 1962), 165–69

8. Ibid., 209, 93–95, 219.

9. Michael Finlayson, "Clarendon, Providence and the Historical Revolution," *Albion*, 22 (1990), 607–32.

10. J. G. A. Pocock, *The Ancient Constitution and the Feudal Law; A Study of English Historical Thought in the Seventeenth Century* (New York, 1967).

11. Ibid., 112, 156, 229–48.

12. This figure is a conflation of the lists in Glenn Negley, *Utopian Literature; A Bibliography* (Lawrence, Kans., 1977); and Lyman T. Sargent, *British and American Utopia Literature, 1516–1975; An Annotated Bibliography* (Boston, 1979). I am indebted to conversations with Jeffrey Brautigam on this subject.

13. Arthur B. Ferguson, *The Articulate Citizen and the English Renaissance* (Durham, N.C., 1965), 135–49, 283, 291.

14. Ibid., 205f., 218f., 252–58.

15. Ibid., 292–305, 311f., 341–62.

16. Joyce Oldham Appleby, *Economic Thought and Ideology in Seventeenth-Century England* (Princeton, 1978), 37–41, 53–60.

17. Ibid., 60–63, 95f.; William Letwin, *The Origins of Scientific Economics; English Economic Thought, 1660–1776* (London, 1963), 81f.; Benjamin Nelson, *The Idea of Usury; From Tribal Brotherhood to Universal Otherhood*, second edition (Chicago, 1969), 95–98.

18. R. H. Tawney, *Religion and the Rise of Capitalism* (New York, 1947), 199–205, 225–29, 162.

19. Letwin, *Origins of Scientific Economics*, passim; Keith Tribe, *Land, Labour and Economic Discourse* (London, 1978), 35f.

20. Stephen L. Collins, *From Divine Cosmos to Sovereign State; An Intellectual History of Consciousness and the Idea of Order in Renaissance England* (New York, 1989), 31f.

21. Christopher Morris, *Political Thought in England, Tyndale to Hooker* (Oxford, 1953), 1, 131.

22. W. H. Greenleaf, *Order, Empiricism and Politics; Two Traditions of English Political Thought, 1500–1700* (New York, 1964), 199–207, 222, 235, 241, 249–57.

23. Figgis, *Divine Right*, 183–87; see also William J. Bouwsma, *The Secularisation of Society in the Seventeenth Century* (Moscow, 1970), 1.5:100.

24. Scarisbrick, *Henry VIII*, 287f., 326.

25. Figgis, *Divine Right*, 231–33.

26. George Boas, *Vox Populi; Essays in the History of an Idea* (Baltimore, 1969).

27. Figgis, *Divine Right*, 242f.; Charles J. O'Neil, "Is Locke's State the Secular State?" *New Scholasticism*, 26 (1952), 424–40.

28. Figgis, *Divine Right*, 148–57; Greenleaf, *Order, Empiricism and Politics*, 80–93; Gordon J. Schochet, *Patriarchalism in Political Thought; The Authoritarian Family and Political Speculation and Attitudes, Especially in Seventeenth-Century England* (Oxford, 1975), 116–54, 215–17.

29. Collins, *Divine Cosmos*, 152f.

30. Tribe, *Land, Labour and Economic Discourse*, 47f.

31. John Dunn, "From Applied Theology to Social Analysis; The Break Between John Locke and the Scottish Enlightenment," in *Wealth and Virtue; The Shaping of Political Economy in the Scottish Enlightenment*, ed. Istvan Hont and Michael Ignatieff (Cambridge, 1983), 119–29.

32. Felix Raab, *The English Face of Machiavelli; A Changing Interpretation, 1550–1700* (London, 1964), 9–15, 100, 53–59.

33. Ibid., 235–46.

34. Samuel I. Mintz, *The Hunting of Leviathan* (Cambridge, 1969), 45.

35. Greenleaf, *Order Empiricism and Politics*, 93.

36. Mintz, *Hunting of Leviathan*, 157–60, 139.

37. K. C. Brown, "Hobbes's Grounds for Belief in a Deity," *Philosophy*, 37 (1962), 336–44; Willis B. Glover, "God and Thomas Hobbes," in *Hobbes Studies*, ed. Keith C. Brown (Cambridge, Mass., 1965), 141–68; Peter Geach, "The Religion of Thomas Hobbes," *Religious Studies*, 17 (1981), 549–58; R. J. Halliday, Timothy Kenyon and Andrew Reeve, "Hobbes's Belief in God," *Political Studies*, 31 (1983), 418–33; Berman, *History of Atheism*, 57–67.

38. Richard S. Westfall, *Science and Religion in Seventeenth-Century England* (New Haven, 1958), 20, 109, 120; Willey, *Seventeenth Century Background*, 177–203.

39. Robert Parsons, *Sermon preached at the Funeral of the Rt. Honorable John Earl of Rochester* (Oxford, 1680), 26.

40. Brian Vickers, ed., *Occult and Scientific Mentalities in the Renaissance* (Cambridge, 1984), 32.

41. Ibid., 9; Edwin Arthur Burtt, *The Metaphysical Foundations of Modern Physical Science*, revised edition (Garden City, N.Y., 1954), 160.

42. Vickers, *Occult and Scientific Mentalities*, 6–10, 34–42.

43. Carolyn Merchant, *The Death of Nature; Women, Ecology, and the Scientific Revolution* (San Francisco, 1980), 192f.

44. Ibid., 202.

45. Ibid., 164–71.

46. Baker, *Wars of Truth*, 359f.

47. Ibid., 235–45.

48. Thomas, *Religion and the Decline of Magic*, 641–47; H. R. Trevor-Roper, *The European Witch-Craze of the Sixteenth and Seventeenth Centuries, and Other Essays* (New York, 1967), 176–82; Thomas S. Kuhn, *The Structure of Scientific Revolutions* (Chicago, 1964), 147, 157.

49. Willey, *Seventeenth Century Background*, 35–37; Franklin L. Baumer, *Religion and the Rise of Scepticism* (New York, 1960), 113f.

50. Burtt, *Metaphysical Foundations*, 201; Jones, *Seventeenth Century*, 125; Charles Coulston Gillispie, *The Edge of Objectivity; An Essay in the History of Scientific Ideas* (Princeton, 1960), 116. James Turner makes a similar point about the eagerness with which religious spokesmen adjusted religion to new currents of scholarship in nineteenth-century American history: *Without God, Without Creed: The Origins of Unbelief in America* (Baltimore, 1985).

51. Margaret C. Jacob, *The Cultural Meaning of the Scientific Revolution* (New York, 1988), 77–80.

52. Willey, *Seventeenth Century Background*, 152.

53. Michael MacDonald, *Mystical Bedlam* (New York, 1981); idem, "Religion, Social Change, and Psychological Healing in England, 1600–1800," *Studies in Church History*, 19 (1982), 101–25.

54. James Howard Robinson, *The Great Comet of 1680; A Study in the History of Rationalism* (Northfield, Minn., 1916), 112 n.2.

55. Thomas F. Gieryn, "Distancing Science from Religion in Seventeenth-Century England," *Isis*, 79 (1988), 585.

56. Marjorie Nicolson, *Science and Imagination* (Ithaca, 1956), 223–27.

57. Gillispie, *Edge of Objectivity*, 73; Herbert Butterfield, *The Origins of Modern Science, 1300–1800*, revised edition (New York, 1965), 58–66, 129–37.

58. Thomas Franklin Mayo, *Epicurus in England (1650–1725)* ([Dallas], 1934).

59. Burtt, *Metaphysical Foundations*, 258f.; Koyré, *Closed World to the Infinite Universe*, 221–34; Westfall, *Science and Religion*, 73–105.

60. E. J. Dijksterhuis, *The Mechanization of the World Picture* (Oxford, 1961), 491.

61. Willey, *Seventeenth Century Background*, 212f.; Gillispie, *Edge of Objectivity*, 166–69; deGrazia, "Secularization of Language," 319–29.

62. Kuhn, *Structure of Scientific Revolutions*, 93.

63. Butterfield, *Origins of Modern Science*, 181f.

64. Michael Hunter, *Science and Society in Restoration England* (Cambridge, 1981), 182–86.

65. Stuart Clark, "The Scientific Status of Demonology," in Vickers, *Occult and Scientific Mentalities*, 362, quoting John Cotta; also 351–62, 369.

66. Jeffrey Burton Russell, *Mephistopheles; The Devil in the Modern World* (Ithaca, 1986), 80, 156.

67. Slack, *Impact of Plague*, 26–48.

68. Ibid., 48f.; cf. 231f.

69. Ibid., 238–54, 339f.

70. J. E. G. de Montmorency, *State Intervention in English Education; A Short History from the Earliest Times Down to 1833* (Cambridge, 1902), 10–58; Joan Simon, *Education and Society in Tudor England* (Cambridge, 1966), 186f.; John Lawson and Harold Silver, *A Social History of Education* (London, 1973), 84.

71. Curtis, *Oxford and Cambridge in Transition*, 23–30; Simon, *Education and Society*, 73, 291–97, 145–49, 168; Lehmberg, *Reformation of Cathedrals*, 298.

72. Simon, *Education and Society*, 196, 240f., 265, 322–29, 101.

73. de Montmorency, *State Intervention*, 68, 93–96.

74. W. A. L. Vincent, *The State and School Education 1640–1660 in England and Wales* (London, 1950), 97–101.

75. Lawson and Silver, *Social History of Education*, 191.

76. de Montmorency, *State Intervention*, 170–79.

77. Pruett, *Parish Clergy*, 126; Holmes, *Augustan England*, 70f.; Lawrence Stone, "The Educational Revolution in England, 1560–1640," *Past and Present*, 28 (1964), 69–71.

78. Foster Watson, *The English Grammar Schools to 1660; Their Curriculum and Practice* (Cambridge, 1908), 34f., 63f.; A. Monroe Stowe, *English Grammar Schools in the Reign of Queen Elizabeth* (New York, 1908), 110, 147–56; W. A. L. Vincent, *The Grammar Schools; Their Continuing Tradition, 1660–1714* (London, 1969), 86–90.

79. Anthony Grafton and Lisa Jardine, *From Humanism to the Humanities; Education and the Liberal Arts in Fifteenth- and Sixteenth-Century Europe* (Cambridge, Mass., 1986), 139–45, 168.

80. JoAnn Hoeppner Moran, *The Growth of English Schooling, 1340–1548; Learning, Literacy, and Laicization in Pre-Reformation York Diocese* (Princeton, 1985), 183.

81. Quoted in Randolph Trumbach, *The Rise of the Egalitarian Family* (New York, 1978), 257, 262f.

82. Ian Michael, *The Teaching of English from the Sixteenth Century to 1870* (Cambridge, 1987), 138, 158–60, 246.

83. Norman Sykes, *From Sheldon to Secker; Aspects of English Church History, 1660–1768* (Cambridge, 1959), 200–202.

84. Curtis, *Oxford and Cambridge in Transition*, 64–77, 122–24, 268. See also Vincent, *State and School Education*, 82f.

85. Wilber Samuel Howell, *Logic and Rhetoric in England, 1500–1700* (Princeton, 1956), 10f., 147, 391; Gilman, *Iconoclasm and Poetry*, 45.

86. Under bishops Bancroft (in 1608–10), Laud (1630–40), and Sheldon (1667–69).

87. David A. Pailin, *Attitudes to Other Religions; Comparative Religion in Seventeenth- and Eighteenth-Century England* (Manchester, 1984), 45–62, 132–36.

88. Ibid., 3–32; Margaret T. Hodgen, *Early Anthropology in the Sixteenth and Seventeenth Centuries* (Philadelphia, 1964), 171, 202.

89. Willey, *Seventeenth Century Background*, 133; John Redwood, *Reason, Ridicule and Religion; The Age of Enlightenment in England, 1660–1750* (Cambridge, Mass., 1976), 30; Berman, *History of Atheism*, 76–78.

90. Paul Hazard, *The European Mind, 1680–1715* (New York, 1963), 252–65, 295–300.

91. Frank E. Manuel, *The Changing of the Gods* (Hanover, N.H., 1983), 48f.

92. Roger Lee Emerson, "English Deism 1670–1755; An Enlightenment Challenge to Orthodoxy" (Ph.D. dissertation, Brandeis University, 1962), 32.

93. G. E. Aylmer, "Unbelief in Seventeenth-Century England," in *Puritans and Revolutionaries; Essays in Seventeenth-Century History Presented to Christopher Hill*, ed. Donald Pennington and Keith Thomas (Oxford, 1978), 27–34, 42.

94. Ibid., 23–27, 36; Michael Hunter, "The Problem of 'Atheism' in Early Modern England," *Transactions of the Royal Historical Society*, fifth series, 35 (1985), 144, 154; Berman, *History of Atheism*, 70. See also Perez Zagorin, *Ways of Lying; Dissimulation, Persecution and Conformity in Early Modern Europe* (Cambridge, Mass., 1990), 291–309.

95. Hunter, "Problem of 'Atheism'," 149f.

96. Manuel, *Eighteenth Century Confronts the Gods*, 7–12; idem, *Changing of the Gods*, 29; Redwood, *Reason, Ridicule and Religion*, 54.

97. Manuel, *Eighteenth Century Confronts the Gods*, 71f.

98. Manuel, *Changing of the Gods*, 39–46.

99. Robert Burton, *The Anatomy of Melancholy* (New York, 1977), 3:379–92; Thomas Jackson, *A Treatise Containing the Originall of Unbeliefe* (London, 1625), 17–20; Thomas Fuller, *The Holy State and the Profane State* (New York, 1938), 2:379–81.

100. Redwood, *Reason, Ridicule and Religion*, 37–39.

101. Hillel Schwartz, *Knaves, Fools, Madmen and that Subtile Effluvium; A Study of the Opposition to the French Prophets in England, 1706–1710* (Gainesville, Fla., 1978), 31–70; MacDonald, "Religion, Social Change, and Psychological Healing," 119.

102. Tom McArthur, *Worlds of Reference* (Cambridge, 1986), 75–84.

12. Religious Responses to Secularization

1. See C. John Sommerville, *Popular Religion in Restoration England* (Gainesville, Fla., 1977).

2. [Richard Allestree], *The Causes of the Decay of Christian Piety* (London, 1667).

3. Lukes, *Individualism*, 32–35.

4. Jones, *Revolution of 1688*, 54f.

5. Lukes, *Individualism*, 107; Bossy, "Some Elementary Forms of Durkheim," 3–18.

6. S. N. Williams, "John Locke on the Status of Faith," *Scottish Journal of Theology*, 40 (1987), 591–606.

7. Damrosch, *God's Plot and Man's Stories*, 4, 11, 262.

8. David Cressy, "Books as Totems in Seventeeth-Century England and New England," *Journal of Library History*, 21 (1986), 92–106.

9. Davies, *Worship and Theology*, 3:50.

10. David D. Hall, *Worlds of Wonder, Days of Judgment; Popular Religious Belief in Early New England* (New York, 1989), 26, 237.

11. Burke, *Popular Culture*, 226.

12. Philip Edgecumbe Hughes, *Theology of the English Reformers* (Grand Rapids, Mich., 1965), 121–58.

13. Ibid., 132.

14. Cross, *Church and People*, 72.

15. Nuttall, *Holy Spirit*, 22–26; Davies, *Worship and Theology in England*, 1:234, 295; 2:138; Norman Pettit, *The Heart Prepared; Grace and Conversion in Puritan Spiritual Life* (New Haven, 1966).

16. William Haller, *The Rise of Puritanism* (New York, 1957), 15–27, 142.

17. Lawrence Stone, *The Causes of the English Reformation 1529–1642* (New York, 1972), 139.

18. Jones, *Seventeenth Century*, 116–18, 134f., quoting Robert Ferguson.

19. Davies, *Worship and Theology in England*, 1:300; 2:141, 496–501; Mills, *Speaking in Tongues*, 186.

20. Davies, *Worship and Theology in England*, 1:300, 386; 2:282.

21. See David Cecil, comp., *The Oxford Book of Christian Verse* (Oxford, 1940), and Donald Davie, comp., *The New Oxford Book of Christian Verse* (New York, 1988).

22. Barrington R. White, *The English Separatist Tradition; From the Marian Martyrs to the Pilgrim Fathers* (Oxford, 1971), 15, 42, 160–69.

23. Cross, *Church and People*, 210.

24. Charles E. Whiting, *Studies in English Puritanism from the Restoration to the Revolution, 1660–1688* (London, 1931), 447–70; James Fulton MacClear, "The Birth of the Free Church Tradition," *Church History*, 26 (1957), 99–131.

25. Michael R. Watts, *The Dissenters* (Oxford, 1978), 289–303; Douglas Lacey, *Dissent and Parliamentary Politics in England, 1661–1689* (New Brunswick, N.J., 1969), 108f., 245f., 309.

26. Watts, *Dissenters*, 290; Geoffrey F. Nuttall, "Assembly and Association in Dissent," *Studies in Church History*, 7 (1971), 289–309.

27. See the definition of movement in John Wilson, *Introduction to Social Movements* (New York, 1973), 8.

28. Bosher, *Making of the Restoration Settlement*, 32–37; John W. Packer, *The Transformation of Anglicanism, 1643–1660* (Manchester, 1969), 72.

29. See More and Cross, *Anglicanism*.

30. Sommerville, *Popular Religion*, 33–59.

31. Edward Lake, *Officium Eucharisticum*, eighth edition (Dublin, 1683), sig. A4.

32. Beveridge, *The Excellency and Usefulness of the Common-Prayer*, 2:561.

33. William Stanley, *The Faith and Practice of a Church of England Man*, third edition (London, 1688), 179–82.

34. Ibid., 19.

35. See C. John Sommerville, "Anglican, Puritan, and Sectarian in Empirical Perspective," *Social Science History*, 13 (1989), 109–35.

36. J. Wickham Legg, *English Church Life From the Restoration to the Tractarian Movement* (London, 1914), 281–303; F. W. B. Bullock, *Voluntary Religious Societies, 1520–1799* (St. Leonards on Sea, Sussex, 1963), 109–30, 157f.

37. Stanley, *Faith and Practice*, 68, 75, 87, 99f.

38. Tina Isaacs, "The Anglican Hierarchy and the Reformation of Manners, 1688–

1738," *Journal of Ecclesiastical History*, 33 (1982), 394; Dudley W. R. Bahlman, *The Moral Revolution of 1688* (New Haven, 1957), 14–66.

39. Garnet V. Portus, *Caritas Anglicana* (London, 1912), 10–20.

40. Bullock, *Voluntary Religious Societies*, 144–57.

41. [Matthew Tindal], *The Nation Vindicated, From the Aspirations cast on it in a late Pamphlet* (London, 1711), 1:43f.; Bahlman, *Moral Revolution*, 37, 83–97; Isaacs, "Anglican Hierarchy and the Reformation of Manners," 391–441.

42. C. F. Secretan, *Memoirs of the Life and Times of the Pious Robert Nelson* (London, 1860).

43. Portus, *Caritas Anglicana*, 52, 65f., 134–36.

44. Bullock, *Voluntary Religious Societies*, 159, 234f.

45. Ibid., 199–201.

46. Marjorie Reeves, *The Influence of Prophecy in the Later Middle Ages; A Study in Joachimism* (Oxford, 1969), 6, 82–87, 322, 377.

47. Thomas, *Religion and the Decline of Magic*, 396–403; Rupert Taylor, *The Political Prophecy in England* (New York, 1911), 120–32; Jonathan K. VanPatten, "Magic, Prophecy, and the Law of Treason in Reformation England," *American Journal of Legal History*, 27 (1983), 16–23.

48. Katherine R. Firth, *The Apocalyptic Tradition in Reformation Britain, 1530–1645* (Oxford, 1979), 9–69, 252f.

49. Lamont, *Godly Rule*, 13–26.

50. Thomas, *Religion and the Decline of Magic*, 142–50, 124–28, 429, 486; Ernest Lee Tuveson, *Millennium and Utopia; A Study in the Background of the Idea of Progress* (New York, 1964), 71–99.

51. John F. Wilson, *Pulpit in Parliament* (Princeton, 1969), 195.

52. Blair Worden, "Providence and Politics in Cromwellian England," *Past and Present*, 108 (1985), 97.

53. Paul Christianson, *Reformers and Babylon; English Apocalyptic Visions from the Reformation to the Eve of the Civil War* (Toronto, 1978), 242f.

54. J. C. Davis, *Utopia and the Ideal Society; A Study of English Utopian Writing, 1516–1701* (Cambridge, 1981), 33–35, 163, 196, 336.

55. Lamont, *Godly Rule*, 111, 126; Harry Rusche, "Prophecies and Propaganda, 1641 to 1651," *English Historical Review*, 84 (1969), 768f.; Hill, *Antichrist*, 135, 142, 172.

56. J. F. C. Harrison, *The Second Coming; Popular Millenarianism, 1780–1850* (New Brunswick, N.J., 1979), 6–10, 208.

57. A. Tindal Hart, *William Lloyd, 1627–1717* (London, 1952), 176–78, 245f.

58. Lamont, *Godly Rule*, 106; idem, "Richard Baxter, the Apocalypse and the Mad Major," *Past and Present*, 55 (1972), 68–90; Bernard Capp, "The Millennium and Eschatology in England," ibid., 57 (1972), 156–62.

59. Clarke Garrett, *Respectable Folly* (Baltimore, 1975), 121–43, 226; Jack Fruchtman, Jr., *The Apocalyptic Politics of Richard Price and Joseph Priestley* (Philadelphia, 1983), 13; Harrison, *Second Coming*.

60. Tuveson, *Millennium and Utopia*, 139f.; W. H. Oliver, *Prophets and Millennialists* (Auckland, 1978), 240.

61. Christopher Hill, *The World Turned Upside Down; Radical Ideas During the English Revolution* (New York, 1973), 111–20, 140f., 165, 190.

62. Ibid., 184, 147.

13. Antecedents, Causes, and Conclusions

1. Eisenstein, *Printing Press*, 79.

2. J. H. Hexter, *Reappraisals in History* (London, 1961), 41.

3. Turner, *Without God, Without Creed*, xiiif.

4. Packe, *Edward III*, 288–98; Hudson, *Premature Reformation*, 508f.; Michael Wilks, " 'Reformatio Regini'; Wycliff and Hus as Leaders of Religious Protest," *Studies in Church History*, 9 (1972), 109–30; Aston, *England's Iconoclasts*, 105–43, 154f.

5. Hudson, *Premature Reformation*, 513, 68.

6. H. F. Westlake, *The Parish Gilds of Medieval England* (London, 1919), 36.

7. Margaret Aston, *The Fifteenth Century; The Prospect of Europe* (London, 1968), 141.

8. Hudson, *Premature Reformation*, 110–15.

9. Thomson, *Transformation of Medieval England*, 288–96; Margaret Harvey, "Ecclesia Anglicana, cui Ecclesiastes noster Christus vos prefecit; The Power of the Crown in the English Church During the Great Schism," *Studies in Church History*, 18 (1982), 229–41.

10. Hudson, *Premature Reformation*, 510.

11. See Colin Williams, *Faith in a Secular Age* (New York, 1966), 50; Peter Homans, "Transcendance, Distance, Fantasy; The Protestant Era in Psychological Perspective," *Journal of Religion*, 49 (1969), 205–27; Guy E. Swanson, *Religion and Regime; A Sociological Account of the Reformation* (Ann Arbor, 1967).

12. See above, chapter 2, n.48.

13. Harry J. Ausmus, *The Polite Escape; On the Myth of Secularization* (Athens, Ohio, 1982), 46; Shiner, *Secularization of History*, 36.

14. See Wilson, *Religion in Sociological Perspective*, 55–77.

15. Hill, *Society and Puritanism*, 79, 84.

16. Thomas, *Religion and the Decline of Magic*, 642–46, 650f., 661–68.

17. Joseph Frank, *The Beginnings of the English Newspaper, 1620–1660* (Cambridge, Mass., 1961), 271f., 77, 89, 93, 107, 120, 125, 196, 248.

18. James Sutherland, *The Restoration Newspaper and its Development* (Cambridge, 1986), 18.

19. J. A. Downie, *Robert Harley and the Press; Propaganda and Public Opinion in the Age of Swift and Defoe* (New York, 1979), 3, 23, 28, 40, 55.

20. *British Mercury*, 2 August 1712, quoted in G. A. Cranfield, *The Development of the Provincial Newspaper, 1700–1760* (Oxford, 1962), 9f.

21. Henry L. Snyder, "The Circulation of Newspapers in the Reign of Queen Anne," *The Library*, 23 (1968), 206–35.

22. Cranfield, *Development of the Provincial Newspaper*, 13–27, 176.

23. Aytoun Ellis, *The Penny Universities; A History of the Coffee-Houses* (London, 1956), 33, 45–49, 86, 89–93, 192, xiv.

24. Ibid., 24.

25. Walter Graham, *The Beginnings of English Literary Periodicals* (London, 1926), 8–16, 24, 44.

26. Quoted in Willey, *Seventeenth Century Background*, 214.

27. Bennett, *Tory Crisis*, 308.

28. All quoted in G. R. Balleine, *A History of the Evangelical Party in the Church of England* (London, 1909), 20f.

29. Richard Baxter, *The Autobiography of Richard Baxter* (London, 1931), 26.

30. Stoye, *English Travellers Abroad*, 35f.

31. Sommerville, *Popular Religion*. Specifically, the declining categories included A3–5, B12, D7–8, F7, G9, H4, I14–20, J5, J7, while rising categories included A1, B3, C1–3, C6, D10, H5, H7, I6–7.

32. Devendra P. Varma, *The Gothic Flame* (New York, 1966), 210–18.

Index